FACES OF
EVEREST

सगरमाथा

ༀ ཇོ་མོ་གླང་མ

FACES OF
EVE

Major H P S Ahluwalia

REST

Vikas Publishing House Pvt Ltd

New Delhi Bombay Bangalore Calcutta Kanpur

VIKAS PUBLISHING HOUSE PVT LTD

5 Ansari Road, New Delhi 110002
Savoy Chambers, 5 Wallace Street, Bombay 400001
10 First Main Road, Gandhi Nagar, Bangalore 560009
8-1/B Chowringhee Lane, Calcutta 700016
80 Canning Road, Kanpur 208004

1V02A0508

ISBN 0 7069 0563 6

Book designed by Aravind Teki

Art works: Vikas Studio

Printed at Thomson Press (India) Ltd., Faridabad

Acknowledgements

Albert Eggler for extracts from the book, "The Everest–Lhotse Adventure", George Allen & Unwin Ltd., U.K.; Brigadier General Bruce for extracts from the book, "Assault on Mount Everest, 1922", Edward Arnold Publishers Ltd., U.K.; Chris Bonington for extracts from the books, "Everest South West Face" and "Everest the Hard Way", Hodder and Stoughton Ltd., U.K.; Eric Shipton for extracts from the book, "That Untravelled World", Hodder and Stoughton Ltd., U.K.; George Leigh Mallory, Norton and Odell for extracts from "Fight for Everest, 1924", Edward Arnold Publishers Ltd., U.K.; Howard Bury and Mallory for extracts from the book, "Mount Everest, the reconnaissance 1921", Edward Arnold Publishers Ltd., U.K.; Lord John Hunt for extracts from the book, "The Ascent of Everest", Hodder and Stoughton Ltd., U.K.; Sir Edmund Hillary for extracts from the book, "Nothing Venture, Nothing Win", Hodder and Stoughton Ltd., U.K.; "The Times", London for the extracts; "Himavanta", Calcutta for the extracts; B. L. Gulatee for his Technical Paper No. 4 "Mount Everest, its Name and Height"; Sir Sidney Burrard for his Professional Paper No. 26 "Mount Everest and its Tibetan Names".

Survey of India for photographs on pages 9, 10, 11 & 12 and like sketches on pages 7, 14 & 27; Royal Geographical Society for photographs on pages 22, 23, 25 & 31 and line sketches on pages 14 & 27; Himalayan Mountaineering Institute on pages 28 & 29; Swiss Alpine Foundation on pages 60 & 61; Hari Dang for photographs on pages 52 and 54; Lt. Col. Balwant Sandhu for photographs on page 53; Norman Dyhrenfurth for photographs on pages 77, 78, 83, 84, 86, 132 & 134; Chris Bonington for photographs on pages 112, 151, 152, 154, 183, 184, 185, 186, 191, 192, 197 & 198 and for sketches on pages 182,

188, 189 & 190; Japanese Alpine Club for photographs on pages 115, 116, 118, 119, 120 & 122; Dough Scott for photographs on pages 142 & 143; Italian Expedition for photographs on pages 156, 159 & 160; Mrs Eiko Hisano for photographs on pages 155, 166, 167, 168, 170 & 171; People's Republic of China for photographs on pages 174, 175, 177, 178 & 180 and Indian Mountaineering Foundation for all photographs of 1960, 1962 and 1965 Indian Everest Expeditions.

Survey of India; Ministry of External Affairs; Director General of Observatories (Climatology and Geophysics), India; Swiss Alpine Foundation; Royal Geographical Society; American Alpine Club; People's Republic of China; Japanese Alpine Club; Embassy of Nepal, New Delhi.

Indian Air Force for the cover photograph.

Contents

List of Illustrations

LIST OF LINE SKETCHES

"Let nobody suppose that Everest is an easy mountain; it is not. And at all times it is dangerous, as the sad toll of life in the Ice Fall, the West Cwm, and on the Lhotse Face bears witness. Whenever the wind is blowing strongly it is impossible to move along the summit ridges, and that means on most days in the year. And it is well that this should be the case, for man should be humble before the greatest works of nature.
Lord John Hunt

Foreword

Forty-three attempts in fifty-seven years (1921–77), thirteen successful expeditions, fifty-six people including two women stepping on its coveted summit, forty-seven making the supreme sacrifice of laying down their lives in the attempt—that in a nutshell is the statistical record of Everest. One might conclude that after so many ascents, climbing Everest would be considered a commonplace adventure and the mountain would have lost its charm. But the lure of this peak has not diminished. Everest continues ever to beckon. So irresistible is the call of the loftiest of earth's pinnacles that unless booked five or six years in advance, a team has no chance of making an attempt.

The mountain has a very special significance for us in India. When it was first climbed by Tenzing with Edmund Hillary, it immediately led to the setting up of our first Training Institute at Darjeeling. The maiden attempt of the Indian Mountaineering Foundation was the expedition to Cho Oyu in 1958. Many people thought us mad to send inadequately trained mountaineers with little experience to this difficult peak, but they climbed Cho Oyu. The very next attempt was in 1960, on Everest. With a team of quite green mountaineers it was a surprise that they nearly pulled it off. On the morning of May 25 a team of three left their camp (27,600) for the summit. The weather was bad and deteriorating fast. Strong winds and powder snow made visibility poor and the going increasingly difficult. It took many hours to reach the foot of the South Summit (28,300'). Further progress became extremely difficult and hazardous. The climbers were forced to retreat when they were less than 700' from their goal.

We were convinced that now nothing but the highest prize in mountaineering would suffice for the country. The second expedition to Everest in 1962 was also beaten back, again due to impossible weather conditions, when the summit team was only 400' short of the peak. The experience proved that the stumbling block was not will or capacity but weather. Next time, luck must turn. But the earliest booking available was 1965. We could not afford to fail again. Accordingly, intensive preparations were made. The best of our mountaineers were selected. They were given special training and helped to acquire that extra degree of toughness and insight that brings the highest achievement.

Wireless communications were organised from Delhi to Kathmandu, to the Base Camp, and on the basis of line of sight, to the Last Camp. Weather data were collected twice a day by the expedition at the Base Camp and the Last Camp reached and sent back over the wireless to Delhi. A special cell made the necessary "interpolations" and prepared the forecasts which were broadcast twice a day and they proved to be extremely reliable.

This time it was victory. Not one but four teams reached the peak on May 20, May 22, May 24 and May 29. The mountain presented all its hazards, but the climbers were sure of the weather—and of themselves. Never before had four successive parties triumphantly attained such an objective. Of the twenty climbers who had reached the peak by 1965, nine were Indians and one of them had done it twice. Sonam Gyatso at forty-two and Wangyal at twenty-three were the oldest and the youngest that had so far reached the top. We had taken a wireless set up to the Ridge Camp at 28,000′.

The achievement stirred the country. Mountaineering received a tremendous boost both from the Government and from the people. From one or two expeditions a year to peaks of about 20,000′ and above, the number of Indian expeditions to high peaks rose to fourteen or fifteen within five years and has now reached the annual total of thirty-five to forty. Many difficult virgin peaks have been climbed, including Nilkantha, Hathi Parbat, Shivling, Changabang, Sakang, and Saser Kangri. Kanchenjunga has been climbed by the more hazardous East Ridge for the first time. Everest, which has provided the motive and inspiration, has come to have a very special place in our hearts.

For nearly seven decades after the discovery that it was the highest mountain, Everest remained closed though there were surreptitious attempts at reconnaissance of its approaches. The saga of Everest in the twenties brings to mind legendary names like Howard Bury, Mallory, Irvine, Bruce, Norton, Somerville, Finch and Odell, while the heroes of the thirties include famous mountaineers like Hugh Ruttledge, Frank Smythe, Eric Shipton, and Tilman.

Of all the attempts on Everest, the pre-monsoon one by the Swiss in 1952 needs mention not only for breaking the trail from the South Ridge but also for very nearly making it to the top. Given better oxygen equipment and reasonable weather, Lambert and Tenzing would have stolen a march on the British. The very next year came the British Expedition in which Hillary and Tenzing reached the peak and became the world's first Everesters. It was in the fitness of things that a British expedition should have been the first to succeed. From 1921 British mountaineers had returned relentlessly again and again, suffering setbacks and casualties, but never giving up, never accepting defeat.

There are scores of books written on Everest. Here is another one but it is different. It does not tell the author's story but the story of the others, not of one or two successes or failures but of all the successes and failures. Beginning with an account of the Survey of India's explorations of the Everest region from 1849 to 1855, it gives an up-to-date account of every expedition including the little known Chinese attempts. The book makes a valuable contribution with its weather forecast charts prepared by taking the mean meteorological averages for the last 30 years. It presents all the faces and moods of this mountain in all its majesty, nobility and ruthlessness.

xvi   The author, Major Ahluwalia, belongs to that band of select men who have had the privilege of communion with Chomolungma. Like his other Indian comrades, he approached the mountain with humility and a spirit of devotion and reverence. On the summit he left a picture of Guru Nanak, a rosary, and a personal offering of his own watch.

Within a few months of his return from Everest, Ahluwalia became a casualty in the military operations in Kashmir. A sniper's bullet paralysed him and almost shattered his life. He was promptly evacuated by helicopter and then rushed by a special plane to Delhi. His life hung by a thin thread for several weeks. I saw him arrive and visited him often as he lay in bed for many long months. I watched his parents and many friends immersed in silent prayer. It was his internal strength, his indomitable courage, his fighting spirit and his strong will to live that saw him through the grave crisis. When he emerged half paralysed, and was at Stoke Mandeville Hospital for rehabilitation, the famous Dr. J. J. Walsh who looked after the handicapped from all over the world, told me that in his long years at the hospital rarely had he seen a man endowed with so much courage and will power. Maj Ahluwalia is a recipient of the Government of India's Arjuna Award and Argentine's Condoro-de-Oro. He is a member of the All India Council of Sports and the Indian Mountaineering Foundation and President of the Delhi Mountaineering Association. His book *Higher Than Everest* has run into four editions and has been translated into many languages. His other publications are *Climbing Everest*, *Trisul Ski Expedition* and *Hermit Kingdom*.

I can think of no better person for writing *Faces of Everest*. It is the result of nearly five years, painstaking research, perseverance, and single-minded labour. I am sure that this encyclopaedic book will be of interest to every mountain lover and of special value to those who want to know about the challenges of Everest.

H.C. Sarin
PRESIDENT
INDIAN MOUNTAINEERING FOUNDATION

*Treating alike pleasure and pain, gain
and loss, victory and defeat*
—Bhagvad Gita.

Introduction

I have had the unique privilege of participating in three Everest Expeditions—all Indian—in 1960, 1962, and 1965—as a member, as Deputy Leader, and as Leader. In 1962, along with two colleagues—the late Sonam and Hari Dang, I missed the summit by 100 m. and had to spend three nights at a height of 27,650′—two nights without oxygen. In 1965 the weather gods were kind and we had unprecedented success, putting on the summit nine climbers in four parties, including Major Ahluwalia. I have seen Everest in various moods, furious in bad weather and strong winds, and smiling in calm and sunny periods. But each trip up the mountain presented a fresh and new challenge.

Everest demands extreme physical stamina, top technical skill, indomitable courage and perhaps in a much greater measure mental endurance because of several months of privation and hardships. Also indispensable for success is good luck with weather.

Anyone who challenges Everest undergoes a great spiritual transformation. In the struggle to reach the highest peak in the world one conquers oneself. During the process of reaching greater heights one gradually sheds petty involvements and a materialistic outlook, and when one reaches the highest point on the earth a metamorphosis takes place in the climber, changing him for life.

The saga of Everest has been told in several books, and every year new volumes are added to the already growing literature on the subject. But Major Ahluwalia's book makes a special contribution. In one volume he has included all that is important about Everest.

It is a creditable effort, for the job could not have been an easy one. Major Ahluwalia has taken great pains to contact leaders of expeditions all over the world, including the Chinese. He also took a trip to Dehra Dun and dug into the archives of the Survey of India to reach the inside story of early accounts of Everest.

Why was Lord Hunt chosen as the leader of the 1953 British expedition when Eric Shipton was more experienced? Why did Mallory choose Irvine as his summit partner when Odell was much more experienced? Among the unauthorised entries into Tibet is also included Eric Shipton's party of 1952 which included Hillary. Is it true that the Chinese, after the 1960 expedition, carved a route on a half-ton jade piece in China for purposes of publicity? Major Ahluwalia has brought to light these and other facts.

Major Ahluwalia was one of the younger members of our expedition to Mount Everest in 1965. He was full of enthusiasm, and possessed unusual will power and indomitable courage. He finally succeeded in reaching the summit in the last party. His success came in the wake of an avalanche which had run down the slopes of Lhotse burying precious bottles of oxygen in camp III. I cannot forget the grim struggle that he undertook in reaching camp III from the Advanced Base Camp with the help of the available sherpas and recovering the oxygen bottles which we had all given up for lost.

As Fate would have it, only four months after his remarkable feat to the roof top of the world, he became paralysed.

But rising above his personal trauma, he has emerged as a missionary to promote and spread mountaineering. In 1971, he took over from me the reins of the Delhi Mountaineering Association when I left for Bombay to take up my assignment with Air India. He has since provided competent and inspiring leadership to the Association. Of the books he has written subsequently *Higher Than Everest* has proved a best seller among mountaineering books in India, and has been translated into other languages. *Faces of Everest* will be welcomed by libraries all over the world and will be read with interest by mountaineers and mountain lovers.

Captain M. S. Kohli
Leader, 1965 Indian
Everest Expedition

Memories of Everest

Tenzing and I stepped on the summit of Everest on May 29th 1953. I felt no great surge of joy and exaltation—only a mixture of more subdued feelings. There was a quiet satisfaction that we had finally made it; a tinge of surprise that I, Ed Hillary, should be standing here on top when so many good men had failed. Behind it all my brain constantly churned out its familiar mental arithmetic—how many litres of oxygen did we have left? Could we get down safely?

Back on the South Col, it was good to be able to tell my close friend George Lowe our news of success. The South Col is no place for wild enthusiasm. "Thought you probably had," he told me quietly "have a cup of soup." Next day we wearily descended the Lhotse face to the Western Cwm and in one of the few emotional moments we were able to confirm to John Hunt that his expedition had been successful. But I still found it difficult to take the matter very seriously. Perhaps I was just tired—we'd done the job, now we should rest.

We came down the Western Cwm and the ice fall and there was small pleasure in it, but the security of Base Camp was very pleasant, even though the tents and surroundings had become very sordid after a couple of months of occupation. It was now 2 June—four days after the ascent—and someone idly tuned the radio to the BBC in London. The news was being read in ponderous tones and I suddenly realised that the man was talking about us. For the first time a shock of excitement went through me. "My God!" I thought, "we've climbed Everest!"

The period after Everest was an exciting time for all of us with much talking, many functions, and a great deal of socialising. But I soon tire of such things. I have never enjoyed dwelling on the past and I have proved somewhat reluctant to even attend reunions of any sort. As the years went by I was almost continuously involved in one expedition after another and they all tended to blend together in a whole experience.

Intellectually I could recall the success on Everest and know how important a part it had played in my life—but there was little emotion about it. There had been so many other adventures, so many other friendships. Certainly the gods had smiled on me in 1953 and I was thankful for that but it was now just history. It was the turn of other mountaineers to get their excitement and fulfilment on Everest. I gain my challenges on other mountains, on the Antarctic continent, on rivers, and in working for the welfare of the people of the Himalayas. Everest has moulded my life, but that was a quarter of a century ago . . . and there is much to do in the present.

Sir Edmund Hillary

Preface

[signature]

Photography has been my favourite hobby since childhood and it was my interest in photography which first took me to the mountains. To capture their grandeur and majesty in pictures is, I think, an apt expression of one's love for the hills.

The story of this book began a few years ago when I visited the Survey of India Office, Dehra Dun, and studied some old, absorbing, and little known accounts of the discovery and naming of Everest. After this preliminary study I carried out further research to select relevant and essential material and present it to the reader in a brief and interesting narrative. As the years roll by, people are likely to forget the great Everest adventure and the many heroic expeditions which preceded and followed the first ascent of the mountain. It has been my endeavour to bring the history of these expeditions up-to-date and preserve it for future generations.

Faces of Everest vividly portrays the highlights of the Everest drama and gives up-to-date information about each expedition. I am grateful to a number of individuals and organisations for their assistance in the production of this book. Besides those mentioned in "Acknowledgements" I would like to express my special gratitude to Norman Dyhren-furth, Brigadier Gyan Singh, and Chris Bonington who provided valuable material relating to their expeditions. I would also like to thank Lord John Hunt for allowing me to quote a passage from his foreword to the book, *Everest the Hard Way*. I am indebted to H.C. Sarin for his foreword and to Capt. Mohan S. Kohli for his preface to the book. My sincere thanks are also due to Sir Edmund Hillary for his poignant note.

Harbans Lal Tandon gave me much useful help in tabulating data for the book and keeping my records in order. I am grateful to K. B. Malla, Ambassador, Royal Nepalese Embassy for providing me with the latest information on the booking and tarrif rates for Mount Everest. Finally, I must thank Chris Briggs of North Wales for helping me obtain some old and rare photographs of pre-war Everest expeditions.

The photographs used in the book belong to the period around 1850 to 1975 and if some of the reproductions attract the reader's notice to their age, I hope the reader will understand.

The story of Everest as I have endeavoured to relate here is not complete. It goes on and on and as the time passes the roll of honour of those whom the mountain permits to set foot on its peak will continue to increase and so will the roll of those who are left buried on the shoulders of Everest.

Major H.P.S. Ahluwalia

Facing: Tenzing on the Summit
29 May 1953

1

The Discovery of Mount Everest

Few people are aware of how the world's highest and most famous mountain got its name. It was during 1849 to 1855 that the Himalayan peaks in Nepal were first surveyed by the Survey of India. No one imagined that one of the peaks surveyed was the tallest in the world. Mount Everest was not prominently visible as it was hidden by a lower peak which lay in front of it. At that time Kanchenjunga was considered the highest mountain in the world. Since most of the peaks observed by the surveyors did not have any local names, Roman numerals were allotted to them. Mount Everest and Gauri Shankar were given the numerals XV and XX respectively.

The methods of computing the heights of mountain peaks were not sufficiently advanced in the mid-nineteenth century. As a matter of fact, altitudes were not calculated with any degree of accuracy till much later. The question of atmospheric refraction was being investigated by scientists and that played an important part in the calculation of altitudes. When the results of the calculation were finally announced at the end of 1855, it became known that peak XV was 29,002' above sea level (sometimes the height was also mentioned as 29,141' but was never accepted). It was then officially announced by the Surveyor General that it was the highest peak of the world. The calculation of the height was accepted as scientifically accurate at that time.

The peak is situated on the Nepal-Tibet border at latitude 27° 59′ 16″ and longitude 86° 55′ 40″. The mountain range at this highest point is formed of sedimentary calcareous and metamorphosed sandstone. The final pyramid composed of dark calcschist is very compact and dips northwards at 30°. The group is estimated to belong to the Triassic or Jurassic period (20 to 30 million years ago). It has a conspicuous, broad, light-brown band of rock known as the Yellow Band, which extends along the base of the pyramid. Stone

1

pieces brought back from the summit of Mount Everest were analysed and the results have proved beyond doubt that it was once under water. Studies of the Himalayas also reveal that they are still rising due to continuing pressure exerted by the hard crust of the earth from the north and the south. It is for this reason that the Himalayas have grown approximately 2,000 m. during the last 20,000 years. It is observed that the average growth is about a meter for every 10 years. Everest itself has grown taller by about 8 m. during the last 100 years.

After having found the highest mountain in the world a search began for an appropriate name, and the matter was debated for nearly ten years. During this period the Surveyor General considered all the local names which could possibly be used. Many names were suggested but they were all rejected. Col. Andrew Waugh, the then Surveyor General of India (in consultation with his deputy, Col. Henry Thullier and Radhanath Sikhdar, Chief Computer), decided to name the peak after his predecessor, Sir George Everest, who had contributed a lot to the Geodetic Survey of India. He was the dominant figure of the great trignometrical survey and believed in great accuracy. The name was accepted by the Royal Geographical Society of Britain. Col. Andrew Waugh wrote to Col. Henry Thullier, Dy. Surveyor General in March 1856:

> I was taught by my respected chief and predecessor, Col. George Everest, to assign to every geographical object its true local or national appellation.... But here is a mountain, most probably the highest in the world, without any local name that we can discover, whose native appellation, if it has any, will not very likely be ascertained before we are allowed to penetrate into Nepal, and to approach close to this stupendous snowy mass.
>
> In the meantime, the privilege, as well as the duty, devolves on me to assign to this lofty pinnacle ... a name whereby it may be known among geographers, and become a household word. In testimony of my affectionate respect for a revered chief, in conformity with what I believe to be the wish of all the members of the scientific department over which I had the honour to preside, and to perpetuate the memory of that illustrious master of accurate geographical research ... I have determined to name this noble peak ... Mount Everest.

The appellation *mount* was chosen by Waugh for a single definite peak and not a massif. *Everest* was changed to *Mount Everest* a year later. However, the naming of the highest mountain did not go unchallenged. Brian Hodgson, formerly a political officer in Nepal and an able linguist and scientist, claimed that the "newly found" peak was none other than *Devadhunga* or *Bhairathan*, names well-known in the ancient literature of Nepal. Waugh spent considerable time investigating these claims and wrote to the Asiatic Society that "the names appear to appertain to some peaks near the Kuti Ghat, but as the position of that Ghat is uncertain ... there is no point of departure for our investigations. The evidence only shows that there is a peak called *Bairoa* or *Deodhanga* considerably to the east of Kathmandu, but there are many peaks. We have nothing on which to have a verification."

Another controversy arose over the name of Gauri Shankar. The German brothers Adolf, Herman, and Robert Von Schlagintweit conducted scientific investigations in Tibet, Sikkim and Central Asia, where Adolf was later murdered in Kashgar. During their stay between 1855 and 1857, they made observations from Sikkim and announced that Everest was called *Gauri Shankar* in Nepal, and *Chingopanari* in Tibet. This caused a great sensation. The Royal Geographical Society in London supported them and dis-

Facing: A typically colourful
Tibetan girl

The wisdom of the age is reflected in this Tibetan's face

A beautiful Nepalese belle

agreed with the Survey of India. Thus the name *Gauri Shankar* came to be adopted in maps as the highest mountain in the world till as late as 1900. Later, their sketches and observations were closely scrutinized by the Survey of India and it was discovered that the observation stations of the German brothers hid Mount Everest from their view. From Phalut they had seen Makalu and from Kaulia they had seen Gauri Shankar. Mount Everest appeared very small from their observation post as compared to these two mountains and remained unnoticed.

The legend of Gauri Shankar and the name persisted for about half a century. It was only in 1903 that Capt. Wood entered Nepal and made observations from two stations and established that Mount Everest and Gauri Shankar were two different peaks, 36 miles apart. The explorations carried out between 1906 and 1908 in Tibet by Sir Sven Hedin and the subsequent publication of his work brought out many interesting facts. He wrote:

I do not wish to rob the English surveyors of their discovery in 1852, but I feel compelled to bring to light the true facts of the forgotten part. In 1921 the Mount Everest expedition under Col. Howard-Bury found that the Tibetans have the name Tchomo Lungma for Mount Everest, and the official instructions from Lhasa to the local district Tibetans informed the latter that the English expedition wished to visit their mountain Tcha-mo-lung-ma. Now this correct Tibetan name Tchomo Lungma appears as Tchoumou Lancma on maps which were prepared from native information by French Jesuits in Peking in 1717, and these maps were printed by D'Anville in Paris in 1733. If the resemblance between the new name Tchomo Lungma and the old name Tchoumou Lancma is held to be merely an accidental similarity in sound, I must then draw attention to the agreement in the geographical position of the name between the latest English maps and the old French maps. On modern maps the latitude of Mount Everest is 27° 59' and on D'Anville's map the latitude of Tch mou Lancma is 27° 20', the modern longitude east of Ferro, 104° 55' and D'Anville's longitude was 103° 50'. This is surprisingly accurate when one remembers that the Peking calculations were made at the beginning of the 18th century.

Commenting on his observations, Sir Sidney Burrard of the Survey of India wrote:

The evidence produced by Sven Hedin to prove the identity of D'Anville's range of mountains Tchoumou Lancma with the Mount Everest of modern geography is certainly very interesting, his investigation has earned our gratitude. But as in some ways his outlook is different from my own, I am venturing with all respect to analyse his conclusions. The two main conclusions which Sven Hedin reached in his books are: (i) The highest peak in the world, which the English claim to have discovered in 1852 was shown on French maps 119 years previously. (ii) The real Tibetan name of Mount Everest, namely Tchomo Lungma, which the English did not succeed in finding until the 20th century, was known to the Jesuits in Peking 190 years before.

These conclusions should be impartially considered; the highest peak of the earth is beyond the reach of nationalism. In his review of Sir Sven Hedin's book, Sir Burrard wrote:

The interest that now attaches to Mount Everest is due only to its great height. The Lamas and Jesuit Fathers discovered that the whole of this region was mountainous, and that it abounded in ranges and peaks, but their maps show that they were unaware that any mountain of exceptional height was standing here. In fact they knew no more about Mount Everest than the Tibetans themselves knew. Nothing was known about

5

Mount Everest, until it was observed by a theodolite from the plains of India in 1849. Until that observation was made, the world was ignorant that their highest mountain was standing here.

The question then arises, who discovered Mount Everest? A popular story which, unfortunately, has gained ground and appears in many books on Everest is that the Chief Computer, Radhanath Sikhdar, rushed into the room of the Surveyor General's office breathlessly exclaiming, "Sir, I have discovered the highest mountain in the world." Burrard in his book has effectively contradicted this version and proved that the above words could not have been uttered then.

While working on this book, I visited the Survey of India office in Dehra Dun and for several days went through all the available files and records on Everest, through the kind courtesy of Col. Dalal, the then Deputy Surveyor General. I am fully convinced from the facts available that the Chief Computer, Radhanath Sikhdar, was at that time in the Calcutta office of the Survey of India. He was posted in 1849 and continued there and had no hand in the computation of the height of Everest. Radhanath Sikhdar, a very able computer, worked under Sir George Everest and was highly praised by him. He joined the Survey of India on a salary of Rs 30 a month and rose to be the Chief Computer, which was a great achievement.

In 1950, immediately after the Independence of India, a great controversy started and at one stage pressure was brought on the then Prime Minister by Bengal that Mount Everest should be renamed Mount Sikhdar as it was stated then that Sikhdar's contribution to the discovery of the highest mountain was much more than that of Sir George Everest. This question also came up for discussion in the Indian Parliament but did not yield any fruitful results. Firstly, Sikhdar had no hand in the computation of the readings of Everest, and moreover, a computer is not the real discoverer. It is only a surveyor making observations in the area who can justifiably be called the real discoverer. According to the records available with the Survey of India: "Mr. Hennessey was engaged on all the computations for determining the positions and heights of the principal peaks of the Himalayan range including Mount Everest. He saw Mount Everest when he was engaged on the North East longitudinal series. Mr. Armstrong is one of the gentlemen by whom Mount Everest was observed."

During my visits to the Survey of India, Dehra Dun, I did visit the various branches where the calculations were conducted and made my notes perhaps on the same table on which the computation readings were made over a hundred years ago.

Five Tibetan names for Mount Everest were familiar in the region of Everest. They were found to be: Chome Kankar (mentioned by Col. Waddell and Sarat Chandra Das, 1904), Chholungbu (mentioned by Surveyor Natha Singh, 1907), Chomo Lungmo (mentioned by Gen. Bruce, 1909), Chomo Uri (mentioned by Col. Howard-Bury, 1921), and Chomo Lungma (mentioned by Col. Howard-Bury, 1921). *Chomo* is a Tibetan word corresponding to the Sanskrit word *Gauri* which means goddess. Everest is known as *Chomolungma* by the Tibetans and *Sagarmatha* by the Nepalese today. The official name used by the Tibetan authorities in Lhasa for Mount Everest was Tcha-mo-Lungma. Sir George Bell, the British representative at Lhasa, who received the first passport in the form of permission for the first Mount Everest expedition wrote:

When the Dalai Lama gave me the permission for the Mount Everest expedition to take place, a week or two after I had reached Lhasa, he handed me a paper on which was written in Tibetan, 'To the west of the five treasuries of Great Snow (in the juris-

The HIMALAYAN area embraced by the arms of the RIVER KOSI

1. As represented on D'Anville's map, 1733

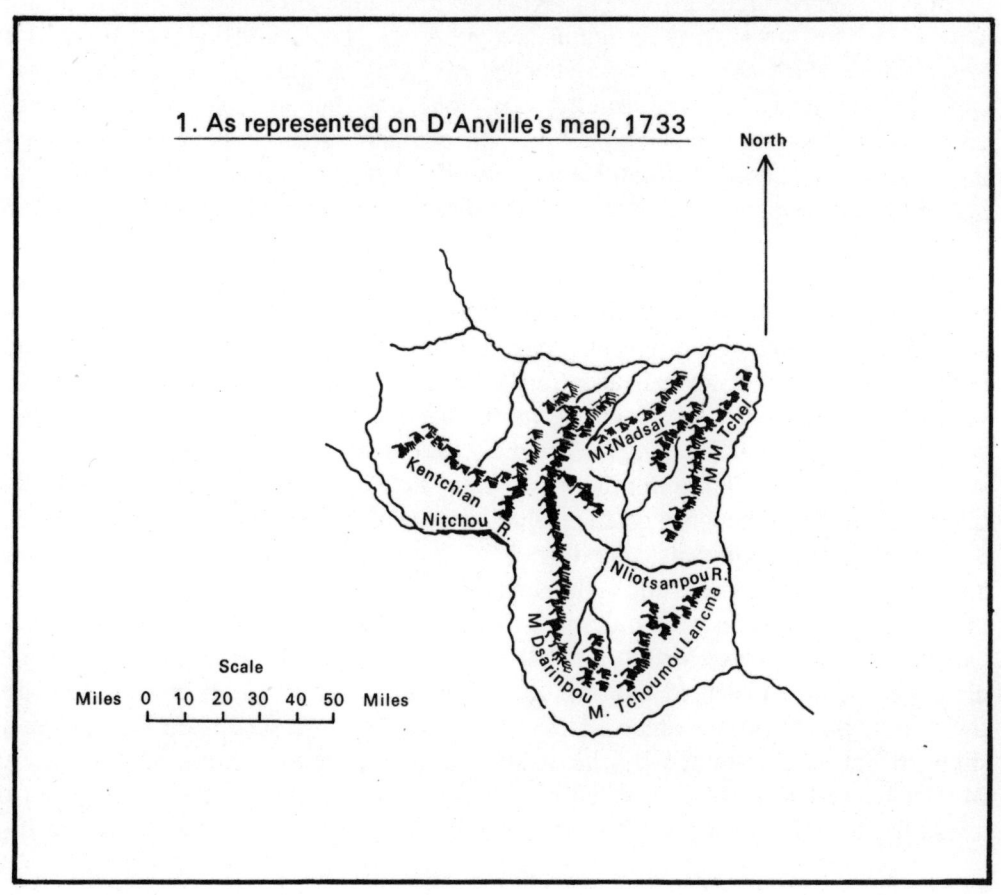

2. As represented by the Survey of India, 1926

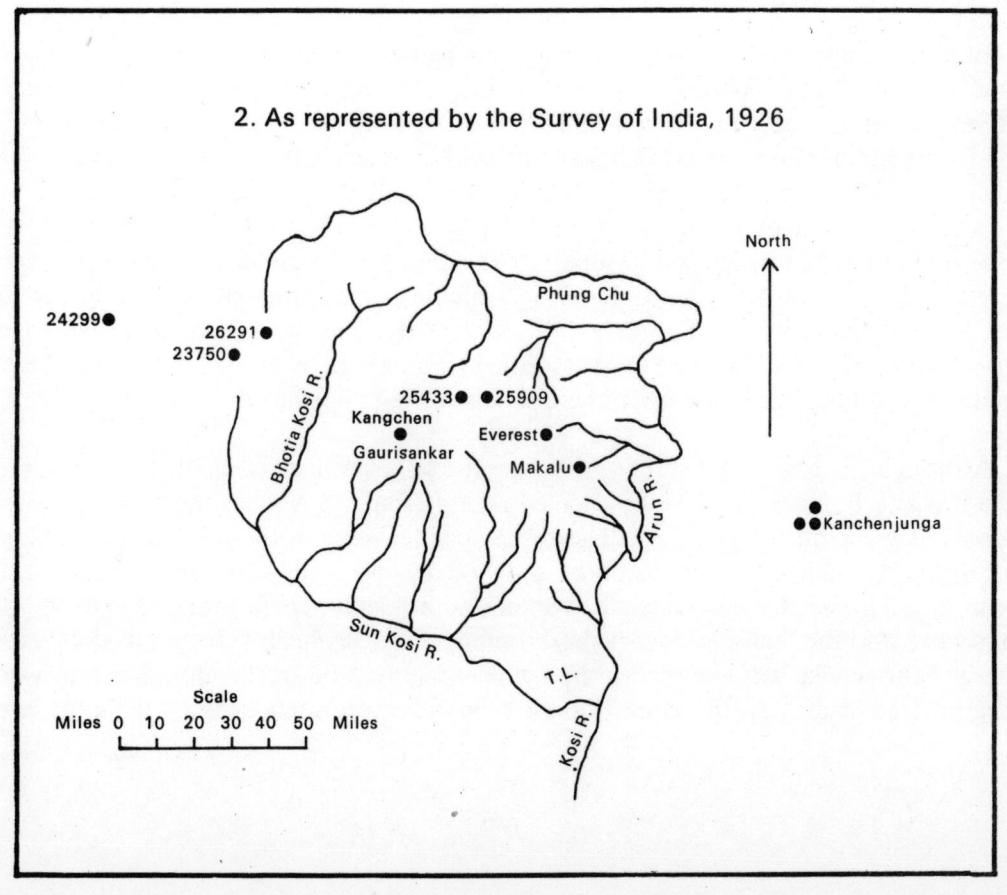

diction of 'White Glass Fort' near 'Rocky Valley inner monastery') is the Southern District where birds are kept (*Lho-Cha-ma-lung*) [*Lho*-south]'. Later on in Lhasa one of the Dalai Lama's secretaries who was in attendance on my party, a man of exceptional knowledge and intelligence, told me that Cha-ma-lung is short for *Cha-Dzi-ma-lung-pa*, which means 'the district where birds are kept'. He told me that in the time of the early Tibetan kings, 650 to 800 A.D. a large number of birds were fed in this district at the expense of the king. Now *lung* in *Cha-ma-lung* means a district that has a valley or valleys in it, and it often means just a valley. It cannot be applied to a mountain summit, nor would a bird sanctuary be on the top of a mountain. In fact *Cha-ma-lung*, which is a common contraction from *Cha-Dzi-ma-lung-pa* cannot be the name of a mountain. Nor did the Dalai Lama or his Secretary use the name in that sense. I never heard *Chomo-lung* or *Chomo-Lungma*. People would be very likely to change *Cha-mo* into *Cho-mo,* for the latter occurs in mountain names such as *Cho-mo Lha-ri* or *Chomo Kangkar. Cho* means Lord amongst gods and *Cho-mo* is the corresponding feminine gender. In the Dalai Lama's paper, it was clearly *Cha* and not *Cho.* The maps on the previous page of Mount Everest were prepared by Sir Sidney Burrard. One was copied from a Lama's survey and the other from a modern map. In comparison, the Lama's map has many errors; the position of the sacred peak of Kailash was in error by 85 miles in latitude. Sir Burrard observed that such an error can sufficiently displace Mount Everest from the crest of the Himalayas to the plains of India. He also observed that the Lama's map followed the rivers and laid down their courses; the modern map shows the same rivers. The maps do agree closely in shape which is determined by the sources of rivers. It can safely be assumed that Mount Everest was not discovered by any individual observer or computer but that it was the combined effort of the two and the credit should go to the Survey of India.

SIR GEORGE EVEREST

Born on 4 July 1790 in Greenwich, England, he was the second son, and his father was a solicitor to both Greenwich and Chelsea Hospitals. George Everest had a brilliant academic career and it was in 1806 that he came to India in the service of East India Company. He later joined Bengal artillery. Few years later he went to Java to make the survey of the island for the Governor, Sir Stamford Raffles. He returned to India in 1818 and began his work in the Survey of India. After working in India for a few years he left for England for a brief period to supervise the design and purchase of new instruments. On returning to India he was employed in Calcutta organising the workshop for field units. In 1830 he became the Surveyor General of India and conducted the grand trignometrical survey. In 1832, he came to Mussoorie bringing a great arc 500m from the Central Himalayas and bought a house which became his summer headquarters for the succeeding ten years.

Although his main interest lay in the great arc, he was responsible for the surveys of Madras and Bombay. In 1834, he selected Dehra Dun and Agra as the base line to start his detailed work on the great arc. The same year he went to the hills of Kedar Kanta and Chour. He made observations of the snow peaks and made sketches of their profiles. He continued his work even during the winter and hot summers in India. Due to the strenuous work and the long journeys he had to undertake, his health started to deteriorate. Once in February he was confined to bed with inflammation in the hip joint which crippled him. He wrote: "To the astonishment of my medical attendants ...after the appli-

Sir George Everest

Karma Valley

Everest South East Peak

Mount Everest (actual summit invisible)

MOUNT EVEREST, NORTH O

Ph

First phot

North Col

North Peak

NORTH PEAK, FROM HLAKPA LA

Wheeler

erest from North

A.S. Waugh, I.T. Walker and Henry Thullier

Maj. E.O. Wheeler

Everest Arc Theodolite

cation of some hundreds of leeches, fomentations administered night and day for several days in succession, a due abstraction of blood from cupping and a course of gruel, did I begin to recover the use of the limb, and by the end of February was again able to walk about."

George Everest became fellow of the Royal Society which paid rich tributes to him remembering the "journeys through vast and magnificent forest where, more to be dreaded than tiger or hyena, lurked the deadly typhus which prostrated him and his whole following . . . . For months he was so weak that he had to be supported by two men while taking his observations at the great theodolite, and could not reach out his hand to the screw of the vertical circle without assistance . . . . The chief was so indefatigable that his contemporaries spoke of him as Neverest." George Everest was promoted to the rank of Lt. Colonel in 1838 and his salary rose from Rs 1,700 to Rs 2,000.

Everest once refused to cross into Gwalior without due ceremony. He wrote angry letters to the Resident who refused to interfere. He then broke all rules and wrote directly to the Darbar for which he was severely reprimanded by the Supreme Government. In 1843, he handed over the charge of Surveyor General of India to Waugh who had joined him to work on the Great Arc in 1836. He returned to England in 1844 where he started the second Great Arc work which was published in 1847.

Immediately after returning to England he married Emma, daughter of Thomas Wind. They had six children but unfortunately none of the Everests' descendants survived. Everest was offered Knighthood on his retirement but he refused. He was again offered the Knighthood in 1861 which he accepted perhaps on persuasion by his friends. Among his other publications were "Instruments and Observations for Longitude for Travellers on Land" published in 1859. He died in 1866.

SKETCH-MAP OF MOUNT EVEREST AND THE RONGBUK GLACIERS.

From surveys by Major Wheeler, with Route and Camps of the 1922 Expedition added by
Colonel Strutt.

2
Reconnaissance and Early Attempts

Everest is like a pyramid with the South, the North West, and the North East Ridges as its great faces. During the years preceding World War II, all the expeditions went by way of the North-East Ridge which descends from the summit to the North Col and rises again to join the North peak. It was only in 1893 that Gen. Bruce (then Captain) and Sir Francis Younghusband suggested that an expedition should be sent to Mount Everest but the plans did not materialise. British authorities then were not able to persuade either the Tibetan authorities or the Nepalese Government to allow mountaineers to enter their territories. In 1905, Lord Curzon, as the Viceroy of India, tried his best to gain entry into Tibet but did not succeed. In 1913, a young Indian Army Captain, J. B. L. Noel, entered Tibet in disguise and went to within a short distance of Everest. In March 1919, he read a paper before the Royal Geographical Society describing his journey and also made the suggestion that a fully-equipped expedition be sent for surveying the Everest region. This was promptly accepted by the Royal Geographical Society and the Alpine Club.

Towards the end of December 1920, Sir Charles Bell, who was in Lhasa on a special mission, succeeded in obtaining the consent of the Tibetan Government to the entry of an expedition to Mount Everest. Preparations were at once undertaken to organise such an expedition. Lt. Col. Howard Burry was chosen the leader. The party consisted of mountaineers, a surgeon, and some members of the Survey detachment party of Survey of India. It was a full scale reconnaissance party with no intentions of attempting the peak. Their main object was merely to explore the area with a view to finding a possible route to the summit and to conduct a full survey of the region. The expedition was sponsored by the Royal Geographical Society and the Alpine Club who joined forces to form the Mount

Everest Committee. The team included H. Raeburn, Dr. A. M. Kellas, G. L. Mallory, G. H. Bullock, and Dr. A. F. R. Wollaston. The Survey Detachment comprised: Maj. H. T. Morshead, Maj. E. O. Wheeler, Surveyor Lalbir Singh, Surveyor Gujjar Singh, Surveyor Torabaz Khan, photographer Abdul Jalil, and Dr. A. M. Heron, geologist.

The expedition of 11 members and 16 Khalasis and menials left Darjeeling on 13 May 1921. For transport they had a hundred mules. The expedition had a setback in the death of Dr. Kellas and the forced return of another member who fell ill. The party halted at Shekar, a small town situated 5 miles north of Phung Chu, on the edge of the levelled plane of barley fields. The town derives its name from the monastery, Shekar Chote, situated at the top of a rocky hill. The monastery has its white walls ranged one upon the other, making it a fine piece of architecture. In full moonlight, the white walls of the monastery glowed as though transparent and lighted from within, a beautiful sight in the wilderness which was all the more impressive when the lamas joined in prayers with their long pipes and great drums.

The expedition, after passing Pong Valley, reached a village called Tilangli which was its headquarters for the next six weeks. They completed reconnaissance of the area to the north-east and north-west approaches to Everest. The weather during this period remained inclement and it was with great difficulty that outdoor work could be done. Mallory and Bullock carried out a reconnaissance in the Karta valley and Major Wheeler in the Rongbuk valley. When the weather improved, the advance base camp was set up in the Karta valley. Camp I was established at a height of 20,000'. The expedition pushed forward setting up camp II at 22,200' at the head of the Karta glacier.

Mallory made a very significant contribution and was soon to become one of the most

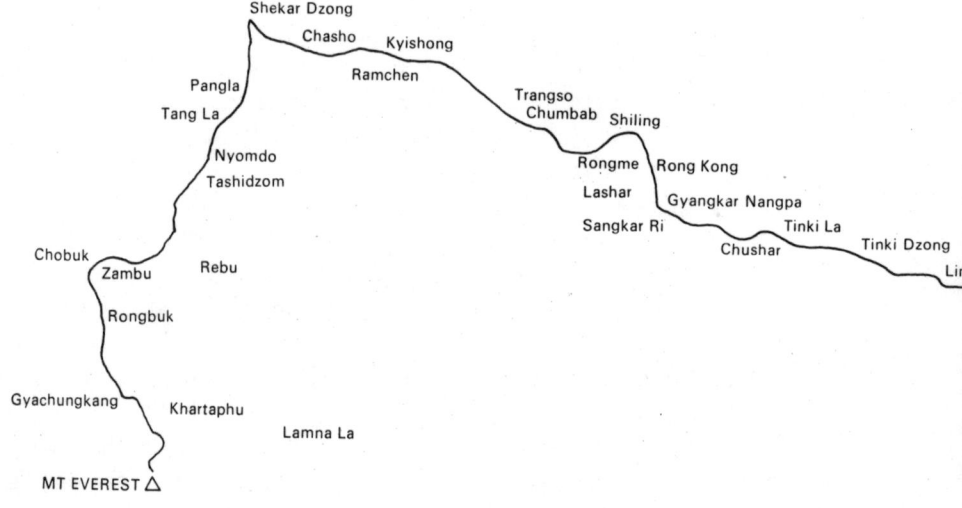

famous of Everesters. He had climbed, on this expedition, to a high pass called Lho La, from where he looked across into the valley that was later to become the Western Cwm from which all the post-war expeditions were to pass. The word "cwm," a Welsh word, was perhaps given by him as he was a frequent climber in Wales. Mallory and his companion reached a height of 23,000′ on the North Col. Above this were the rocks of the North-East ridge, which they presumed were negotiable, but they were not equipped at that stage to negotiate them. The weather deteriorated and there were very high winds. A number of members became victims of high altitude effects and the party left the mountains reaching Darjeeling on 16th October. This expedition had done a lot of work in the field of mountaineering and in the survey of the area. Mallory in the book *Men against Everest* wrote:

> In all it may be said that one factor beyond all others is required for success. Too many chances are against the climbers, too many contingencies may turn against them. Anything like a breakdown of the transport will be fatal; soft snow on the mountain will be an impregnable defence; a big wind will send back the strongest; even so small a matter as a boot fitting a shade too tight may endanger one man's foot and involve the whole party in retreat.
>
> The climbers must have above all things, if they are to win through, good fortune, and the greatest good fortune of all for mountaineers, some constant spirit of kindness in Mount Everest itself, the forgetfulness for long enough of its more cruel moods, for we must remember that the highest of mountains is capable of severity, a severity so awful and so fatal that the wiser sort of men do well to think and tremble even on the threshold of their high endeavour.

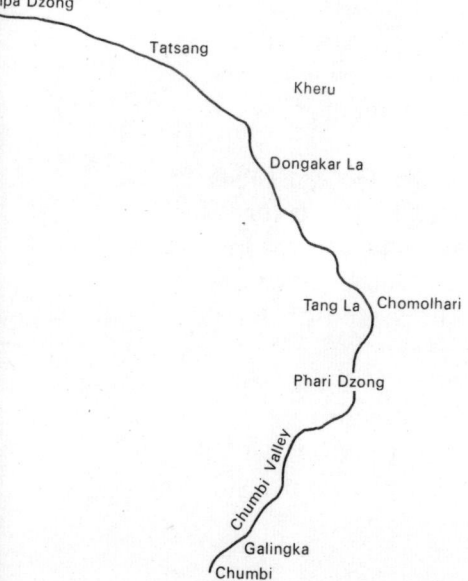

1922 EXPEDITION

The year 1922 should be considered a milestone in the history of Mount Everest, as it was in this year that the first full-scale expedition was sponsored by the British to attempt the peak. The expedition was led by 56 year old Brigadier-General Charles Bruce. It included Mallory, Maj. Morshead, Col. E. T. Strutt, Lt. Col. E. F. Norton, Dr. T. Howard Somervell, Capt. Geoffrey Bruce (cousin of the Brigadier), Capt. George Finch and Capt. John Noel. This team of thirteen Englishmen, 16 Nepalese, 100 Tibetan porters, and over 300 animals left Darjeeling in late March, on a 250 mile journey to the mountain base. Brigadier-General Bruce in his book *The Assault of Mount Everest*, 1922, wrote:

> The object of the expedition of 1922, of course, was the actual attack on the mountain in an attempt to climb it; but no great mountain has ever succumbed to the first attempt on it, and therefore it is almost inconceivable that so tremendous a problem as the ascent of Mount Everest should succeed at the very first effort.

The expedition followed almost the same route as the previous expedition of 1921, except that, instead of going to Tingri from Shekar, they went to Rongbuk which was a four days' march. They set up base camp on the Rongbuk glacier at a height of 16,000' adjacent to the Rongbuk monastery. Rongbuk, the highest monastery in the world, has a shrine dedicated to Everest and the Lamas offer their prayers to the Goddess mother of the earth. Rongbuk means, "the valley of precipices or steep revines." The Rongbuk valley is extremely sacred and no animal is allowed to be slaughtered.

The expedition approached the mountain *via* the East Rongbuk glacier and the North Col. On 10 May Mallory and Somervell, who were the strongest climbers in the party, set out from the base camp and reached North Col after a difficult climb of three days. A camp at North Col was set up with four tents at a height of 23,000'. It was on this expedition that oxygen was first used. From 23,000', the members of the assault party— Maj. Morshead, Mallory, Somervell, and Norton—climbed along the shoulder of the North East ridge and reached a height of 25,000' where they pitched their camp. The weather deteriorated and it became very windy. There was heavy snowfall at night.

The summit party, in spite of all the hazards and restless night, set out for the summit next morning. Maj. Morshead had to drop out as he was unwell, while the others conti-nued climbing. The three summiters, after having reached a height of 27,000', found the weather most unfavourable and they decided to return. Their decision to return was also due to the fact that Morshead was all alone in the camp and they were worried that he may not survive the night if left alone. On reaching the North Col they discovered that they had no fuel and so there was no other alternative but to swallow cold liquid to assuage their acute hunger. Under these circumstances, they hastened down to camp III where they discovered that Morshead was suffering from acute frost-bite.

Meanwhile, the second assault party, consisting of Geoffery Bruce, George Finch, and Sherpa Tejbir left for the summit. They pitched their camp at 25,000'. It was for the first time that oxygen was used by a summit party. They were constantly faced by the high winds; wrote Finch: "It was impossible to work in the open for more than three or four minutes at a stretch, so profound was the exhaustion induced by this brief exposure to the fierce, cold wind."

Around 26,000' Tejbir collapsed and had to be left behind, while Finch and Bruce continued their climb. The oxygen apparatus started giving them trouble and they soon discovered that their oxygen was exhausted. They were now standing at almost 27,000'

18

A renowned Khampa from Tibet

A colourful Nepalese feeding her child

A rich merchant woman, Dolma, from Solo Khumbu

and were terribly exhausted. They struggled on for another 300′ but they knew that they had reached the limit of their physical endurance, but their achievement was noteworthy as they went higher than any man had been. The team, still not satisfied, launched another attempt. The new summit party consisted of Mallory and Somervell, with a support party of 14 high altitude porters. While they were 600′ below camp IV they were struck by an avalanche. Mallory and Somervell had a narrow escape but seven of their porters died on the spot and others had heavy injuries. The expedition was terribly shaken and was called off. Mallory in the book, *Assault on Mount Everest*, 1922, recounted:

> For a second or two, I seemed hardly to be in danger as I went quietly sliding down with the snow. Then the rope at my waist tightened and held me back. A wave of snow came over me and I was buried. I supposed that the matter was settle. However, I called to mind experiences related by other parties; and it had been suggested that the best chance of escape in this situation lay in swimming. I thrust out my arms above my head and actually went through some sort of motions of swimming on my back.
>
> Beneath the surface of the snow, with nothing to inform the sense of the world outside it, I had no impression of speed after the first acceleration—I struggled in the tumbling snow, unconscious of everything else—until, perhaps a few seconds later, I knew the pace was easing up. I felt an increasing pressure about my body. I wondered how tightly I should be squeezed, and then the avalanche came to rest.

1924 EXPEDITION

In 1924, the British undertook another expedition destined to become one of the most famous in mountaineering history. The team included Mallory, Col. Norton, and a number of newcomers. It was in this expedition that Mallory and his companion Andrew Irvine, an Oxford undergraduate and the youngest member of the expedition, left for the summit as the last assault party on 6 June. While Odell was the obvious choice, Mallory chose Irvine as his companion. Irvine was the youngest, the least experienced member of the expedition. He was also suffering from "mountain throat" but he was a genius in fixing mechanical things and it was for this reason that Mallory decided to have him as his companion so that in case of any difficulty with the oxygen apparatus Irvine could fix it. This, to Mallory's mind, was an extremely important factor.

Mallory and Irvine reached camp V with great difficulty and sent back a note through their porters saying that there were no winds and things looked hopeful. On 7 June, the climbers left for camp VI with Odell staying back at camp V. Everything was perfect that day. They reached camp VI safely, slept very well, and were up at six in the morning. The weather was good except that mist had started forming. Odell wrote: "In a sudden clearing of the atmosphere above me I saw the whole summit ridge and finally the peak of Everest unveiled . . . they were moving one at a time over what was apparently moderately difficult ground."

While they were climbing well around 28,000′ on the ridge of the summit they suddenly disappeared in the mist and never re-appeared. Odell along with the other members made a thorough search for a couple of days, but there was no sign of Mallory and Irvine. They searched the entire area and were utterly disappointed. Odell, all by himself, went above camp VI to search for Mallory and Irvine. In the book *Fight for Everest,* 1924, Odell wrote:

*Rongbuk monastery
and Mount Everest*

*ory and Norton approaching
their highest point, 1922*

This upper part of Everest must be indeed the remotest and least hospitable spot on earth, but at no time more emphatically and impressively so than when a darkened atmosphere hides its features and a gale races over its cruel face. And how and when more cruel could it ever seem than when balking one's every step to find one's friends? After struggling on for nearly a couple of hours looking in vain for some indication or clue, I realized that the chances of finding the missing ones were indeed small on such a vast expanse of crags and broken slabs, and that for any more extensive search towards the final pyramid a further party would have to be organised. At the same time I considered, and still do consider, that wherever misfortune befell them some traces of them would be discovered on or near the ridge of the north east Arete. I saw them on that ridge on the morning of their ascent, and presumably they would descend by it. But in the time available under the prevailing conditions, I found it impossible to extend my search.

Whether they met with disaster after reaching the summit or before, or died on the way up or coming down, are questions which remain unanswered. Odell, however, is of the view that it is due to their being overtaken by night. Even if they had not climbed to the summit, it is not failure by any means; rather it is a failure rich in glory and it is a courageous display of their spirit which will continue to inspire mountaineers.

After this expedition, Tibet was closed to foreigners for nine years and it was only in 1933 that permission was granted for a third British Expedition. The 1933 Expedition was led by a very experienced Alpine and Himalayan climber, Hugh Ruttledge. He had a strong team of 14 climbers, prominent among whom were Frank S. Smythe, Eric Shipton, J. L. Longland, Wyn Harris, Lawrence Wager, and E. Birnie. The expedition left Darjeeling in mid-April and established camp II at 21,000' on the East of Rongbuk glacier. The weather turned bad and the expedition could only establish camp IV. Later there was a brief spell of good weather and the expedition established camp VI on 29 May at a height of 27,400'. This camp was 600' higher than Mallory's camp VI of 1924. The expedition's hopes were frustrated by bad weather, which continued unabated, forcing the expedition to make a hasty withdrawal. On return, they came across some remnants of Mallory and Irvine's camp VI such as a folding candle and lantern and an electric torch which still worked. There was a strong blizzard and the climbers had great difficulty coming down. The expedition also came across an ice-axe which was later identified as Mallory's, lying about 60' below the crest of the ridge. The expedition had to return because of the early break of the monsoons which whipped the mountain with all its fury.

1935 RECONNAISSANCE

Eric Shipton led a small reconnaissance party of seven men to survey the Western side of Everest and the Nyonno Ri range. The party was climbing in mid-July and reached North Col. Shipton decided to continue his climb and to see what the conditions were like up there during the monsoon season, and in case of favourable conditions the party was to attempt the summit. But unfortunately, the bad weather continued and the party had to retreat to camp III and wait there. The conditions never improved. There was a massive avalanche just below the crust of the fall which completely changed the snow conditions. The climbers thought better to continue their explorations on lesser heights and not to endanger the entire party with possible avalanche.

It was on this expedition, some 300 yards above their camp II, that they found a body which was apparently that of Maurice Wilson, who had vanished on this mountain a year

The first summit party

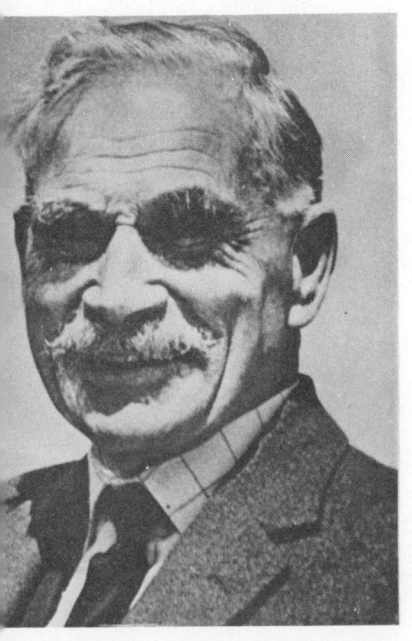

W. H. Tilman

Andrew Irvine

George Leigh Mallory

ago while making a solo attempt on Mount Everest. Wilson firmly believed that with the help of yoga he could reach high altitudes if he starved himself for three weeks. By doing so, his mind would establish direct contact with his soul, he believed. In such a state, he would be free of spiritual and bodily ills and this would give him super-strength which would carry him to the summit of Everest without any difficulty. He was no mountaineer and his plan was to go in a small aeroplane and crash-land in the Everest region as high as possible and then walk the final distance to the summit without any difficulty. With this in mind, he bought a small aeroplane and took off for India but was stopped at Cairo and sent back. He later succeeded in reaching Darjeeling and paid a very high amount to the sherpas who smuggled him into Tibet on the pretext that he was a member of the 1933 expedition and was there only to retrieve old equipment. He proceeded to North Col with rations of only rice water and succeeded on his own in reaching camp II. After taking some rest he took the help of sherpas and reached camp III, where he found some food dumps of the earlier expeditions including chocolates, biscuits, and sardines. He had no training and did not even know how to use the ice axe which he had brought with him. He tried his very best, but was beaten back and could not proceed further up the slopes of the North Col. He was later discovered by Shipton's party, dead in the tattered tent with his diary, which recorded his implicit faith in yoga. He had died two months after leaving Rongbuk. The Chinese expedition of 1960 discovered Wilson's body and filmed it, and later the film was shown in Europe.

1936 EXPEDITION

The expedition was led by Hugh Ruttledge with members: Shipton, Smythe, Wyn Harris Wigram, Warren, Gavin and Oliver. This was the strongest team ever to go on Everest after 1924. The team left Darjeeling in March and by April set up camp III and then camp IV. It was for the first time that an expedition was equipped with radio and was constantly receiving weather warnings from Darjeeling. Although the expedition faced bad weather due to early monsoons, they remained in the mountains upto the first week of June, but had no luck. None of the members could climb beyond 21,000' due to constant bad weather.

1938 EXPEDITION

Large expeditions had been sent so far but now it was decided to send a small party of a few hand picked climbers supported by a team of strong sherpas. The team consisted of Smythe, Warren, Oliver, Odell and a newcomer, Peter Lloyd with Harold Tilman. After opening camp III on 18 May they reached North Col on the 24th. Since the weather was extremely bad, the members faced great difficulty going up. Shipton and Smythe, along with porters, went down to explore the possibility of making a flank attack from the west while the rest of the party pushed up to occupy camp IV. Tilman along with a sherpa tried to open camp V, but had to return from a height of 24,500' because of bad weather. He later joined Shipton's party and established camp III at 21,500'. This expedition also, like the previous one, did not have much success and reached only as far as 27,200'. After this expedition the war broke out and all mountaineering activities stopped and Everest was left in peace.

In 1947, however, there was another unauthorised attempt on Everest. This was by Earl C. Denman, a Canadian by birth who was living in South Africa. In 1947 he made

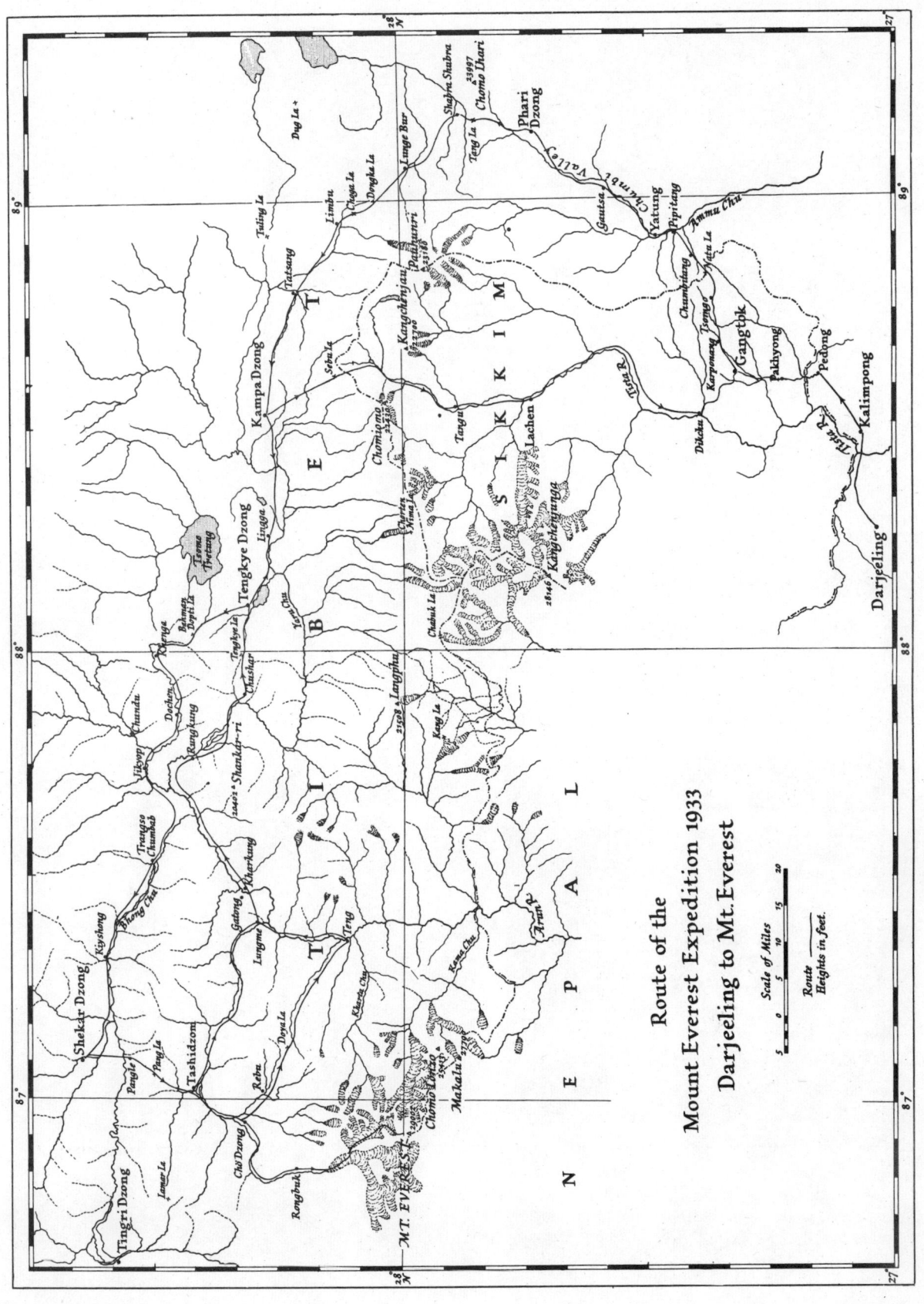

Route of the
Mount Everest Expedition 1933
Darjeeling to Mt. Everest

Scale of Miles

Route
Heights in feet.

Eric Shipton

H. Ruttledge

Lt. Col. E. F. Norton

Shekar monastery in Tibet

Members of the Expedition, 1924.
Hazard   Hingston   Somervell   Beetham   Shebbeare
J.G. Bruce   Norton   Noel   Odell

THE ROUTE TO THE SUMMIT FROM THE NORTH

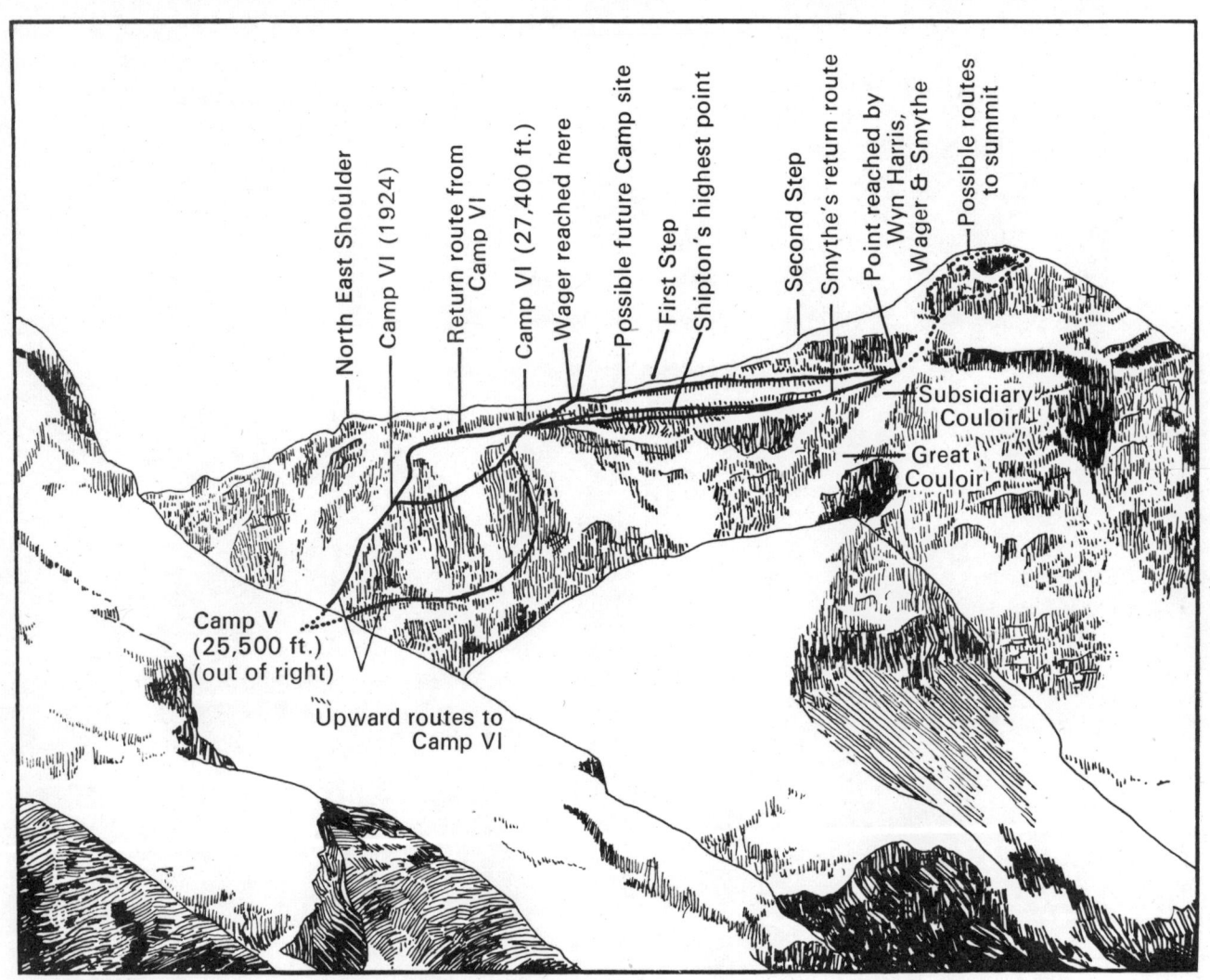

North East Shoulder

Camp VI (1924)

Return route from Camp VI

Camp VI (27,400 ft.)

Wager reached here

Possible future Camp site

First Step

Shipton's highest point

Second Step

Smythe's return route

Point reached by Wyn Harris, Wager & Smythe

Possible routes to summit

Subsidiary Couloir

Great Couloir

Camp V
(25,500 ft.)
(out of right)

Upward routes to
Camp VI

The Expedition at Base Camp.

Left to Right, Back Row: Major Morshead, Captain Geoffrey Bruce, Captain Noel, Dr. Wakefield,
Mr. Somervell, Captain Morris, Major Norton.
Front Row: Mr. Mallory, Captain Finch, Dr. Longstaff, General Bruce, Colonel Strutt, Mr.
Crawford.

his way to Tibet in quite the same manner as Maurice Wilson, without any permit and in disguise. He had acquired some experience in climbing in Africa. He had strong will power and could stand considerable hardships. He took two sherpas with him. One was Tenzing, who later climbed the summit of Everest. They had a minimum of equipment, and taking advantage of ideal snow conditions they reached the southern slope of Everest. Since he was ill-equipped, the sherpas refused to accompany him any further but he continued with his attempt, even without a sleeping bag, but was forced to abandon the attempt due to cold and harsh winds. Although his records did not tally with those of Tenzing, it seems he got to a height somewhere around 23,000'. Denman became very sad for not having achieved his goal. He later wrote a book, *Alone to Everest,* which made him very popular.

3

1951 Reconnaissance
1952 Swiss Expedition

After the war ended the British began to revive their efforts through their mission in Lhasa, for possible permission by the Tibetan authorities to allow a British expedition to Mount Everest. Because of the deteriorating situation created by the Chinese Communist armies who had entered in almost every part of Tibet, it became certain that perhaps there would never be any foreign expedition approaching the mountain from the North route. Meanwhile, the Nepalese Government relaxed their rules and started allowing climbing and scientific expeditions to the Nepal Himalayas. The first party to enter the Everest region from the Nepalese side was an American team consisting of Charles Houston and Bill Tilman in autumn 1950. They explored the area around Khombu glacier but did not have time to conduct a study of the ice fall below the Western Cwm. The party came to the conclusion that the chances of ascent from this side were negligible. Even Eric Shipton, after studying the available records with recent aerial photographs, believed that there was hardly any chance of opening the route to Everest through the ice fall. It was only the reconnaissance of 1951 which proved otherwise.

The Himalayan Committee, which was nothing but an old Everest Committee, lost no time and applied for the permission for the British expedition in 1951 to investigate the route from this side. The permission was granted. The expedition was led by Eric Shipton who had just arrived after completing his assignments in China with other members of the team—Bill Murray, Michael Ward and Tom Bourdillon. The team left England on 18 August. They were joined in Nepal by two New Zealanders, Edmund Hillary and Earle Riddiford, who were already climbing in India. They entered Nepal from Jogbani, a rail head in India. They reached Namche Bazar on 22 September. On 30 September they began their reconnaissance on the glacier and managed to climb up to 20,000 on the glacier. They were able to look into the Western Cwm and realised that there was a possible route through the Western Cwm on to Lhotse face and then to the summit via South Col and the South Summit.

For three days it snowed heavily and the party could not climb any further. The team returned in November and, instead of coming back to Jogbani they came back to Kathmandu. This reconnaissance of the possible route to Everest conducted by this expedition created a worldwide interest in the public, as it was for the first time that a route from the Southern side was observed. It was on this expedition that the first photographs of the footprints of the Yeti were taken. Shipton had described them as slightly longer and broader than those made by mountain boots. It had three broad toes and a broad thumb to the side. The Yeti remains a mystery till today.

This reconnaissance was very important in the sense that the information brought back by them led mountaineers to believe that there was a route to the summit of Everest which would have its own hazards and disappointments. The party firmly believed that the route looked easier and probably safer than the traditional route from the Tibetan side. The British hoped to make a full scale attempt to climb Mount Everest in 1952 but were disappointed when they discovered that the Swiss had already been granted permission to climb it. There was however, an offer to have a combined expedition under the joint leadership of Eric Shipton and Dr. Wyss Dunant. The Himalayan Committee did not agree to such a joint venture, as it would have been a total failure. Joint ventures with mixed nationalities can never work smoothly because of the physical and psychological stresses peculiar to the Everest climb. Eric Shipton was totally against the joint ventures.

1952 SWISS EXPEDITION

In 1949, the Swiss Foundation for Alpine Research approached the Nepalese Government for permission to climb Mount Everest. Permission was granted towards the end of 1951 and the Swiss started preparations for a full-scale expedition for 1952. They first wanted to send a joint Swiss-British expedition to Mount Everest but the idea was soon abandoned, as a combined party of the Swiss and the British would become very large and unwieldy. There was hardly any time to co-ordinate administrative and other matters, particularly when the Swiss preparations were at a very advanced stage. The other important factor would be divided leadership.

The Swiss team under the leadership of mountaineer-cum-skier, Wyss Dunant along with Flory, Lambert, Dittert and others, left Kathmandu in early April. The expedition had much better equipment than the British, including lighter oxygen apparatus. The team also included a tough sherpa, Tenzing. They made brisk progress and established camp IV at 21,150′, and camp V at 22,630′. The weather was extremely good and the first summit party of Lambert and Tenzing accompanied by Flory and Aubert set up camp VI at 25,840′ on South Col.

The weather was good and it seemed that there was every chance of success for the summit party. Raymond Lambert and sherpa Tenzing were the first pair to set off for the summit camp accompanied by Flory and Aubert. The party established camp VII at 27,550′. It was not possible for all four of them to go to the summit and they had to decide as to which two of them would be the best to make the summit. Aubert, who is considered a fanatical mountaineer, insisted that Lambert and Tenzing stood the best chance to reach the summit and as such they should be the chosen ones. Flory fully agreed with Aubert's decision. It was a great sacrifice for them particularly when they were

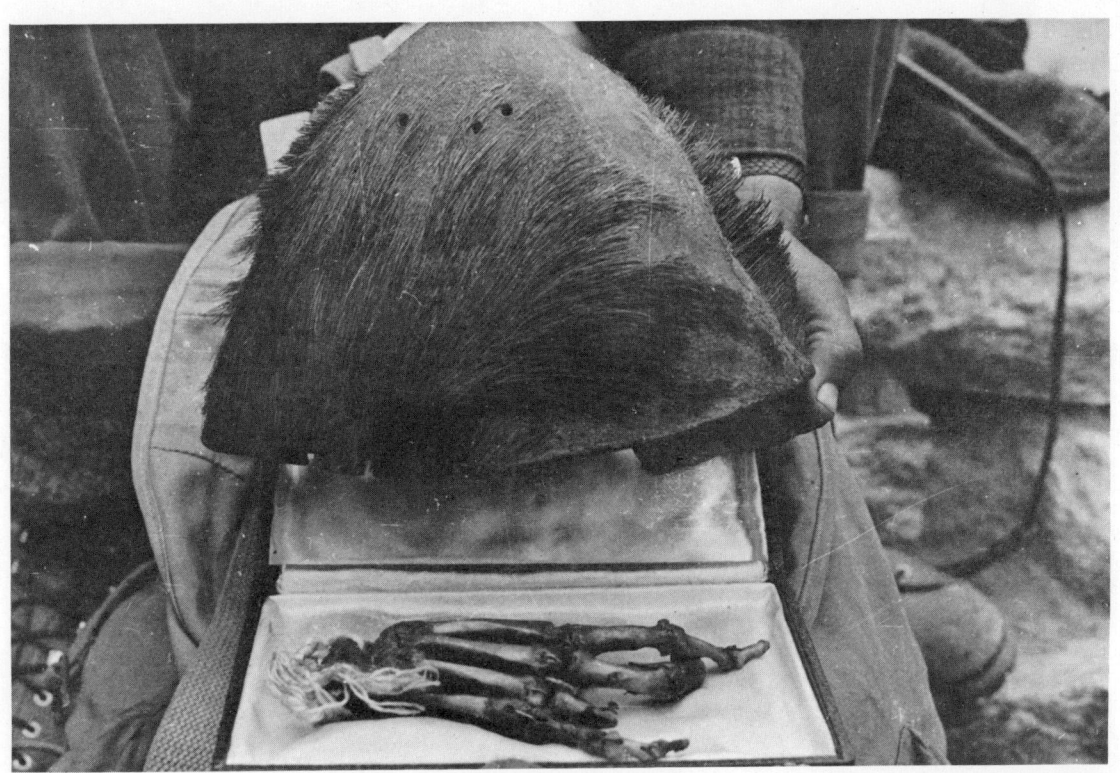

Yeti scalp and palm

Raymond Lambert

Facing:

Overleaf: Over 180° wide-angle lens view of the Khumbu glacier with the Everest massif in the back-ground from Kala Pattar.

Sunrise on Kangtega around the Everest region

within reach of the summit. Flory described this dramatic moment as follows: "It is a moving moment, this parting at more than 27,500'. Our comrades appreciate our sacrifice, and cannot restrain themselves from embracing us, sobbing. Is all this the effect of the altitude?" On 28 May, while Lambert and Tenzing left for the summit, Flory and Aubert started moving down without looking back either at the summit or the summit pair. Raymond Lambert and Tenzing slowly and cautiously fought their way up. Everything seemed good and they reached 28,210'. It was the highest point any man had climbed so far. They could not go any further as they were utterly exhausted due to altitude affects, and in spite of their best efforts they could not climb. Utterly disappointed, they started their downward journey and on 29 May they reached camp V and collapsed in their tents. The second assault party which was led by Dittert also became a victim of high altitude sickness and returned. Dittert wrote:

> Our breath became ever shorter as the height increased. When we had passed 25,600' we stopped again, hoping as we always did, that a rest would allow us to recover our strength a little. This was an illusion. At that height a man does not regain his powers, and each minute that passes reduces his physical strength. Even the strongest body is weakened. When you sit down, you feel better. Your breath comes more easily and slowly. But when you get up again, pick up your pack and resume the climb, you find to your dismay that you are hardly better than before you halted. Then you must summon all your will-power, for each step becomes an effort, a torture . . . .
>
> We climbed like automata repeating a hundred times the self-same movements. The slightest false footing, the least extra effort exhausted us and nearly halted our progress; for each such extra effort took from us six, seven, perhaps eight very rapid and irregular breaths.

It was a great disappointment, particularly, when they had to return after reaching within almost 800' from the summit. Raymond Lambert appropriately summed up the attempt:

> Each Everest expedition learns a little more about the way in which the mountain may eventually be conquered, and certain well-defined lessons emerge from our experiences this year. Not the least interesting, perhaps, is the conclusion we reached that the best ages for Everest climbers are between 30 and 43.
>
> We have learnt more about the benefits of long acclimatization. Thanks to our reconnaissance in the Western Cwm, all the members of our expedition stayed in good physical condition at heights up to nearly 26,000'. Some of the benefits of this acclimatization were lost by the too lengthy gap between Camp V, in the Western Cwm (22,630'), and Camp VI, on the South Col (25,840'). To make this journey we had to climb more than 3,000' in a single day, leaving us too exhausted, in the rarefied atmosphere of those extreme altitudes, to make a successful final assault. For the success of any future attempt along the same route, an intermediate camp must be established, at somewhere about the 24,000' level, allowing climbers to set out for the assault in better condition.

1952 POST-MONSOON EXPEDITION

The Swiss were up again in the mountain for a second expedition under the leadership of Dr. Gabriel Chevalley. The party now consisted of Raymond Lambert, Ernst Reiss,

Gustav Gross, Arthur Spohel, Jeam Brizio and sherpa Tenzing. On 10 September, the party left for Namche Bazar with 250 porters. Two porters died due to exposure on the way. The expedition established its base camp on 2 October and camp V on 26 October. The expedition had more bad luck when the young sherpa, Mingma Dove, died in the ice fall and three more sherpas broke their bones and were evacuated. By now strong winds started blowing in the area, but Lambert, Reiss, and Tenzing with seven sherpas set up camp VIII on 19 November. The weather further deteriorated. They waited for two days but the weather did not improve and they decided to return, bitterly disappointed.

1952 RUSSIAN EXPEDITION

An Italian Alpine review, *Scarpone*, reported of the Russian attempt to Mount Everest in winter 1952. When the Russians learned that the second Swiss expedition was leaving in winter of 1952 after the failure of the first, they apparently resolved to make a determined effort to anticipate them. The London *Times* reported that the expedition consisting of 35 experienced climbers and five scientists including Professor Yondomnov, a geologist, and Dr. Dengmuarov, a specialist in the study of human physiology at high altitudes, left Moscow on 16 October. The team was led by Dr. Pawel Datschnolian, an Armenian.

Five army aircrafts transported the expedition equipment first to Novosibirsk, then to Irkutsk and finally to Lhasa. From there the approach march was longer than was expected and the expedition is stated to have left Nasulan, its base to the north of Everest, a month later. It is stated to have returned to Nasulan on 27 December, having failed in its objective with a loss of 6 of its members at a height of 26,800'. Among the 6 killed were Dr. Datschnolian, who was regarded as one of the best Russian climbers, and Kazhinsky, Alexandrovich, and Lanitsov, who had vast experience and had made a number of ascents in the Caucasus.

Datschnolian is said to have been in daily contact with Moscow by means of a portable wireless transmitter and his last message was that the assault party had established camp VIII at 26,800'. The message also stated that the members were in a fit condition and they expected to reach the summit within the two following days subject to weather conditions. After this no more messages were received and Moscow immediately ordered a search. Search parties explored the mountain, going as high as possible for 18 days, but found no trace of the missing men. Finally the search was abandoned because of the arrival of winter. A further search was made in the following spring but without any fruitful results. It is assumed that the members of the assault party were swept away by an avalanche not far from camp VIII. The expedition and its organisers are said to have come under heavy criticism in Russia. It was alleged that the expedition was sent out rather rashly with outdated equipment.

4
1953 British Expedition

In early June 1952 while the Swiss were making their first bid on Everest, Eric Shipton, Charles Evans, Bourdillon, Earle Riddiford and George Lowe were trying to climb Cho-Oyu from the north-west face to serve as a trial run for the forthcoming British expedition to Mount Everest in 1953. The party wanted to climb Cho-Oyu from the Tibetan side. There were heated discussions among the members to enter Tibet without permission for climbing Cho-Oyu and the possible danger of being apprehended by the Chinese.

Eric Shipton was particularly concerned. The younger members felt that the risk was well worth it as they would be able to have a view of the Tibetan side of the mountain, and in any case they did not feel that the Chinese soldiers were competent enough to climb beyond 17,000'. The team entered Tibet by crossing the Nangpa-La and travelled upto the Kyetrak and established camp at 21,000'. The route seemed difficult and the members retreated across the Nup-La and visited the North side of the Everest, and saw the Rongbuk glacier and the traditional camp sites of the earlier expeditions from the Tibetan side. This was an interesting experience and since the Nepalese Government was not that strict as they are today, they did not show any concern at the British having crossed into Tibet. Hillary was excited about this sojourn, and in his book *Nothing Venture, Nothing Win* he wrote:

> We had many exciting moments—our first glimpse down valley of the renowned Rongbuk Monastery; getting to Camp I (still littered with old batteries and other rubbish from the early British expeditions), and the sight of the famous North Col and its snow approaches—which in all honesty didn't look terribly difficult. For five days we galloped around the lower slopes of Everest but there was always one nagging thought—in these warm conditions what was happening to the Nup La?

43

On their return the selection for the 1953 expedition began. On the question of leadership it was always assumed that Eric Shipton would be the leader of the 1953 expedition. He had been to the Everest five times and was the most experienced mountaineer having climbed more than any other climber. It was also a well known fact that Eric Shipton disliked large expeditions, and the publicity they carried, particularly those climbing Everest. It had now become an issue of national importance. He also thought that since he has already been to Everest five times he would now hand over to a younger mountaineer. So he asked the Committee to consider these aspects before they decided as to who was to be the leader of the expedition. The next man to Eric Shipton would be Charles Evans, about whose climbing abilities Eric Shipton had the highest opinion. John Hunt was considered as an organising Secretary at this stage. Eric Shipton in his book *That Untravelled World* writes:

> We had a frank discussion, and John told me that he did not feel able to accept the position unless he were made deputy leader. While I understood his point of view as a high-ranking Army officer, I could not, of course, agree to his terms, since I had already nominated Charles Evans as my deputy. Also, it was clear to both of us, and admitted, that our approach to the enterprise, both practical and temperamental, was so fundamentally different that we would not easily work together. We parted, however, on friendly terms.

Preparations for the expeditions began at the Royal Geographical Society on 11 September. A meeting of the Himalayan Committee was convened, a most important meeting in the history of British mountaineering. To quote Eric Shipton:

> I was surprised to find that the first item on the agenda was the 'Deputy Leadership', and still more so when I was asked to go out of the room while this was discussed. An hour later I was recalled and told that John had been appointed 'Co-leader' with me. Then, for the first time, it dawned on me that there must have been a great deal of backdoor diplomacy since the last meeting, of which I had been totally unaware. It seemed particularly strange to me that I should have been expected to accept the proposal, especially remembering the views expressed the previous winter on the subject of joint leadership by most of the Committee and by myself. In declining, I told the Committee that if they wished to reconsider their former decision regarding the leadership, they were, of course, free to do so. I then withdrew for a still longer period. I returned to be told that it had been decided to appoint John Hunt in my place.

This was a great disappointment to Eric Shipton whatever his views on large scale expeditions. Shipton further writes: "The influences which caused the Committee's *volte face* are still obscure .... I was far from pleased to withdraw from this despised limelight; nor could I fool myself that it was only the manner of my rejection that I minded."

This decision was not welcomed by some members who were expected to participate in the expedition and wrote to the committee resigning from the expedition. They were persuaded, however, to join as it was a national venture. About the selection Sir Edmund Hillary in his book writes:

> Then came the bombshell; I read in the newspapers with disbelief that Shipton had been replaced with a new leader—Colonel John Hunt—someone I had never heard of. The report said he was a distinguished soldier with a couple of Himalayan trips

American expedition—Camp IV

Dawa Norbu at South Col

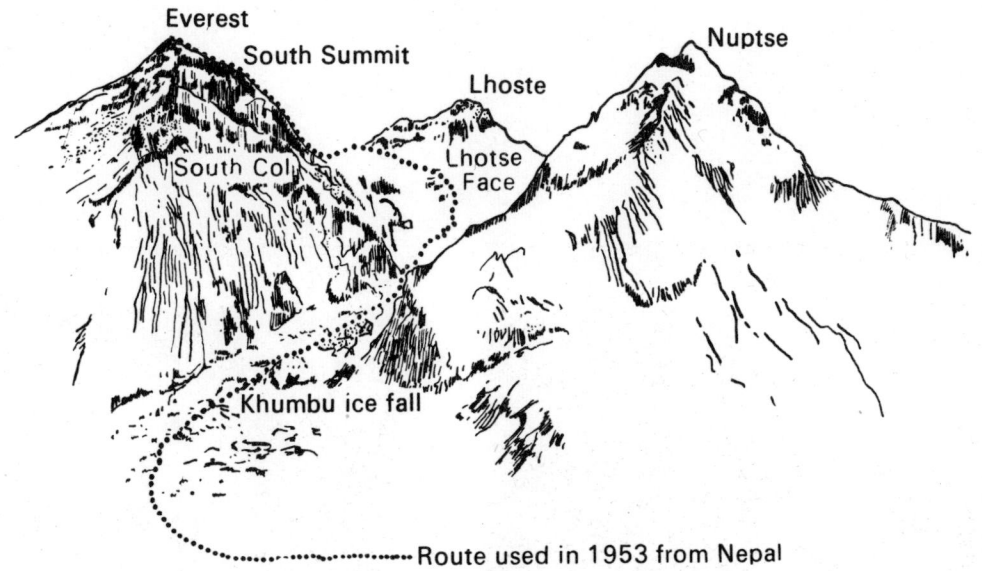

Everest
South Summit
Lhoste
Lhotse Face
South Col
Nuptse
Khumbu ice fall
············· Route used in 1953 from Nepal

to his credit. 'Everest will be unthinkable without Shipton,' was my immediate reaction, 'and who wants an Army man anyway?' I seriously considered pulling out of the party.

Since it was going to be a national venture and it would be a very big expedition with big publicity, the Committee might have been of the opinion that perhaps Eric Shipton would not be happy as he disliked large expeditions with big publicity. The Himalayan Committee's decision later turned out to be correct as Col. Hunt proved himself to be a brilliant organiser and an able leader who brought glory to his country.

Col. John Hunt, aged forty-two, had served as Chief Instructor at the wartime Commando mountain school and had served in Egypt, Italy, Greece. He had the distinction of commanding a Brigade of the famous 4th Indian Division and was known to be a first rate climber. With Col. John Hunt as the leader, the other members of the party were G. C. Band, T. D. Bourdillon, R. C. Evans, A. Gregory, W. G. Lowe, C. W. F. Noyce, Dr. L G. C. Pugh, T. Stobard, Dr. M. P. Ward, M. H. Westmacott, Major G. C. Wylie, E. P. Hillary, and Tenzing. This was the eleventh expedition of the British and in selecting the team, Lord Hunt recalls, "I felt that one of the most important matters to be decided was the choice of the members of the expedition. The climbers had to be young, fit, and of course, skilful. It was no less important, I thought, that they should get on well with each other. They would have to live together, often in unpleasant conditions, for many weeks. We could not afford to take men who might argue with one another. We had, in fact, to form a *team*.

The expedition left Kathmandu on 10 March 1953 with 350 porter-loads weighing nearly 8 tons. After a long, though pleasant, climb from the Dudh Kosi valley, it arrived at Thyangboche, where it was to spend a few days acclimatising. The team spent five days climbing nearby peaks of about 20,000′. As planned, the expedition opened the route through the ice fall by the end of April. Lord Hunt in his book, *Ascent of Everest* wrote:

In the upper part of the ice fall we faced several problems. The massive blocks of ice were so loosely poised that the collapse of one of them would have crushed anyone   47

Lord John Hunt

Sir Edmund Hillary

near. At one point we had to climb down into a trough sixty feet wide. On the far side of the trough, we climbed up through a great jumble of huge blocks of ice, all looking as though they would crash down at any moment.

Beyond this we had to pass two lofty blocks of ice. One rose sheer for forty feet, and was called by us the 'Nut cracker.' There was a hollow space below it when we chipped steps, there was a wierd rumbling noise as pieces of ice fell into the black depths below. It sounded as if a train were passing beneath our feet, and was eerie and frightening to listen to.

At last we established camp at the Western Cwm. The route through the ice fall was opened by Hillary and his team who had been in this area with Shipton in 1951. Bourdillon had designed a new oxygen apparatus with an open circuit system which was also tested and found functional. Indeed, one of the sherpas trained in the use of oxygen apparatus went so far as to say that using oxygen made climbing feel like going downhill.

All supplies were now moved to the advance base camp at the head of the Cwm. By 3rd May the party was able to establish a camp at the base of the Lhotse face. Then began the arduous task of opening a route through the hard blue ice of the Lhotse face. There were many problems. The weather was bad. Snow fell so thickly that tracks vanished almost as soon as they were made. The wind was so strong that it nearly swept the climbers off the mountain side. The job was completed on 21 May and the camp was established there.

According to the strategy of the team, two pairs of climbers moved to the South Col. It was then planned that one pair would attempt the summit directly from the South Col camp while the other would establish the last camp as high as possible on the South East ridge. Lord Hunt in *The Ascent of Everest* wrote:

On 23 May, we climbed to Camp 7, half-way up the Lhotse Face. Here, the wind howled round our tents all night. But, using oxygen, we managed to sleep. Next day, we began the long traverse to the South Col. It was a terribly hard climb. In the lead were Charles Evans and Tom Bourdillon, breaking the trail through the crust of snow, while I followed with the two sherpas, all of us heavily laden. The sherpas soon got very tired; after every few paces we had to rest while they recovered.

Not until 4 p.m. did we reach the top of the Geneva Spur. Above us, across the hollow of the South Col, rose the South summit of Everest. And at our feet was the wide, icy plateau we knew as the South Col. We went down the slope to level ground, where there were splashes of colour among the stones; these showed where the Swiss Camp VII had been.

The ground was stony, and was partly covered with sheets of bare, bluish ice, for the snow here had been hardened by the wind until it was little different from ice. And it was the wind that made the Col so bleak and desolate. When we tried to put up our tent, the wind snatched at it as though playing tug-of-war with us. For over an hour we fought to put up that single tent.

We had taken off our oxygen sets to give us more freedom. But now, trying to breathe the thin air, we found we had no more strength. Once I tripped and fell, and lay for five minutes before I was able to get up again. But at last the tent was ready. By 5.30 p.m. a second tent was put up. Charles Evans, Tom Bourdillon, and I were in one; the two sherpas were in the other. We lay amid all our gear to recover from this terrible struggle. And, outside, the great wind tore angrily at the tent walls.

It was not possible for us to be ready in time to try for the top next day. Food had to be sorted out, and, even more important, the oxygen apparatus had to be prepared. All this would take a long time and Tom and Charles needed to start very early if they were to get to the summit. So we rested, put up a tent for myself, and made ready for our great day.

The next day the summit party was delayed by the oxygen valve which stuck due to low temperature in Evan's oxygen apparatus. The support party, however, continued to climb and reached 27,350′ in spite of the blockage in Col. Hunt's oxygen tube. This was a great achievement. On the way they came upon the remains of the little tent left by Tenzing and Lambert, the Swiss climber, exactly a year before. The canvas had been ripped away by the wind and only the metal poles, with tattered pieces of orange cloth, remained. The support party consisting of Col. Hunt and Da Namgyal made their way down after leaving their oxygen cylinders for Hillary and Tenzing who were the second summit pair.

Meanwhile, the first summit pair continued their climb and reached the top of the South summit, a height of 28, 720′. Since it was late in the evening, the weather and their depleting oxygen supply forced them to turn back when they were barely 500′ below the summit. They were extremely hopeful that the last 500′ would not pose any problem for the second summit party and they seemed extremely hopeful about their success. But unfortunately the weather deteriorated.

On 28 May, the weather improved and the summit pair consisting of Hillary and Tenzing left South Col. with the support party of Lowe, Gregory and Ang Nyima. After reaching a height of 27,900′ at 2.30 p.m. they decided to camp while the support party returned to South Col. On 29 May at 4 a.m. Tenzing and Hillary began their historic climb. It would be appropriate to quote here Hillary's account of the ascent :

We looked with some interest at the ridge ahead. It was certainly impressive and even rather frightening. On the right, great twisted cornices—everhanging masses of snow and ice—stuck out like twisted fingers over the 12,000′ drop of the Kang-chung Face. Any move on to these cornices could only bring disaster. From the cornices, the ridge dropped steeply to the left until the snow merged with the great rock face sweeping up from the Western Cwm.

The steep snow slope between the cornices and the rock precipices seemed to be composed of firm, hard snow. If the snow proved soft, our chances of getting along the ridge were few indeed. If we could cut a trail of steps along this slope, we could make progress.

We cut a seat for ourselves just below the South summit and removed our oxygen apparatus. As our first partly-full bottle of oxygen was now exhausted, we had only one full bottle left. Eight hundred litres of oxygen at three litres per minute? How long would it last? I estimated that this should give us four and a half hours. Our apparatus was now much lighter, weighing just over 20 lb., and as I cut steps down off the South summit, I felt a sense of freedom and well-being.

In a number of places the overhanging ice cornices were very large indeed, and in order to escape them I cut a line of steps down to where the snow met the rocks on the west. It was a great thrill to look straight down this enormous rock face and to see, 8 000′ below us, the tiny tents of camp IV in the Western Cwm. Scrambling on the rocks and cutting handholds on the snow, we were able to shuffle past these difficult portions. After an hour's steady going we reached the foot of a rock step some 40′

Mountain flora provide a colourful sight near Lobuje

high. The rock, smooth and almost holdless, was a barrier beyond our feeble strength to overcome. I could see no way of getting round it or the west. But fortunately another possibility of tackling it remained.

On its east side was another great cornice; and running up the full forty feet of the step was a narrow crack between the cornice and the rock. Leaving Tenzing to belay me as best he could, I jammed my way into this crack. Then, kicking backwards, I sank the spikes of my crampons deep into the frozen snow behind me and levered myself off the ground.

Taking advantage of every little rock hold, and all the force of knee, shoulder, and arms I could muster, I literally cramponed backwards up the crack, praying that the cornice would remain attached to the rock. My progress although slow, was steady. As Tenzing paid out the rope, I inched my way upwards until I could reach over the top of the rock and drag myself out of the crack on to a wide ledge.

For a few moments I lay regaining my breath, and for the first time really felt the fierce determination that nothing now could stop us reaching the top. I took a firm stance on the ledge and signalled to Tenzing to come up. As I heaved hard on the rope, Tenzing wriggled his way up the crack, and finally collapsed at the top like a giant fish hauled from the sea after a terrible struggle.

The ridge continued as before: giant cornices on the right; steep rock slopes on the left. The ridge curved away to the right and we had no idea where the top was. As I cut around the back of one hump, another higher one would swing into view. Time was passing and the ridge seemed never-ending.

Our original zest had now quite gone, and it was turning more into a grim struggle. I then realised that the ridge ahead, instead of rising, now dropped sharply away. I looked upwards to see a narrow snow ridge running up to a snowy summit. A few more whacks of the ice-axe in the firm snow and we stood on top.

My first feelings were of relief—relief that there were no more steps to cut, no more ridges to traverse, and no more humps to tantalize us with hopes of success. I looked at Tenzing. In spite of the balaclava helmet, goggles, and oxygen mast— all encrusted with long icicles—that concealed his face, there was no disguising his grin of delight as he looked all around him. We shook hands, and then Tenzing threw his arm around my shoulders and we thumped each other on the back until we were almost breathless. It was 11.30 a.m. The ridge had taken us two and a half hours, but it seemed like a lifetime.

The success of this team was largely due to the previous British expeditions who were the pioneers in selecting and investigating the possible routes to the summit. Credit must go to Gen. Bruce's party of 1922 and then to Eric Shipton for his very valuable survey in 1935 and his subsequent reconnaissance of 1951 which had explored the new unknown South-West side of the mountains, and last, but not least to Col. John Hunt for providing able leadership. If it were not for Col. Hunt, the results may not have been so spectacular.

The fifties saw new achievements in the history of mountaineering; the first "Eight Thousander" (above 8,000 m.) the Annapurna (26,504'), was climbed by Maurice Herzog and Louis Lachenal. In 1953 Herma Buhl climbed Nanga Parbat (26,660')—a lone effort which is unparalleled; then came the success on K2 the second highest mountain in the world 28,253' by the Italians in 1954. In the same year the sixth highest mountain, Cho-Oyu (26,870') was climbed by Herbert Tichy. Kanchenjunga, 28,168', the third high-

Facing: Rhododendrons

est mountain, was climbed in 1955. In the same year, Makalu 27,790′, the fifth highest mountain, was climbed. Then came the Swiss expedition of 1956 which climbed both Lhotse and Mount Everest.

5
1956 Swiss Expedition
1960, 1962 Indian Expeditions

The Swiss Foundation for Alpine Research was founded in 1940. The Foundation had sent a number of expeditions abroad, notably to the Himalayas (1940, 1947 and 1950), the Karakorum (1947), Tibesti (1948), Nepal (1949) and Baffin Island (1950 and 1953). It came into prominence with its two expeditions to Everest in 1952. It was established with the object of promoting explorations and research in areas outside Europe including both the Arctic and Antarctic regions, and financed, equipped, and made arrangements for these. The Foundation works directly under the Swiss department of Internal Affairs.

The third Swiss expedition to Everest was composed of climbers and scientists. The team was led by Albert Eggler, a noted climber, who has to his credit the traverse of the Weisshorn in the Valais by its North Ridge, Mont Blanc by the Brenva, the Aiguille des Grands Charmoz, the Ecrins, the East Ridge of the Bietschhorn and the Fiescherhorner. His most reliable partner on the rope had been his wife, Lucie, with whom he had done extensive climbing. A notable member in the team was Ernst Reiss who had already reached a height of 26,600 on Everest in the autumn of 1952 with Raymond Lambert and Tenzing.

The members of the team were Ernst Schmied, Adolf Reist, Ernst Reiss, Fritz Muller, Jurg Marmet, Fritz Luchsinger, Eduard Leuthold, Hansrudolf von Gunten, Hans Grimn, and Wolfgang Diehl. The total expenditure incurred was £30,000 (360,000 Swiss Francs), which was raised by the Foundation. Each member of the expedition had contributed a large sum. The team under the guidance of Marmet, a young engineer and oxygen expert, developed a new system which greatly reduced the problems of oxygen which had plagued early expeditions. The team carried 160 oxygen bottles, containing one thousand litres each.

After having a very tough acclimatization at Thyangboche monastery, the expedition established the base camp on 7 April, and the work to open the camp beyond began with full vigour. Each member of the team was fit and climbed a number of small peaks during the acclimatization period. On 12 April Schmied worked in the Khumbu ice fall and opened the way to the Western Cwm. On 18 April, Reist and Hansrudolf von Gunten opened the route up to camp II on the way to the Western Cwm. On 16 April, Reiss and Ernst Schmied pushed ahead from camp II to a height of 22,000' in the Cwm. Camp III was opened at the base of the western shoulder to Everest, at 21,300' On 23 April, for the first time, Reist and Gunten spent their first night at camp III, which was called the advance base camp. Camp III was to be used as a springboard for assaulting both Lhotse and Everest. Soon the advance base camp became the nerve centre of all expedition activity.

The work on opening the route beyond, began on 1 May and a camp at the base of Lhotse face at a height of 23,000' was established. Fritz Luchsinger, Reiss, and the leader spent the night at this camp. It was from this camp that the expedition started using oxygen at the rate of half a litre per minute. Next morning the team moved up to the Lhotse face opening the route and fixing the ropes for a possible route upwards. The team succeeded in reaching almost 650' above the last camp and dumped all equipment. The work beyond was taken over by Gunten and Reist, who succeeded in opening a route up to 24,900' and had to turn back because it was getting very late. Camp V was established at this height and reconnaissance of the route beyond was taken in hand.

On 9 May Schmied and Luchsinger established camp VI at approximately 26,250' and spent the night there. It was in this expedition that a cable hoist was installed to facilitate lifting of the loads. It started snowing, the winds became strong and the weather deteriorated. It was confirmed that the monsoon had broken. The bad weather persisted but 14 May showed some signs of the clouds lifting. There was a party already at camp III which was coming down, but due to the lifting of the clouds, the party stayed on and confirmed that the weather had cleared up in the higher regions. This improvement in weather hastened their movements as already planned and the party at camp III started reopening the routes ahead. On 20 May, Schmied, along with two sherpas, opened camp VI. The leader along with the other members reached camp V. Albert Eggler writes:

> If the weather did not deteriorate, we would have to make our decisive effort in the next few days. We were already in the second half of May, the monsoon had sent ahead a number of its messengers and might easily set in with full force any day now. We would have no time to waste.

The position of their camp VI was shifted to South Col. and the leader rearranged the climbing.

It was decided that before attempting Everest, they would have a go at Lhotse from the South Col camp over the ridge. The party moved to camp VI on the 15th when the weather started to deteriorate again. But the summit pair comprising Luchsinger and Reiss left South Col on 18 May in spite of gale and high winds and the pair reached the Lhotse groove. By 2.30 p.m. the wind had increased and the face was also covered with an unbroken cloud of snow and there was mist all around. They were crossing the last cliff below the summit and were moving to the summit by the left hand crest and by 3 p.m. they reached the summit. It was difficult climbing *via* South Col over the North route which consisted of cliffs and large chimney towers which were all situated above 26,000' Reiss described his

climb:

At last we climbed out over the little depression between the summits and were in sunshine once more. The last bit to the summit looked terribly steep. We had to get over one more band of greenish rock and then we were only a rope's length, at an inclination of about 60° below the summit of Lhotse. The *neve* was as tough as sheer ice, and we were determined not to take a single risk in such an exposed position. I cut a row of steps, which necessitated hundreds of strokes of my ice-axe. Just below the crest of the ridge I hacked out a large stance in the snow-cap and leaned my head against the face of the mountain in an effort to recover from my exertions.

Fritz joined me on the stance, where we crouched, waiting for a momentary lull in the wind. Then we hauled ourselves up over the crest, which was almost as sharp as a knife-blade, and looked down into the smother of cloud covering the eastern and southern faces of the mountain. We were on the summit of Lhotse.

After having succeeded on Lhotse, the morale of the team rose high and they now diverted their energy with full vigour to Everest. Everything was set and the team was now ready for an assault. Although the 22nd morning had a slight snowfall and mist, the sun came up. Schmied and Marmet left with four sherpas for the higher camps. The team passed the site on the South East Ridge where Lambert and Tenzing had pitched their camp on 26 May 1952. The party chose a place on the ridge at a height of approximately 27,550' for their last camp. It was almost 5 p.m. and the support party of sherpas returned to South Col after establishing the camp.

Marmet and Schmied had a tough time as there had been snowfall at night which resulted in the tent collapsing over them. Schmied was gasping for breath. Marmet, who was an expert on oxygen, gave him a strong dose of oxygen at almost four litres a minute which relieved Schmied's suffocation. The tent, which was full of snow, was cleared. As it was nearing 3.30 in the morning it started to light up. Snow which had drifted into the tent had covered the cooker and the food, which meant that extra labour and time would be required to dig up the cooker and to boil the water for drinking.

This delay may have hampered their reaching the summit, so they decided to start for the summit without breakfast. Why they did this is best explained in their own words:

To wake up at 27,550 feet on Everest's summit ridge and find the morning clear was such a unique bit of luck that, after weeks of training, we felt we could face the prospect of having to tighten our belts for a day. We would probably have plenty of opportunities for breakfasting later on in life and the chance of climbing Everest seemed to us worth more than any breakfast.

It was 8.30 in the morning when they moved for the summit still debating whether to turn back or to go ahead as there was a gale blowing. But they kept moving. They negotiated the steep and narrow ridge and at 11 o'clock they reached the last steep slope which would take them to the summit. The wind had died down and there were prospects of bright weather. They also left their half-consumed oxygen cylinders there.

It was about noon when they reached the South Summit. They soon negotiated Hillary's Chimney and there was nothing now to prevent them from reaching the summit and soon they stood on top of the highest mountain in the world. It was a victory well deserved by the Swiss. They were on the summit for almost an hour. The cloud started forming and they had to rush down. It was 5 p.m. when they reached the last camp. While they moved down, Reist and Gunten prepared to move to the summit the next day. They reached the summit at 11 in the morning—a clear day without any winds. On 29 May, the

Crossing the Yellow Band

*The members of the expedition. Seated,
in front left to right: Leuthold, Diehl, Reist.
Behind them: Luchsinger, Eggler, Grimm.
Standing: Schmied, Marmet, von Gunten,
Reiss; half-hidden by von Gunten is
Pradham*

Dolf Reist on the summit

Albert Eggler

*Hansrudi von Gunten on the
summit of Everest*

expedition left the base camp on their return journey. The expedition had done extremely well, not only in climbing Everest but also Lhotse which was a great achievement for any country.

1960 INDIAN EXPEDITION

With Tenzing's climbing Everest, a new chapter in the history of Indian mountaineering began. The Himalayan Mountaineering Institute at Darjeeling was opened and for the first time basic and advance training in mountaineering began to be imparted to youths in India. In 1958, the Indian Mountaineering Foundation came into being by launching its Cho-Oyu expedition which was a great success. The Foundation launched its first Everest Expedition to Mount Everest under Brig. Gyan Singh in 1960. Brig. Gyan Singh had barely five months in hand to select the team and be fully prepared with the equipment for the mountain.

In October/November 1959, he took a team of 25 climbers to Mount Kabru in Western Sikkim on a pre-Everest expedition. He had Tenzing as his guide and adviser. As a result of this pre-training, 12 climbers were selected, but the final team comprised the following 23 members: Keki F. Bunshah, Lt. M. S. Kohli, Capt. Narinder Kumar, C. P. Vohra, Flt. Lt. A. K. Chowdhury, Sonam Gyatso, B. D. Misra, Rajendra Vikram Singh, Nawang Gombu, Da Namgyal, Ang Temba, Flt. Lt. N. S. Bhagwanani, Capt. S. K. Das, Flt. Lt. A. J. S. Grewal, Capt. A. B. Jungalwala, Lt. S. C. Nanda, C. V. Gopal, S. U. Shankar Rao, Sohan Singh, Naik Balakrishnan, Om Prakash Vaid, and Dhanbir Rai. Brig. Gyan Singh writes that it was "with a feeling of humility blended with a spirit of challenge that I began to plan for the expedition. To face this gigantic task, I had to fall back on what I had learnt at the Staff College. The Instructor had mentioned that the processes of methodical thinking as taught in 'Appreciation of a Situation' could be applied to planning of any kind. I, therefore, started examining my problem on the lines of a military operation."

The next three hectic months were spent in getting the equipment together. The Indian ordnance factories undertook the manufacture of the special clothing required. Apart from the mountaineering equipment, the expedition needed 75 pullovers, 200 pairs of stockings, 450 woollen shirts and 70 pairs of climbing trousers. For this a few hundred yards of fabric and over 500 lbs of wool was obtained from Punjab. When the material arrived, Tenzing distributed the wool to Sherpanis and Nepalese women who are very quick at knitting. For a few weeks in January and February, practically every Sherpani and Nepalese woman in Darjeeling was knitting frantically for the expedition.

The expedition assembled in Delhi and then left for Jaynagar, a border town between India and Nepal. On 6 March, the expedition left Jaynagar with 19 tons of baggage carried by 800 porters. The team was ceremoniously sent off by Tenzing. Brig. Gyan Singh recalled:

> The next three weeks were the most pleasurable part of the Everest pilgrimage for me. If there were no restrictions on space I would have liked to relieve and share with the reader in detail the unforgettable experiences of the happy and carefree days of the approach march to our objective. The young mountaineer is understandably bent on achievement. Challenge, heights and headlines often form the basis of his motivation and the burning urge for the unattainable. But as he mellows with age, his values change. Maturity slowly converts him from a mountain climber to a lover of the mountain.

On the way we met many hill-folk—Rais, Limboos, and Newars who follow the Hindu religion or the Buddhist. Tamangs and sherpas have one thing in common, they are all friendly and hospitable. A Tamang girl comes up with a pot of milk and a dozen eggs in a basket. Placing these offerings on the ground she greets me with folded hands. This is a local custom for welcoming guests and she expects nothing in return for this heart-warming gesture. How can one forget such charming people?

On the twelfth day of the march, the team arrived in Namche Bazar and later at Thyangboche Monastery. The next day they reached Pangboche where they stayed two weeks for acclimatization. An advance party under K. K. Bunshah, the deputy leader, went ahead and established the base camp. After the main party arrived, the work on opening the route beyond began. Camp I was established on 10 April and camp II on 13 April at 20,000' and by 16 April, the expedition had established camp at the base of Lhotse face. By 28 April they had set up camp at 25,000' and on 9 May the South Col camp. It was remarkable to reach this height in such a short time. With a bit of luck the expedition would have made the summit within a week but as luck would have it the weather deteriorated. In the words of Brig. Gyan Singh:

Weather seldom works on a strict schedule. It certainly did not seem to do so now when we wanted it to. Soon after South Col was reached, it took a turn for the worse again. We were ready to send up supplies to stock Camp VI, but snowstorms and gales made progress very difficult. We even had to vacate the high camps to save rations and fuel. In any case, there was no point in wasting ourselves under such strenuous conditions. So a minimum number of men were left at the advance base and most of us come down to the base camp.

It was still snowing heavily on 19 May. Every mountain, including the ever-frowning Lhotse, was clothed in white. Even at the base camp there was a thick blanket of fresh snow. A decision had been made by Brig. Gyan Singh about the advance. The two summit teams of three men each and their supporting parties were asked to reach the advance base camp at the earliest, to take advantage of any break in weather. 20 May was bright and clear but the team did not move due to the danger of avalanches. The first summit party consisting of Sonam Gyatso, Capt. Kumar, and Nawang Gombu left for the summit. The summit team reached South Col on the 23rd and last camp on the 24th. On 25 May, the summit team left the last camp with the wind threatening to blow hard. An extract from Brig. Singh's diary describes the situation:

A strong gust of wind almost knocked them over; they would soon learn to lean into the wind to keep their balance. With deliberate movements, they fastened the nylon climbing rope to their waists, Gombu in front, Kumar in the middle and Sonam bringing up the rear.

It is nearly 7 a.m. Crystals of dry snow stung the faces of climbers as strong winds whipped them up. Not an ideal day to accept this high challenge. Visibility was becoming poorer and poorer. Occasionally, an odd patch of cloud drifted past well below them. The climbers' progress was painfully slow. Sonam's gas mask had started giving trouble. Moisture from his breath had frozen and blocked the oxygen inlet valve. Gasping for breath, he tugged the climbing rope. The party had to halt and scrape off the obstruction.

It was nearly 11.15 and they were still at the foot of the south summit at 28,300'. No more than 700' yet to go. Brains were foggy. They sat still for some minutes, then

Gombu broke the silence and pointed out that to go further would be a grave risk. The other two nodded their heads in dejected agreement. Once the issue was broached, the conference did not take long to come to the unanimous decision about the only course left open to them. Down-hearted and gloom, they decided to return without reaching their goal, which was so near and yet so far. The attempt was abandoned.

They moved very slowly down, at snail's pace. After what seemed like an eternity, they reached South Col. Late in the afternoon, dehydrated and exhausted. They were taken care of by their comrades of the support party. The following day they reached safely down to the advance base.

The second summit team remained pinned down at the South Col. The monsoon's advance guard was already in the Everest region. On 27 May, it was apparent that they had just enough time to come off the mountain before the whole massif was enveloped in a dark shroud. Instructions went out to all men in the higher camps to close in at the Base Camp without delay. A strong party was detailed to look after the withdrawal route in the ice-fall. "To say that we were not disappointed would be incorrect," said Brig. Gyan Singh. "Our hearts were heavy. Everyone hopes and works for success. But we know Gombu, Sonam Gyatso and Kumar had done their best and when you have done your best, you can do no better."

1960 CHINESE EXPEDITION

While on 25 May, due to gusts of winds and deterioration in bad weather—the Indian expedition had to return, the Chinese Everest expedition of 1960 claimed to have reached the summit from the Tibetan side. They are reported to have hoisted the red flag and placed a bust of Mao Tse-tung on the summit. They had further reported that since they climbed at night, they were unable to take pictures. It was later reported that as a proof of having reached the summit, a photograph was offered which was later found to have been taken at 8,700 metres. This started a bitter controversy and long-winded discussions in various mountaineering journals.

A detailed examination of the photograph revealed that it was an enlargement of a single frame from one of the Chinese documentary films taken on the expedition. The film was shown in London in October 1962 and later withdrawn. As a result of a thorough examination of the photograph, it was found that the height of the camera from where the photograph was taken was 8,500 metres and not 8,700 metres as claimed.

Shin Chan-chun in 1961 published a report on the expedition in the *British Alpine Journal*. Some of the important facts are reproduced below:

On 25 May 1960, three young Chinese mountaineers reached the summit of Mt Everest by the difficult northerly route ... and started on the most dangerous and arduous journey in the history of mankind. The summit was reached at 04.20 hours Peking time on 25 May 1960, and a flag, a bust of Mao Tse-tung, and a document giving the names of the party and the date were deposited. It was too dark to take any photographs, but nine geological specimens were collected as a present for Chairman Mao Tse-tung.

The success of the Chinese expedition is due to our having adhered to Mao Tse-tung's thoughts on strategy: to disregard difficulties strategically but to give them careful consideration tactically. We succeeded because we were able to profit by the experiences of mountaineers from other countries, particularly from the progressive

Soviet Union. Other reasons for our triumph were our firm belief in the victory of the revolution; the collective spirit of solidarity, friendship and brotherhood which our team so conspicuously displayed, their nobility of character, and the Communist precept of putting "side before self."

To commemorate this great success of the expedition, a jade stone carving of Everest along with 41 mountaineers at various stages of their climb was produced. The carving was done on a green jade found in the province of Honan. It was 5 feet long and weighed $2\frac{1}{2}$ tons. It is also understood that the entire carving was done by 18 skilled craftsmen and it took them over $2\frac{1}{2}$ years to complete this work.

1962 INDIAN EXPEDITION

Having failed in 1960, it was decided to have a broader base of talent to select the next team from. With this in view, the Indian Mountaineering Foundation sponsored three expeditions in 1961: Annapurna III, Nilkantha, and Devisthan-Maiktoli. From these expeditions a new team was selected comprising Maj. John Dias, Lt. M. S. Kohli, Sonam Gyatso, C. P. Vohra, Flt. Lt. A. K. Chowdhury, Capt. A. B. Jungalwala, Gurdial Singh, Hari Dang, Capt. Mulk Raj, K. P. Sharma, O. P. Sharma, Suman Dubey, Dr. A. N. D. Nanavati and Capt. M. A. Soares. The team left on 17 February via the same route as the first Indian Everest Expedition. Towards the end of March, the base camp was established. During the first week of April, a route through Lhotse face was opened. On 28 April, while crossing an ice gully, Sherpa Nawang Tshering was hit in the stomach by a stone which came hurtling down the Lhotse face. Before he could be evacuated, he died.

With bad weather and loss of life, progress was greatly hampered and the team could only establish camp VI on South Col on 1 May. In spite of bad weather, John Dias personally led a ferry of 6 climbers and 17 sherpas to complete the stocking of the last camp. On 26 May the summit party comprising the Deputy Leader, Mohan Kohli, Sonam Gyatso, and Gurdial Singh moved up to South Col. They found the wide expanse of Col littered with angular fragments of frost, shattered rock and rubbery sheets of green and blue ice. But the worst was the 70-knot gale that greeted them and threatened to uproot their Jamet and Meade tents. The winds continued unabated during the night and on the 27th morning. The logic of the weather proved conclusive. The thought of proceeding to the last camp was soon given up and the summit party, with the support team, prepared to spend another night at the treacherous and hostile South Col. Oxygen supplies were, however, limited and the sherpas were persuaded to spend the night without it. The weather forecast that evening announced: "Thunderstorm or snow showers with high winds. Monsoon to strike the Everest region around 1 June."

The morning of 28 May was bright and clear. The summit trio supported by Hari Dang, and 7 sherpas under Sirdar Ang Tharkay of Annapurna fame, moved up to establish the last camp. Among the sherpas was Phu Dorji who later climbed Everest with me in 1965. The team had hardly left the South Col camp when one of the sherpas suffered a mild heart attack and had to be evacuated. A little later Gurdial Singh also returned as he was not feeling well. The party reached the last camp in the afternoon of 28 May. The support party left for South Col after establishing the last camp at 27,650′.

By the afternoon of 28 May, the summit trio was at their last camp. This team missed the summit by a sheer 100 m. and had to spend three nights at the last camp without oxygen—a feat unparalleled in the history of Himalayan mountaineering. The drama of these three days and three nights is best described by Mohan Kohli:

As Ang Tharkay, Phu Dorji and the other Sherpas left us, wishing us good luck, the three of us settled down in the small Hillary tent which opens to only one side. The tent was pitched on a sloping shelf. We managed to fit in three air mattresses without the pillow-sections, with space to one side on to the two small Butane-gas burners and a bag of snow with three cylinders of oxygen each.

After an early dinner, consisting of roast chicken, sattu (flour of parched gram) and aerated juices, we set our oxygen supply at one-litre a minute and retired. The night of 28 May, at 27,650' was reasonably comfortable, especially with the prospect of reaching the summit on the 29th, the date on which Hillary and Tenzing had first reached the summit 9 years ago.

The 29th morning, however, saw our hopes shattering. There were howling winds outside the tent and to get out even briefly to answer the call of nature appeared impossible. During the night the tent had slipped a foot or so forcing us to sleep with our legs bent at the knee, with a portion of the tent overhanging.

There were only two alternatives: one to abandon the attempt, the other to spend a day and a night without oxygen, thus conserving the bottles of oxygen each for the summit and to attempt the peak on the 30th provided the weather permitted. We decided in favour of the latter. This decision followed a long debate. The limited oxygen was the bone of petulance, if not of contention.

Somehow, we managed to spend the day without oxygen. The stoves kept burning the whole day and we gulped mug after mug of beverages. But the night was the longest and most painful that I have ever spent in my life in the mountains. Besides the 6 full bottles of oxygen reserved for the summit attempt, there were two other bottles with oxygen to last a couple of hours each. We gave one to Sonam and decided to share the second between Hari and myself, changing the mask at 15 minute intervals. For us the night was an endless agony while Sonam who is known to eat and sleep was calm. Hari was rather uncomfortable and kept moaning except when he was using oxygen.

It was really an amazing experience—no sooner was the mask brought to his face, he was fast asleep. We accused each other of prolonging one's share of fifteen minutes. Anyway, the bottle was soon empty and the remaining part of the night was one long nightmare.

The morning of 30 May was the one that we had been waiting for a long time. It was bright and clear. We were woken up by Sonam's voice, "See brothers, see! What did I tell you? Twenty-one lamas do not pray in vain!" We soon forgot the ordeal of the night and prepared to leave. It was now 5 a.m. By 7 we were outside the tent, in superb weather and ready to leave. We scrambled up the rocks at a good pace, delighted at the prospect of good weather. The winds and the driving snow were now forgotten. The rocks of the South East ridge were covered with soft, driven snow. At 11 the wind started blowing and our speed reduced significantly. We kept on moving however. Just below the last slope leading to the South summit, we dumped our half used oxygen bottles and changed to fresh ones.

The wind speed increased gradually, reducing our hopes of reaching the summit. At 2 p.m. I suggested that we stop and take stock of the situation. Nobody stopped. Finally at 3.30 p.m. I suggested again when we all stopped. Sonam and Hari were keen to continue. I realised that we had been climbing for nearly $8\frac{1}{2}$ hours, going for about a 1000'. The remaining 300' would take at least 2 hours for which the oxygen supply would not last, and with the deteriorating weather we decided to call off the

66

Facing: A sherpa family crossing
a rivulet on the approach march.
Overleaf: Above: On the approach march.
Below: Khumbu glacier.

attempt. We debated the matter and decided to call it a day.

We descended gingerly, changed our empty bottles for the half-used ones at the base of the South summit. We were utterly exhausted. As we approached the steep slope at around 28,000′, Sonam slipped taking with him Hari who was caught unaware. Like a driver who instinctively jams his breaks at the slightest hint of an impending collision, I drove my ice axe into the ice which stopped our fall to the Western Cwm 7,000′ below.

At 8 p.m. it was pitch dark and we were nowhere near our tent. One can write a book on what happened during the next two hours. We knew that if we stopped here, we would be frozen to death. But in pitch dark it was not easy to move. At one time we almost said our last prayers. However, we did not really give up. We took the lead turn by turn, including Hari who was tied to the middle of the rope. At 10 p.m., crawling on all fours, we hit our tent. We could only manage to remove our crampons and slipped into our sleeping bags, without any food or liquid. In fact we were unconscious with exhaustion.

On the 31st morning we waited until 10 a.m. when the heat from the sun brought life to our exhausted limbs, and marched down to South Col. It took us six hours to get down to the vast expanse of the South Col where we met our faithful sherpa Danu, who had anxiously waited for three days for us. He had brought with him juices and tea which we gulped down our parched throats and then stumbled down to South Col and thus ended the drama of the three days and three nights that we had spent close to the summit.

It was indeed a heroic effort against heavy odds. Like the first expedition, John Dias and his brave boys were sent back not by the mountain, but by the weather against which man has no recourse on a mountain of the magnitude of Everest. "We will come back," was John Dias' promise to Everest and this promise was to be kept. Everest was booked by the Americans for 1963 and by the Germans for 1964. So the Indian Mountaineering Foundation booked it for 1965.

THE UNAUTHORISED ATTEMPT

There have been almost four unauthorised attempts or so-called raids on the mountain from the North side. Three were lone adventurers—an Englishman, a Canadian, and a Dane. The fourth was a quartet of three Americans and a Swiss. All these attempts were from the Tibetan side with hardly any food or equipment and no permission. The results were either death by exposure or a retreat. The most recent one was that of the quartet in 1962 which was led by Woodrow Wilson Sayre (grandson of the late U.S. President). The team approached the mountain through Nepal. They told everybody that they were attempting a neighbouring peak of Everest, called Gyachung Kang. Once they were half way up this mountain, they told the sherpas and the porters not to worry as they would go up this peak on their own without their support. From the pass, they quietly crossed over into Tibet and climbed above the North Col. Taking into consideration their inadequate mountaineering experience, the low stock of food and mountaineering equipment, and no sherpa support, having climbed so high was indeed a remarkable feat and all the more creditable because they returned without any fatal accidents.

Their absence caused great anxiety and when the facts were known, the American Ambassador in Nepal had to apologise to the Nepalese Government. Later, Sayre wrote

Left to right: Sherpa Thopke, Da Namgyal, "Brig." Thondup (the cook), Ang Temba, Tenzing Norkay and Nawang Gombu

Brig. Gyan Singh

ossing the Dud Kosi

that it was all fun and games. I do not know why Sayre had to take such a risk when it could have been easy for him to get the permission through normal channels. Such hair-brained adventures bring a bad name to the mountaineering fraternity. This attempt was also responsible to a large extent in the closure of Everest and other mountains immediately after our expedition, and they were reopened only in late 1969.

6

1963 American Expedition

On 10 May 1961 permission was granted for an American expedition to Mount Everest in spring 1963. The leader of the expedition, Norman Dyhrenfurth, organised the expedition with scientific precision intending to investigate certain fundamental problems in glacio-physics, human behaviour, and biology. Out of a total budget of $ 400,000 the greater part was set aside for scientific investigation and for the production of a full length documentary film. The team comprised 19 Americans: Dr. William E. Siri, Allen C. Auten, Barry C. Bishop, John E. Breitenbach, James Barry Corbet, David L. Dingman, M. D., Daniel E. Doody, Norman G. Dyhrenfurth, Dr. Richard M. Emerson, Dr. Thomas F. Hornbein, Luther G. Jerstad, Dr. James T. Lester, Jr., Dr. Maynard M. Miller, Richard Pownall, Barry W. Prather, Dr. Gilbert Roberts, Lt. Col. James Owen M. Roberts, James Ramsey Ullman, Dr. William F. Unsoeld, and James W. Whittaker.

On 20 February, the team left Kathmandu with 27 tonnes of food and equipment carried by 909 porters. The expedition had its first stroke of bad luck on 1 March when the bridge across Likhu Khola collapsed while the porters were crossing it and they fell into the torrent. It was very fortunate that there was no serious accident and they escaped unhurt.

In the village of Junbesi, a badly burned woman was brought into their camp who needed immediate evacuation and hospitalisation. On the request of the expedition, a helicopter evacuated her to the United Missions Hospital where she made a rapid recovery but left the expedition short by $ 2,000 which was the hire charge for the evacuation by helicopter which had to be paid for by the expedition.

The next halt was the village of Ghat in the Dudh Kosi valley, where they had their first encounter with smallpox. One of their porters died and the disease threatened to spread in epidemic proportions. Vaccines were flown with the help of Sir Edmund Hillary's team and the disease was brought under control. The expedition reached Namche Bazar on 7 March and on the 9th they reached Thyangboche.

The High Lama of the monastery developed an unbearable toothache for which the expedition's doctors were called in to pull out five badly infected teeth. On 15 March the expedition left for base camp. There was heavy snowfall which delayed reaching base camp and it was only on 21 March that base camp was established.

In spite of heavy snowfall, Jimmy Roberts was able to handle the sherpas and the porters extremely well, thereby putting the expedition slightly ahead of schedule. According to the original plan, they not only wanted to climb Everest but Lhotse and Nuptse as well. But this was dropped in favour of the West ridge, one of the great remaining challenges of the mountain. Norman Dyhrenfurth writes in his diary:

> Now that we have no more 'camp followers', we talked very frankly about the thing that had been on the minds of all the climbers: the West Ridge, which, if we can pull it off, would be one of the biggest things in Himalayan mountaineering. It was interesting to see how highly motivated the whole group was. There was comparatively little interest in Lhotse and Nuptse, although I had explained to them that initially, when we were trying to raise funds, the idea of an American "Grand Slam" of three peaks had its appeal. But to most of the men that meant very little. In fact, Tom Hornbein, who is such an idealist and so enthusiastic about the West Ridge, declared himself in favour of throwing everything into that attempt, even if it meant jeopardizing success altogether. At this point I had to speak up strongly. I told them that I was in favour of making a serious stab at the West Ridge, or at least a thorough reconnaissance. If it proved feasible, we would push up a line of camps, but at the same time we would build up the South Col route. If the West Ridge proves impossible, we will at least have taken some good pictures of the Tibetan side of Everest from an entirely new point of view. But if the ridge is possible, we could attempt a traverse by having some men go up from the West and come down toward the South Col, and two—or perhaps four—do the same in reverse.

On 22 March, Willi Unsoeld, Jim Whittaker, Lute Jerstad, Nawang Gombu and two Solu Khumbu men entered the ice fall to open the route and return to base camp for the night. The next day, the team consisting of John E. Breitenbach, Dick Pownall, Dr. Gil Roberts and the sherpas Ang Pema and Ila Tsering, went up to improve and continue opening the route from the point from where the first team had left. At 2 p.m. they heard a deafening noise and everything under, around, and above started moving. A huge section of the ice wall had collapsed, burying John E. Breitenbach under tons of ice. He died instantaneously. His team mates suffered minor injuries. This sudden tragedy shook all the members and there was no movement for two days as they had lost a very close and outstanding mountaineer. Norman G. Dyhrenfurth writes:

> Sudden and violent tragedy had struck. During the next two days, while we were trying to find our way back to life and purpose, there was no movement of man in the ice fall. The 25th was spent passing out clothing and equipment, and by the end of the day we were again a team instead of a group of lonely and severely shaken individuals. We had lost a close friend and an outstanding mountaineer, but as deaths go, John E. Breitenbach's was a clean-cut, kindly one.

Norman Dyhrenfurth

By the 28th, the members succeeded in reaching the top of the ice fall and established camp I at 20,000', and camp II was established on 31 March at 21,300'. On personal preferences, the leader divided the members into two teams, one for the West Ridge and the other for the South Col. For the West Ridge, Willi Unsoeld would be in charge of operations, with Tom Hornbein, Barry Corbet, Dick Emerson, Dave Dingman and Barry Bishop. For the South Col operations, Norman G. Dyhrenfurth was himself in charge with Will Siri, Jim Whittaker, Lute Jerstad, Dick Pownall and Gil Roberts as the team mates. The balance of the members, who were not included in either team, were to act as a support team.

On 13 April, the West Ridge party returned to advance base camp after reconnaissance of the West Ridge. The party had succeeded in reaching a height of 25,100' and was fully convinced that there was a route to the summit. They were also aware of the fact that they would be confronted with logistical problems and perhaps a lack of a suitable camp site. However, two members of this party, Dave and Barry Bishop, later got themselves shifted to the South Col party. Barry Bishop was a professional photographer on the staff of the National Geographic Society and did not want to take a chance. On the other hand the South Col party was making sturdy progress. On 14 April, Jim Whittaker Gombu and two sherpas established camp IV at 24,900'. The only portion now left for this party was fixed ropes across the Lhotse Couloir and Yellow Band to open the South Col Camp. At this stage, the planning of the expedition was to continue the build-up on a limited scale, while the major thrust applied to the South Col route. Norman G. Dyhrenfurth wrote: "There were to be two teams of four men each. The first assault group would consist of Big Jim Whittaker, Nawang Gombu (from Darjeeling), Barry Bishop and his sherpa Girmi Dorje (from Solu Khumbu). The second team of Lute Jerstad, Dick Pownall, Ang Dawa and myself would move up one day behind the others in support and make its summit bid after the first team's attempt."

On 16 April the route beyond camp IV was opened and the party reached South Col at 3.30 p.m. The weather, which had been unusually good, began to deteriorate, and stopped further progress on the South Col route. The leader had a difficult decision to make —whether to stop further progress and call everybody to the base camp till the weather improved. After open discussion with the team members, the leader decided to hang on for another date and in case there was no sign of improvement, the members would go down. But fortunately, the 27th was a clear day and activities were resumed in stocking the camp in the South Col and making preparations for the summit team.

The first summit party left camp III followed by the second group the next day. The leader changed places with Barry Bishop as it was important to film the first ascent which would bring them a large income. At camp III, Gombu, Ang Dawa, and Norman G. Dyhrenfurth shared the four-man tent and started using oxygen for sleeping. On 28 April the party moved up to Camp IV supported by 12 sherpas. The next day they reached South Col. It was cold and windy but the night was fairly comfortable as they were on oxygen throughout the night on a one-litre flow to conserve their strength. On 30 April it was extremely windy when the party left for the last camp, followed by Ang Dawa and Dyhrenfurth for filming. The party reached the last camp in the afternoon.

The last camp was established by levelling a small platform at a height of 27,450'. Later they discovered that they were several hundred feet below the 1953 final camp. On 1 May, the first summit party left the last camp. The following account by Dyhrenfurth from the *American Alpine Journal* is reproduced below:

The night was quite comfortable, but on the morning of May 1 there was a gigantic

plume of snow directly above us, with Lhotse and Nuptse barely visible. Makalu was completely blotted out. After a quick breakfast—a cup of hot Jello per man—Big Jim and Gombu were on their way by 6.30. I told them: 'Don't wait for us, we'll come along and see how high we can get. If the weather improves, we hope to reach the South Summit and film you guys on the final ridge.' As we followed the ridge we saw no more than a few feet ahead of us, and I was uncomfortably aware of the fact that my right hand with the ice axe was inside Tibet, with a nearly vertical drop of more than 10,000′ to the Kangchung Glacier. From time to time we looked over our shoulders at Lhotse, barely visible through the driving snow. We were just about even with its summit, then we were above it.

On we went, following the faint tracks into nothingness. It was tough going, with three to four breaths for every step. I started counting steps, with a prolonged rest after every twenty, then after every ten. Suddenly there was a tug on the rope. Ang Dawa's breathing bag was empty, and he seemed to be in trouble. I cramponed down to him to discover that his first cylinder was used up. After changing bottles, we continued to climb.

At a point where the ridge levels off before rising sharply toward the South Summit, half of my oxygen supply was gone, and Ang Dawa helped me change cylinders. I explained to him that this was the end of the line for us, but when I got ready to go down, he looked at me uncomprehendingly: 'Up go, Bara Sahib?' said Ang Dawa, pointing. But I shook my head: 'This is the point of no return. If we go on, we will have oxygen until we're about halfway between the South Summit and the Main Summit. Then we will run out of air, and we will never get down alive. We will also not reach the Main Summit, so we can't even be dead heroes on top!' And I tried to explain that our main function was to take movies as high as possible and to support Big Jim and Gombu. We had carried heavy movie equipment to this point, up to 28,200′, but it was absolutely useless since we couldn't see anything. At last Ang Dawa saw my point of view, and after a very slow and careful descent we reached camp VI around 1.30, completely done in. All the way down, while hanging on for dear life in that terrifying storm, I kept worrying about our summit team. It seemed utterly impossible that the summit could be reached.

And yet, at the very time when Ang Dawa and I decided to turn back, Big Jim and Gombu were kicking steps up the steepest portion of the ridge. Each had deposited one partially-used oxygen bottle at about 28,400′ to lighten his load, confident that one full bottle per man was sufficient to reach the summit and get back again. With Big Jim in the lead at 11.30, they reached the South Summit, where the full force of the storm hit them. Doubt arose in the big man's mind as to whether to go on. Although he had studied the previous photographs of that final ridge, now that he came face to face with it, it looked much steeper and more difficult than anticipated. After a few minutes' hesitation and soul-searching, Big Jim and Gombu dropped down some 30′ to the saddle between the two summits and began climbing up the final ridge.

Carefully they worked their way up between the immense snow cornices which overhang the Kangchung Face on the right, and the rocks on the left. Struggling through the gale, they reached Hillary's Chimney and encountered no difficulties. Soon they were above it, and what followed was a series of humps in the snowy ridge. And then, as Big Jim approached what appeared to be the final dome, he stopped and waited for Gombu to come up to him: "You first, Gombu." "No, you go first," was the small man's reply. Then Jim said, "Let's go together," and side by side they walked fighting to maintain their balance on the storm-swept summit of the world. It was 1 p.m.—almost seven hours after their departure from camp VI.

At the very top Big Jim drove a four-foot aluminum stake to which he had secured an American flag. And then they took pictures of each other holding various smaller flags. Toward the west and the plains of Tibet in the north the view was clear, but to the south and east everything was obscured by the mountain's vast snow plume. After Gombu tied a *kata,* the traditional Buddhist friendship scarf, to the stake, the men began their descent.

The summit party had a terrible time coming down as their oxygen bottles were completely empty. They were completely dehydrated when they reached camp VI and were helped by Dyhrenfurth and Ang Dawa. The next morning they all descended. The second summit party could not, however, go up as scheduled. The attempt had to be postponed because of acute shortage of oxygen and they all went down to base camp. By 4 May most of the team members were down at base camp. The names of the summiters were not given out as they had decided to withhold this till everybody was off the mountain but this was not possible. The pressure from the outside world became unbearable and the leaders had to give the names of the summiters. Dyhrenfurth wrote in his diary: "Everybody contributed, everyone worked together. There are no heroes: The men who first reached the South Col, or those who were the first to open up the ice fall and the Lhotse Face, and others who did many hard and thankless jobs. This is a team effort, and I'll be damned if we're going to have one or two heroes."

As a result of the discussion among the members, a new plan was worked out for two assault teams—one on the West Ridge and the other on the South Col. The traverse on the mountain would also be attempted and a possible meet of the two summit parties on 18 May. Later the date was changed to 21 May. Now, after having climbed the mountain *via* the South Col route, all efforts and man power were diverted to the West Ridge. Most of the equipment and oxygen cylinders required were lifted up with the help of a winch to camp III-W.

By 16 May camp IV-W had been established at a height of 25,100′ near the steep rock. The reconnaissance for camp V-W at a height of 26,200′ was made. This camp was to be established at the base of the snow-filled gully west of the famous great couloir of the pre-war British expeditions. The team was to move on the 17th, but unfortunately they could not do so as on the 16th two of their four-men tents (along with four sherpas, who were sleeping inside at camp IV) were flown away by wild winds towards Rongbuk glacier 6,000′ below. They were lucky to have escaped a very major disaster in which there could have been a loss of lives. The tents, however, were damaged.

On 18 May, Lute Jerstad, Barry Bishop, and three sherpas left advance base camp for the summit. The weather was good and on 21 May they established camp VI. Meanwhile, on the West Ridge side four-men tents were brought up from the lower camp and were pitched at camp IV-W. On 21 May, Barry, Corbet and Auten left for a reconnaissance with their sherpa support, reaching a height of 26,000′. Barry and Auten had reached the very edge of the Yellow Band at a height of 27,200′ which would be a possible camp site. Tom and Willi Unsoeld enlarged the edge to make a possible camp site. As there was not enough time for more than one summit attempt, those who had contributed the most in preparing the route, Tom and Willi Unsoeld, were chosen to be the summit pair on the West Ridge. On the next day they left camp V-W (west) at 7 a.m. Willi Unsoeld wrote for

the *American Alpine Journal* in 1964:

The couloir proved steeper than we had expected, forcing us to move one at a time with constant belays and much step-cutting. Well over an hour was spent on one hairy 40 foot rock pitch requiring two pitons and bare hands. Thus by 10.30 a.m. we were still no yet through the Yellow Band although its major difficulties now seemed to be below us. While switching bottles, we radioed Base for the first time that day, telling Big Jim that the stretch we had come up was so messy that we had to hope of trying to descend it. Jim was greatly unsettled by such talk about a 'point of no return,' but we felt strongly that the way to the South Col via the summit offered much less danger than did a descent to V-W.

Meanwhile Lute and Barry had moved up the southeast ridge to the South Summit. Barry, after a very bad night at Camp VI and the almost disastrous explosion, felt weak and close to exhaustion on the entire ascent. After a much needed rest on the South Summit, they continued along the final ridge on a reduced oxygen ration. And then, shortly before 3.30 they saw the American flag flying from the summit of the world. Placed there three weeks before by Big Jim, the aluminum pole still stood straight and tall, with only the ends of the flag slightly tattered. Tears of emotion and relief came of their eyes as together they stepped onto the summit. For 45 minutes they photographed the world around and beneath them—Lute took the highest motion pictures ever made—and they scanned the West Ridge for any signs of us. They waited, they shouted, but finally as the shadows lengthened, they began the descent.

In bright sunshine and gentle breezes Tom and I had at length crept out of the couloir and onto the upper snowfields of the North Face. The mass of the summit rocks now loomed above us—a mass of such imposing bulk that we were afraid of being unable to find the true top without an extensive search. We even called Base again to ask Jim where the top was and what it looked like, but understandably his puzzled efforts at description didn't help us out much. Then we remembered that Jim had spoken of looking *down* the West Ridge from the summit. Therefore, we had only to follow the crest on up. A long traverse to the right across crumbling slabs and steepening snow slopes brought us finally to the crest of this Ridge, where we could look straight down into the Cwm.

Across the South Face from us and slightly above appeared the South Summit. Ahead the Ridge rose as a twisting rocky spine. Doffing crampons, we attacked this lovely stretch with all the enthusiasm of snow-surfeited rock climbers. To our surprise, unlike the Yellow Band, the gray rock was sound, allowing quite delicate moves on moderately small holds. Or maybe it only seemed sound in comparison to the gravity-matrixed crumble of which so much of the North Face is composed. At any rate, we genuinely enjoyed those several rope-lengths on rock and were regretful when the arête changed back to snow again, demanding crampons for the last few hundred feet. The snow was ideally firm, however, and our progress was steady until just after six o'clock. I suddenly came out at the top of the snow arête only about forty feet from the American flag. As Tom joined me, we threw arms around each other's shoulders marched up to the flag in silence.

What did we feel? What did we think about? What did we do during this culmination of our date with the world's very 'nose-tip?' The actions are pretty well prescribed: pictures and placement of summit objects. The Rev. Andy Bakewell, A. A. C. and member of the first reconnaissance expedition to Everest from the south in 1950, had given me a crucifix to leave on top. I tucked it down inside Gombu's *kata* (Buddhist ceremonial scarf) at the base of Big Jim's flag pole—along with two prayer flags given me by Ang Dorje. Buddhist prayer flags and ceremonial scarf, the American flag, and the cross of Christ all perched together on the top of the world—supported by an aluminum rappel picked painted 'Survival Orange'. ... The symbolic possibilities rendered my summit prayer more than a trifle incoherent.

Feelings and thoughts melted and merged in our climactic moment. My thoughts were heavily weighted with history—the early attempts via the North Col—the drive and vision of such men as Mallory, Norton, Smythe, Shipton and Timan. And the later generation of Everesters led by Hunt, Hillary and Tenzing and including such as Lambert, Evans, Bourdillon, Eggler, Marmet, and Von Gunten. Following these years of effort and achievement appears our own expedition and the tremendous output on the part of the entire team—Sahibs and Sherpas alike—output and sacrifice without which our own summit moment would never have materialized. But dominating such thoughts were the surging emotions which coloured them. Control is thinned by the altitude and the tears came readily—called forth by a wave of gratitude and burst of comradely feeling for each member of the expedition. And behind the expedition—our wives and families—eliciting their own peculiar mixture of guilt and exaltation. Twenty minutes of emotional flux such as this and the marvel is that we still had the starch to even start the descent.

The sun was just disappearing as we left the top afte one last broadcast which was picked up at Camp II. In the short twilight, we raced across the treacherous ridge to the South Summit and from there started down the line of tracks towards Camp VI. Barry Bishop and Lute Jerstad had preceded us to the top by about three hours and we took advantage of their tracks until first the sun and then my flashlight faded into darkness. The blind, stumbling descent became more and more reflex. Belays were set up, a fall was stopped, a route searched out—because we had spent so much of our lives doing just these things. Then echoes from below—then shouts. Must be Dave Dingman and Girmi Dorje in support at Camp VI. Hours later a blacker smudge against the snow below and falling into the arms of ... Lute and Barry?!! What a surprise! They had heard us and waited till we reached them around 9:30 p.m.

Now down again—the four of us together. Terribly tired and Tom the only one with a little oxygen left. Four stumbling tight-rope walkers edging down a knife-edge of snow. Lute falls and is stopped when his chin hooks over the rope stretching between Tom and me. I am supposed to be belaying Barry as I precede him down the ridge. Fatigue engenders strange techniques.

Finally, at around 12.30 a.m., the arête becomes indistinct and Lute thinks it is time to get off the ridge before turning left toward Camp VI. The turning point is crucial—a mistake could land you in the Cwm—and it is too dark to be certain. We bivouac. A simple maneuver—just take off your pack and lie down. Nothing fancy, not even a common huddle. Mostly just fall like logs and wait for daylight. Tom fusses with his feet, complaining of the cold. I report no discomfort in my feet (nor even feeling) and feel secretly proud at my superior cold tolerance.

At dawn they started walking down towards camp VI where they were met by Dave and Girmi. They were later evacuated by helicopter from Namche Bazar. The rest of the team started to trek back to Kathmandu on 25 May with 275 porters.

Facing: Everest South West Face—Camp II
Overleaf: Camp II with Pumori in the
background.
P-86: Jim Whittaker on the summit.

Looking up from a crevasse

Negotiating Ice wall on the Khumbu glacier

Igloo

Ice fall

A Jumbo leap on lhotse face

7
1965 Indian Expedition

The failure of our expedition to Mount Everest in the years 1960 and 1962, when we were beaten back by the fury of the winds, left a burning desire among Indians to make another attempt on Mount Everest. The third Everest expedition was planned for 1965. The leader of the expedition was Lt. Cdr. M. S. Kohli, who had been to Everest in the previous two attempts and was deputy leader of the 1962 expedition where he had the unique experience of spending 3 consecutive nights at the last camp. He had climbed extensively in the Karakoram, had also climbed Nanda Kot, Annapurna III and had led the Nanda Devi East and Trisuli expedition in 1964. The Deputy Leader, Major N. Kumar, had been with the first Everest expedition and had reached a height of 28,300'. He had led a successful expedition to Nilakantha in 1964, where he suffered serious frost bite and later led the successful expedition to Nanda Devi (25,645'). The rest of the team was selected from among the mountaineers of the country.

The selection of members of the team was a difficult task. The first list of 26 climbers was made on the basis of their past experience. These climbers were then sent on pre-Everest expeditions to Mount Rathong in Sikkim, 21,911' as yet unclimbed, in the middle of October 1964. I was lucky to be chosen to participate in this expedition and later was able to climb to the summit of Mount Rathong along with the other members of the pre-Everest expedition. Members were finally chosen for the Mount Everest team on the basis of their performance in the Rathong Expedition. Among the other members selected was Tenzing's nephew Nawang Gombu who had already climbed Mount Everest with the Americans. The other members of the team were: Sonam Gyatso, Gurdial Singh, C. P. Vohra, Major Mulk Raj, Sonam Wangyal, Captain A. S. Cheema, Captain Bahuguna, Captain J. C. Joshi, Dr. Lala Telang, H. C. S. Rawat, Ang Kami, Major B. P. Singh,

Facing: Author and Phu Dorji on the summit
of Mount Everest flying the Indian Tri-
colour and the Nepalese flag with American
pole on the right.
P-89: Camp IV at Lhotse face.

Capt. A. K. Chakravarti, G. S. Bhangu, Hav. Balakrishnan, and Lt. B. N. Rana, Liaison Officer.

On 26 February, the expedition left Jaynagar, a border town between India and Nepal. We carried 25 tonnes of equipment and stores which were distributed among 800 porters to be carried up to the base camp. For higher camps, we had 50 sherpas and most of them had come from the Solu Khumbu area. The long approach march to the Everest provided a great opportunity to get to know one another and also to communicate with and appreciate the sherpas, besides developing one's outdoor hobbies. The understanding that grows up among the members and the sherpas is of great help later when the climb becomes difficult.

Our porters, both male and female, carried an equal amount of load. Each load was very carefully prepared and weighed 60 lbs. Kumar wanted to recruit more female porters than male as he said the women drank less and created less fuss in carrying the loads. There were many female porters in our expedition. In fact, of the 800 porters almost half were female. At times a women porter would carry her husband's load in addition to her own as he would be drinking or was drunk. The women porters from the hills are very strong, hardy and spirited. I remember an incident when a woman porter gave birth to a child. Just for a day or two after delivering the child she did not carry the load, but then resumed carrying the load. This is not very unusual. She probably delivered the baby at a height of about 9,000'.

Camps were set up at Namche Bazar and Thyangboche. We then moved on to the rarefied atmosphere of the Khumbu glacier, and the base camp was established at 17,800'. The first phase of the climb after the base camp was crossing the ice fall. Rising 2,200' from the base to the top, it presented one of the most hazardous stretches of the route. Hillary called it a "tottering chaos," as the route through it is constantly changing. It took ten days to open the route slowly through the ice fall, and camp I was set up at a height of 20,000'.

After camp I was sufficiently stocked, reconnaissance for camps II and III started. On 3 April, a party of four members and three sherpas set out from camp I to open camp II, which was set up at 21,300'. A wireless link with the base camp was immediately established. Camp III was established at 22,300', and although it was considered safe, it was very unpopular with the sherpas. In 1952, during the Swiss attempt, a sherpa was killed in this area by an avalanche. Ever since then a superstition had developed that the ghost of the watchman wandered around that area. Sherpas avoided staying overnight at this camp if they could help it. They complained of being disturbed by a nocturnal visitor — the watchman knocking at their tents. One of our sherpas, Nawang Tshering, refused in 1960 to stay at camp III in spite of very bad weather. Two years later, in 1962, with the second Indian Everest expedition, he was hit by a rolling stone and died in the same area. This only helped strengthen the superstition and the camp, although well stocked, remained "haunted."

The work in opening the route beyond camp IB was undertaken by the Gyatso party, which opened the route up to Geneva Spur. By 13 April they were all set to move the first ferry consisting of Cheema, myself and 15 sherpas to dump loads at South Col (Camp V). 13 April, according to the Indian calendar, happened to be Baisakhi or New Year's Day and was considered very auspicious. Our party had moved to this camp on 12 April. It was decided not to use oxygen at this height, at any rate to start with. Matters were complicated by heavy snowfall, which caused the roofs of the tents to collapse. As soon as the weather improved summit plans were quickly taken in hand again. This could

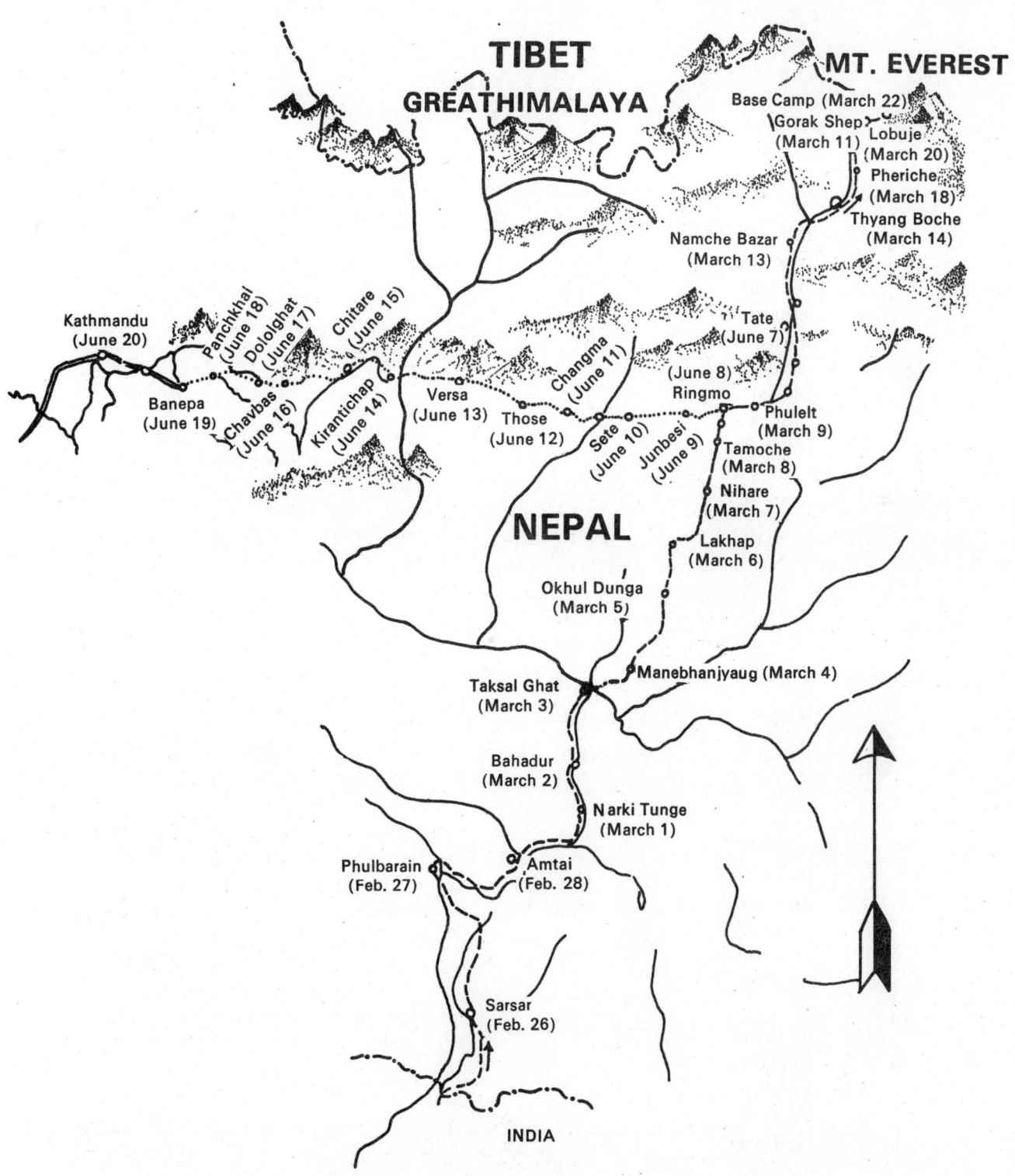

TIBET

GREATHIMALAYA

MT. EVEREST

Base Camp (March 22)

Gorak Shep
(March 11)

Lobuje
(March 20)

Pheriche
(March 18)

Thyang Boche
(March 14)

Namche Bazar
(March 13)

Kathmandu
(June 20)

Panchkhal
(June 18)

Dololghat
(June 17)

Chitare
(June 15)

Tate
(June 7)

Changma
(June 11)

(June 8)

Ringmo

Banepa
(June 19)

Chavbas
(June 16)

Kirantichap
(June 14)

Versa
(June 13)

Those
(June 12)

Sete
(June 10)

Junbesi
(June 9)

Phulelt
(March 9)

Tamoche
(March 8)

Nihare
(March 7)

NEPAL

Lakhap
(March 6)

Okhul Dunga
(March 5)

Manebhanjyaug (March 4)

Taksal Ghat
(March 3)

Bahadur
(March 2)

Narki Tunge
(March 1)

Phulbarain
(Feb. 27)

Amtai
(Feb. 28)

Sarsar
(Feb. 26)

INDIA

be one of the earliest attempts on Everest. The summit party consisting of Gombu and Cheema made rapid progress reaching South Col on 28 April and were ready to move up the next day. But unfortunately, the weather deteriorated. Every member was ordered to withdraw from the mountain. By 1 May, the entire expedition gathered at the base camp. We had some rather unexpected visitors from the North—Chinese soldiers who moved to the Lho-la pass on the Tibet-Nepal border overlooking our base camp. They created quite a stir and gave the impression of having been sent to report on the activities of the camp.

On 14 May, the plume on Everest had vanished, the wind had died down and the weather improved. The time had come for us to move to a higher camp. The summit parties were announced by Mohan, as the leader was affectionately called by his team mates. Gombu and Cheema were the first party followed by Gyatso and Wngyal. The third pair would be Vohra and Ang Kami followed by Rawat and Bahuguna, and the last would be B. P. Singh and myself. It was also decided that the summit pairs would be moved at two-day intervals. This would avoid crowding at the last camp. The first summit party would make an attempt on the 20th, the second on the 22nd, the third on the 24th, and the fourth on the 26th.

This seemed a very ambitious plan on the basis of our existing stock of oxygen cylinders. I was in the last party, so I sat down to assess the oxygen situation. In all we had 150 oxygen cylinders out of which 44 had already been used in an unsuccessful attempt in April. Six cylinders were reserved for medical purposes and only 100 cylinders were left to be used by the summit parties. To make a comparison with the American expedition, it is relevant to note that they had 200 oxygen cylinders and were able to put only six members on top. I wondered how we would be able to support so many with half that stock of oxygen in hand.

On 16 May, the first summit party comprising Cheema and Gombu started their upward journey with their Sherpa support. It was a clear day. The path through the ice fall had changed, and every now and then they had to strengthen the bridges or at places make a new route. They reached camp I at noon. After resting for a while, they left for the advance base camp where the stores, equipment, and oxygen masks were checked and got ready. On the 17th, the party left for camp IV. To save oxygen it was decided that the summit parties would start using oxygen only after reaching camp IV.

Cheema and Gombu reached camp IV at 4 p.m. The camp was in bad shape owing to the foul weather which had prevailed earlier. They re-erected it with the help of sherpas led by Deputy Sirdar Phu Dorji. The weather was now good and the party left the South Col on 18 May. Gombu and Cheema were now fitted with oxygen masks consuming oxygen at the rate of two litres per minute. They passed the Lhotse couloir with the help of fixed rope and reached the Yellow Band. The entire path now led over snow, rock and ice or a mixture of rock and ice. After traversing the Geneva Spur they reached the South Col. Phu Dorji and his party also reached South Col immediately behind them. Together they re-arranged the camp at South Col and erected the tents. Oxygen cylinders were neatly stacked at one end. The oxygen masks and other apparatus were checked.

The wind at South Col continued to blow hard and lashed the tents. Cheema contacted the advance base camp by wireless and gave an "all's well" report. Thereafter the summit party retired into their sleeping bags to have a good night's rest. The consumption of oxygen was reduced to one litre per minute. On 19 May, the pair along with sherpa support, left for the last camp. Cheema in his excitement forgot the juice tin on the stove. They had hardly stepped out of the tent when it exploded and sounded like a gun salute. Nobody was

94

Tengpoche Monastery

Walk through the Phantam Alley

Tiger and Sonam Gyasto

Base Camp

hurt and the party went ahead.

Phu Dorji was entrusted with the task of opening the last camp. The leader had advised him to set up this camp as high as possible. The summit party and the sherpa support led in turns. Early in the afternoon they reached the hump on the ridge which was at an altitude of approximately 28,000′, and decided to pitch the tent on a small area about 70′ below it. This was then declared the last camp on the route to Everest, the highest ever in the history of the mountain. The area around was levelled and the soft snow was cleared. The oxygen cylinders were neatly stacked outside by the sherpas. Phu Dorji and the sherpas, after bidding goodbye to the summit party, left for South Col.

The summit party retired rather early as a hard day was ahead of them. On 20 May at 5 a.m. the pair left for the summit. We were all excited and everyone kept a close watch on the progress made by them. Three observation posts were established by us. They were at the base camp, advance base camp, and at camp IV. From these points with the help of binoculars one could follow in that difficult weather the movements of the summit party. One of the posts reported having seen them moving on the ridge close to the summit, having stayed on the summit for thirty minutes and then coming down, reaching the last camp at 12.45 p.m. The news of the expedition's success was flashed to Delhi without delay. Congratulatory messages soon started pouring in.

On 22 May the second party of the Sonams left the last camp at 6.45 a.m. despite the sufferings of the previous day and night. The wind continued to blow strong, but they kept going and reached the peak after five hours of a most strenuous climb. Sonam's back injury gave him much trouble but he did not give up. While returning from the summit they had some trouble with their oxygen and with difficulty they reached the last camp at 6 p.m. They had no alternative but to spend the night at this camp. The following morning they moved to the lower camps.

The third summit party of Vohra and Ang Kami reached the top at 10.45 a.m. on 24 May and returned to the last camp at 4.15 p.m. Vohra was able to take a film from the top. They too had their share of troubles. On the return journey Vohra's oxygen finished. They spent a very uncomfortable night at the last camp vainly trying to warm their feet. The next day Vohra and Ang Kami came to South Col where they were received by their support party and later moved to the advance base camp.

The fourth summit party comprising B.P., Bogie, Rawat, Dorji and myself was to attempt the summit on the 26th. The 25th morning was bright but chilly. Inside our tents, we were brought the fearful news that there had been a huge avalanche over camp III. Forgetting the tea, Mohan and I rushed outside. What we saw was a frightful sight. The camp, with its colourful tents—luckily unoccupied at the time—had been completely wiped out and nothing was visible except a huge expanse of white. But while there was no loss of life, we had lost something as precious. The cylinders of life-sustaining oxygen which we had carefully conserved and stored in the camp had now been buried under the avalanche. And with them too, it seemed, were buried the hopes of our summit party reaching the top. The leader had no option except to call off the final assault as without the oxygen it was doomed to failure. Could we search for the cylinders, we asked? Such a search seemed both pointless and hopeless as whoever heard of bottles being dug out from under a huge mass of snow? But if we were so keen about it, we might as well make the effort, he said. He gave us four sherpas to assist with the search, and our Nepalese Liaison Officer Rana also accompanied us.

There was no trace whatsoever of the camp when we reached the site after a two-hour trek—there was no recognisable landmark. It was all white barrenness. The avalanche had

99

*Ahluwalia and Harsh Bahuguna with
Namche Bazar merchant*

Mohan Kohli

Cheema and Dr Lala Telang on the medicine counter

poured over our camp in a tide of whiteness. Everything had disappeared under the snow. Only the jet black rocks of the Lhotse Face protruded from the thick white blanket. The icy winds of the South Col howled at us without respite and lashed our faces. It was a massive avalanche, and we were lucky that we were not in camp when it struck. Without wasting much time, we organised ourselves and started digging with the hope that we might find some oxygen cylinders, if not the rest of the equipment. Doubt and determination kept up a running battle in my weary mind.

We kept digging but there appeared to be no sign either of the equipment or the oxygen cylinders. It was tough going. Mind and body fought desperately to conquer fatigue and bitter cold, and to win the race against time. Towards late afternoon, after digging for six hours, I was worn out and depressed. I glanced at the sherpas. They too were downcast. We looked at each other without a word and continued digging. The minutes seemed like years but eventually time—that relentless enemy—entered our calculations. We could not go on like this much longer. And it was at this crucial stage that I happened to glance at the sherpas once again. They were praying. And at that moment God seemed very near. I began to pray. "If not you, Oh God, who will help us?" I began digging again. Suddenly my axe struck an oxygen cylinder. My prayer had been answered and the miracle gave me new life. Slowly we unearthed a few more cylinders. It was at this stage that I felt a fierce determination flow back into me—nothing could stop us from reaching the summit.

We left advance base camp on the morning of 26 May, and when we reached camp IV at a height of 25,000' it was still warm and sunny. We spent the night there and set of for the steady climb to the South Col at 10.15 a.m. Someone has called the South Col "the highest rubbish heap in the world," and the sites of the Swiss, the British and the Americans were all easily recognisable because of the refuse lying around. Phu Dorji and his party caught up with us at South Col. Since B.P. complained of a pain in the chest he returned to the advance base camp with Vohra and party who were returning after the summit climb.

It was 11.30 when we reached our camp site at 27,930' just below Razor's Edge. Wind speed had shot up to about 100 km. per hour as we tried to pitch our tents. Phu Dorji and I were in one tent, Bogie and Rawat in the other. At our evening meal, the steam-heated chicken was not easy to munch. In the cold our jaws worked slowly and I took nearly an hour to get through a few pieces of chicken.

Although there was just space for one tent, since our summit party constituted two ropes, we had to make space for another tent. Here again, like at camp IV, our tent could not fully rest on the ground. We tried to anchor it as best as we could but it kept lifting up from one side with the force of the wind. While my sleep was disturbed to some extent, Phu Dorji kept snoring. To him the lifting of the tent from one end probably felt like a rocking bed which he seemed to enjoy.

After a night's rest, it was 5.30 a.m. when we began the ascent on Razor's Edge. Phu Dorji and I led, with Rawat and Bogie following a few minutes later. The wind was blowing at tremendous speed and there was not much foothold on Razor's Edge. Lashed and buffeted by the wind, I found it difficult to keep my balance. We dug our ice axes in and tightened the ropes but the wind was merciless and kept lashing at us while the cold penetrated to the very marrow of our bones. The going became tough and there were moments when I felt like giving up the struggle. The main ridge had now ended but our path was hardly less hazardous. As we took a turn to the right, we were faced on the left with an unbroken wall of slate rocks. Pressed against the loose, black slate, we clung to whatever handhold or foothold we would manage as we moved across like tiny flies against all that immensity. Below us was a straight fall of some 10,000' into Tibet.

Greatly relieved, we would now have continued the ascent but Phu Dorji spotted a lone figure which was trudging towards us up the rocky part of the path we had left behind. I thought of the Abominable Snowman but Phu Dorji was more realistic. When the figure came nearer we discovered it was Rawat. Waving and panting, he reached us where we sat under the base of the South Summit after repairing the leaking pipe. What had happened to him is best stated in Rawat's own words. Below is an extract from his diary:

Ahlu and Phu Dorji had left. We followed them ten minutes later. I was leading. Bogie was, however, finding the climb very difficult and was taking each step after considerable delay. We had hardly gone fifty or sixty feet from the camp when Bogie sat down and after a while said he could not proceed any farther. He had developed a rash the previous night and kept scratching his body the whole night. He felt weak and exhausted and had to make a lot of effort to take even a few steps. He decided to unrope and asked me to go ahead and join the first rope.

I repeatedly asked myself whether it was wise on my part to continue alone and to leave Bogie all by himself. A quick decision had to be taken. Bogie's condition did not appear very serious and he could wait for us at the last camp. I was prepared to take the risk of a lonely climb. I reasoned that if I experienced any difficulty, I could always come back to the last camp. After a few minutes' deliberation I decided to go on. With a heavy heart I released Bogie from the rope and bade him goodbye.

The wind was blowing at sixty to seventy kilometres an hour. Being alone I was concentrating hard on the climb and took each step carefully on the sharp ice ridge. In my heart were feelings both of urgency and fear. Would I get to Ahlu and Phu Dorji or not, was the vital question. I knew that one slip or one small mistake could plunge me to my death on either side of the ridge. There was nothing to break my fall for a mile or more. Mustering all my courage, I inched my way up. Strong gusts of wind almost swept me off my feet and it became increasingly difficult to maintain my balance.

Once I had to cut the ice with my axe before I could find a place to hook my fingers. When I had gone about half a furlong on the rock I had trouble with my

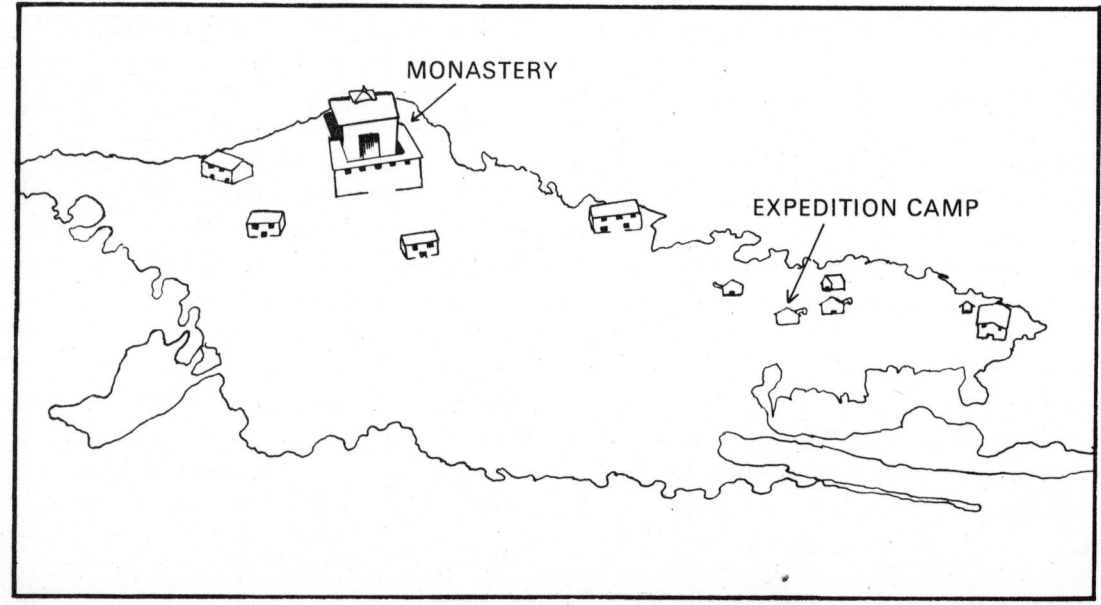

102

Overleaf: Photograph taken from top of a Rocky Peak.

Village near Okaldunga

Om Mani Padme Hum

*The Lama dance at
Tengpoche Monastery*

oxygen supply. I was breathless and did not know what to do. I kept shaking my head and waving my hands to attract Ahlu and Phu Dorji's attention but it did not help. After progressing about a furlong I came to the yellow rocks which I traversed a hundred yards or so. I had now been struggling all alone for almost an hour and a half. And then I joined Ahlu and Phu Dorji waiting for me at the base of the South Summit. I could hardly believe my eyes.

The foremost thought now in my mind was whether we would be able to climb Hillary's Chimney and come back to this place safely after achieving our goal, or would it prove an insurmountable obstacle and rob us of success when it seemed within our grasp. Descending vertically for about 35′ we came to some rocks and a narrow path that led us to the Chimney—an almost vertical obstacle between rock and snow cornice, which I had dreaded ever since I was selected for the expedition.

In fact, negotiating the Chimney proved to be a most hazardous affair. Since I was at the rear of the rope and quite far away from Phu Dorji when he made his final attempt, I could not see the exact holds which he took. Rawat, not being able to push forward from the same place, had moved slowly to the left over a big boulder and thus ascended the top of the Chimney. I being in the corner could hardly see him moving up but tried to follow him. Not realising that I had gone too far left, when I stepped over the big boulder, it started rocking. I knew that with a little more pressure on it, the boulder would fall down along with me and I might possibly also bring down the other two climbers, in which case nobody would be able to stop us during a fall of 8,000′. I must have wasted at least fifteen minutes or more trying to push myself forward.

We now found ourselves perched on an ice platform. From here the slope slackened gradually and there was rock to the left and snow to the right. We followed the path between the two. The climbing was not steep now. There were only humps of rock or snow and often a mixture of both. Breathing, which had never been easy, became even more difficult. We would take a deep breath but it would shorten into a hiccup and we gasped for breath. Would the ascent never end? Each step now was a totally exhausting effort.

The humps undulated endlessly. Sometimes there would be only rock, sometimes a snowy rock or a shoulder of snow. I kept asking myself how much longer and how much farther. Maybe it was far off, maybe we would have to turn back without reaching it. On every climb one is assailed by these doubts, and there comes a time the mind and body dwell on the sheer bliss of going downhill again. I was in such a state. Yet, another part in me urged me to go on. It couldn't be more than a few feet now—perhaps fifty or even less. But the slope led on and on. Heavens, was there no end? And then, suddenly, there was an end—no more little humps, only a white little dome curving slightly above us. Incredible! It was the summit of Everest.

Yes, we were there. Linking arms, we climbed the last few feet together. The tricolour planted by our first summit party was flying, tattered but jaunty. There were other flags too and some souvenirs and offerings left by the summit parties which had come before us.

After spending half an hour on the summit as we began our descent, I thought what a coincidence it was for us to have chosen 29 May for our climb. That was the day on which Hillary and Tenzing had stepped on this very summit, the first time over, 12 years ago to the day.

Of all the emotions which surged through me as I stood on the summit looking over miles of the panorama below us, the dominant one I think was humility. The physical in me seemed to say, "Thank God it's all over." I thought of all the Everesters who had gone before and those who would follow us. The British, the Swiss, the Americans, and my own countrymen. I thought of the few who had tried and triumphed, and the many who had tried and failed. On our way down the pressure in my oxygen bottle reduced considerably and I was running out of oxygen. The wind had arisen from a hum to a moan and then to a roar. Around Razor's Edge my oxygen ran out again. I began to pant convulsively. Snow coated my goggles. My legs would not move and they were lifeless.

I would take a step and feel as if I had run a mile. We descended very slowly, stopping to fight for breath. The wind raged over the ridge from the gulfs of vast space on either side. Hands and feet went numb. It was a terrible, and at times frightening experience. The effort was agonising as I began to gasp—I thought my lungs would burst. I crawled over Razor's Edge, in the teeth of this fiendish gale, sometimes collapsing on my belly. Phu Dorji was in the same plight and could not help me. But we spotted the tents of our last camp; they were no more than a hundred yards away. We thought we might attract Bogie's attention if we shouted "Bogie, oxygen! Bogie, oxygen!" But our cries went unheeded as Bogie had already left for the lower camps. As Phu Dorji and I lurched and floundered down the long slopes, Rawat kept supporting us. At each step we had to take a long deep breath. Phu Dorji took the lead and with much difficulty I made it to the last camp. I can never forget how my companions helped me in those crucial moments. Companionship and friendship are vital factors on a mountain. You can never forget a man who has shared a rope with you. It was 3.30 p.m. when we reached the summit camp.

Due to lack of oxygen we decided not to stay at the last camp but to go down to the South Col. We were so exhausted that night, and because of sleeping without oxygen at South Col, I had terrible hallucinations throughout the night. I imagined that Rawat was trying to close the door flaps of the tent to choke me to death. (Rawat had not moved so much as an inch.) Furious with him, I tore open the door flaps and wanted to tear the walls of the tent too. Then I staggered out collecting whatever discarded oxygen bottles I could find. I did not bother to see if they were full or empty or had just a little oxygen left in them. Like a maniac I continued to collect these bottles till midnight, making a heap of them, and then sat on my bed the remaining part of the night striking a Buddha pose. When Pema Sunder brought a hot mug of tea in the morning, I looked sick and weak. He was amazed to see the mound of oxygen bottles at the entrance of the tent. Rawat told me later how rude I had been to him that night and how I accused him of hiding his pencil torch which all the while I had been using when screwing and unscrewing the regulators of the oxygen bottles.

It is true that lack of oxygen effects different people in varying degrees. There are instances when people have climbed a little higher than 28,000′ without oxygen. One day perhaps a man will reach the highest point on earth without oxygen, but his return may not be safe, I believe, as he would have overstretched the limit of human endurance. He is subjecting himself not only to the lack of oxygen but total dehydration, fatigue and exhaustion and a lack of balance. The lack of oxygen will not only lead to breathing problems but will also effect his mind and vision.

Ang Kami on the Summit of Everest with Indian Tri colour.

Summit ridge with foot marks.

South Col

Ladders in the ice fall

8

1969-70 Japanese Expedition

The Japanese Alpine Club, encouraged by their experiences of climbing Manaslu and Himal Chuli, decided to plan an Everest expedition and made a formal application to the authorities in Nepal. It was in May 1963 that permission was granted for the spring of 1966. In 1965, while we were going to Mount Everest, we met the Japanese team who walked with us for quite a distance during the approach march. This was their pre-Everest training, on expeditions to peaks near Everest. I remember that many members of the team called on us at the base camp. Immediately after our expedition in 1965 the Nepalese Government banned all mountaineering activity on the Himalayan ranges and it was only in March 1969 that the ban was lifted and 38 peaks, including Everest, were again opened to foreigners.

In March 1969 the Nepalese Government also raised the rates of royalty for climbing in the Nepal Himalayas. Anyone who wants to climb Everest has to pay the Nepal Government Rs 10,000. The royalty rates have now almost doubled compared to 1965. The peaks above 26,000′ called for a royalty of Rs 8,000 and those below 26,000′ called for a royalty of Rs 6,000. The Nepalese Government also revised the monthly pay of the Nepalese Government Liaison Officer and the death compensation. The Liaison Officer will now be paid Rs 800 a month plus food and travel expenses, and the death compensation has been raised to Rs 50,000′. The compensation for the death of sherpas and reporters was raised to Rs 30,000.

The Japanese were allowed to climb in 1969 but they also booked the mountain for the spring of 1970, with the object of reaching the summit not only *via* the South-East Ridge, but also from the new route of the South-West Face. It was the first time that any country was to try this face of Everest. To achieve this, the Japanese Alpine Club decided

113

to send two reconnaissance parties—one in the spring of 1969 followed by another in the post-monsoon period of the same year. The Japanese Alpine Club had also decided to carry out some scientific research, such as the study of the human body at high altitudes, geo-physical research, and meteorological observations. The total budget of the expedition, including the reconnaissance parties, amounted to 100 million yen.

In spring 1969 a small Japanese team left to make the reconnaissance of the South West Face of Everest. The team cut a route across the ice fall and reached the Western Cwm from where they had a good look at the face. Some members of the reconnaissance party went slightly further to have a closer look at the Western face to find a possible route to the summit, and concluded that it was feasible. The party included Naomi Uemura who subsequently reached the summit in 1970.

In autumn 1969, the Japanese came back with a larger reconnaissance party compri-sing 12 members including Naomi Uemura, and led by H. Mihashita. The team flew to Lukla airstrip on 4th September and established base camp on 16 September. The camp at the foot of the South West face after negotiating the ice fall was established on 28 September. Thereafter, they pushed forward on the lower slopes of the face and established camp III at slightly above 23,000'. The team cut across a rocky buttress and established camp IV in the middle of the gully at approximately 24,000'. They had great difficulty in carrying out a platform to pitch the tents due to lack of space. Beyond camp IV is the famous gully which runs for about 800' and then divides. One portion runs towards the left of the rock band where there is a narrow chimney and a snow field which emerges into an upper part of the face, ultimately leading towards the South Summit.

The Japanese, having followed the left route, established camp IV at a height of 25,600' on 29 October. M. Konishi and Uemura established a route upto the rock band on 31 October and more members of the team reached the same point to find that the route through the rock band was feasible. This was a great achievement for the Japanese. The weather was extremely favourable to them as they were not unduly troubled by the high winds which are common at this time of the year. During this expedition, the party happened to find the corpse of John E. Breitenbach, of the American expedition of 1963, at a lower part of the ice fall on 24 September. It was later handed over to the family with the help of N. Dyhrenfurth and Barry Bishop. His grave stands on a thickly wooded northern slope of a hill behind Thyangboche Monastery with a magnificent view of Everest, Lhotse, Nuptse and other Himalayan peaks. While the expedition returned, Uemura stayed back in Khumjung to make arrangements for their forthcoming expedition with J. Inoue at Pheriche to carry out meteorological observations.

The 39-member team led by Saburo Matsukuta, aged 70 years, left Japan on 15 February in the following year, with the following members: Shinichi Hirano, Masatake Doi, Masatsugu Konishi, Miss Setuko Watanabe, Takashi Kano, Tadao Kanzaki, Hideo Nishigori, Naomi Uemura, Kiyoshi Narita, Katsuhiko Kano, Yoshiaki Kamiyama, Akira Yoshikawa, Chitoshi Ando, Hiroshi Sagono, Reizo Itoh, Michiro Nakashima, M. D., Koichiro Hirotani, M. D., Shigeo Ohmori, M. D., Masaru Kono, Masayuki Osada, Jiro Inoue, Katsuhisa Kimura, Hirofumi Aizawa, Shigeru Satoh, Masao Harada, Kenji Taira, Toshio Naito, Tokutaro Noguchi, Shozo Tateno, Hiroshi Nakagawa, Saburo Matshkata, Hiromi Ohtsuka, Senya Sumiyoshi, M.D., Yuichi Matsuda, Yoshihiro Fujita, Katsutoshi Hirabaysashi, Teruo Matsuura, Hiroaki Tamura, Hiroshi Nakajima, and 26 sherpas.

The expedition profited greatly by the experience of earlier reconnaissance parties. On 23 March they established base camp and on 4 April, after trekking for 10 days, opened

Facing: Japanese camp at Namche Bazar.
Overleaf: The second team battles strong
winds on the ridge. Makalu is seen in the
centre
P-118: Fixing rope at Lhotse face.

Neomi Uemura on the summit

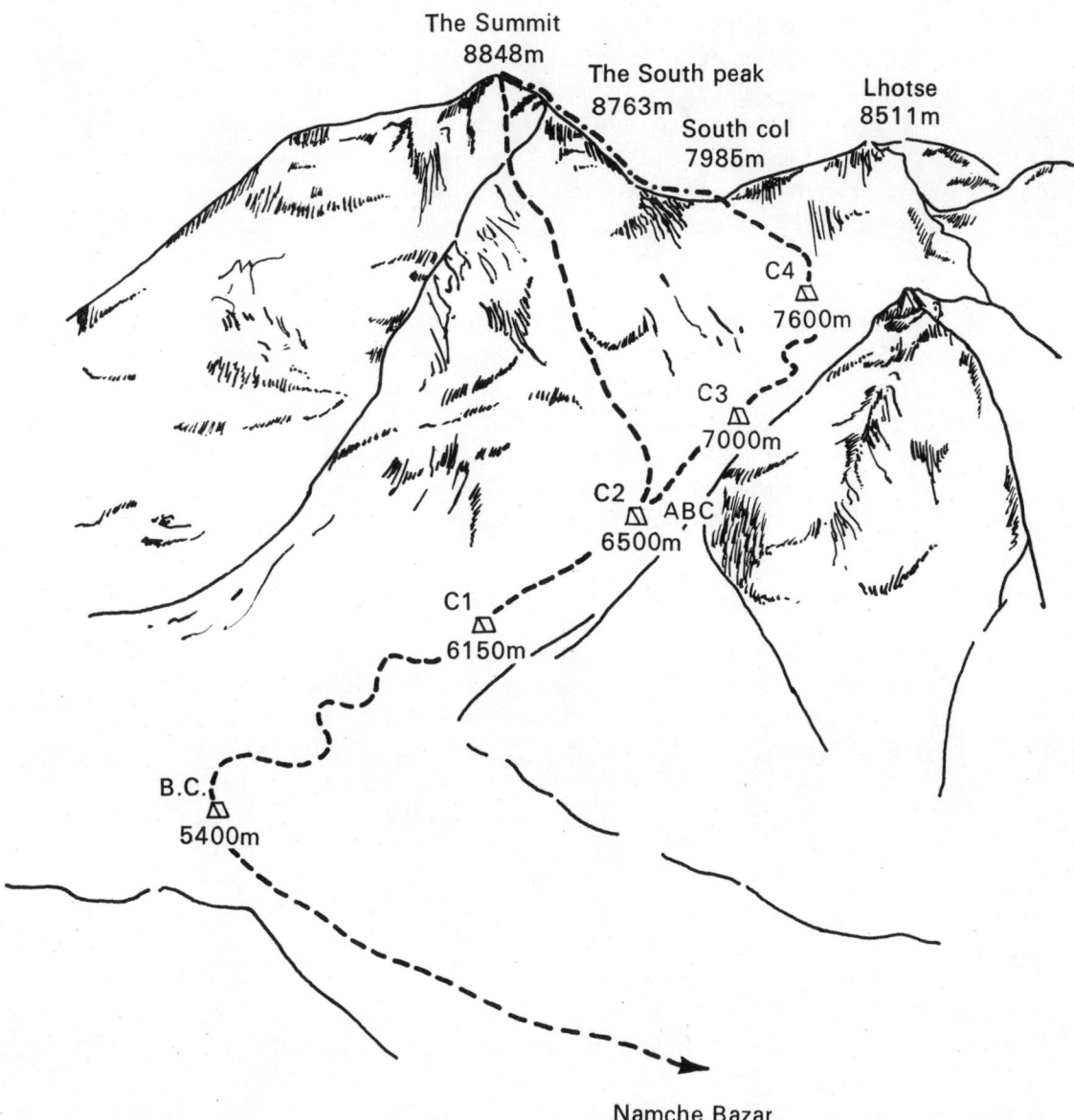

The Summit
8848m

The South peak
8763m

South col
7985m

Lhotse
8511m

C4
7600m

C3
7000m

C2
6500m

ABC

C1
6150m

B.C.
5400m

Namche Bazar

camp I at the head of the ice fall. The expedition was marred by the death of their ice fall porter, Kyak Tsering, who was killed on 9 April, and the death of six sherpas of the ski party. This accident completely shattered their morale. Some of the members also suffered from high altitude sickness which forced them to change the schedule. To facilitate further progress of the expedition, the team was divided into two parties.

On 17 April, after opening the advance base camp, the leader, depending on the performance of the team members, grouped them to form the South West Face team and the South East Ridge team. Both the teams worked independently in opening their respective camps. The progress on the South East Ridge was certainly better than that on the South West Face. By 28th April they had opened camp at South Col, though the South West Face team could only open camp III at 23,000′. The team had planned to make the summit by way of the South Col during early May, but soon discovered that because of the difficulty in carrying loads, they were lagging behind schedule.

123

P-119: South Col
P-120: Matsuura, tied by a red rope to
Uemura, makes way up the South East
ridge.

The expedition suffered yet another loss. Narita, the strongest and youngest member of the expedition died at camp I of a heart attack on 21 April while eating. During this period the situation was discussed at the base camp as the expedition was behind schedule. Due to the death of some members and the increasing sickness of others it was decided to put off the South West Face assault and to concentrate all available manpower in making the ascent from the South East Ridge successful.

On 1 May having gone back to base camp, Hiromi Ohtsuka changed his plans, due probably to pressure from the South West team not to give up the attempt on that face. He made some modifications and his new plan was as follows. Both the South West Face and the South East Ridge projects will be carried out. Forward camp IV (8,000 m.) will be established just below the Rock Band in the South West Face by May 12. The summit attack from the South East Ridge will be carried out twice, on the 11th and 12th of May. Matsuura and Uemura were assigned for the first summit party. The second team was to consist of one member and a sherpa. 350 kg. of equipment and food would be carried up by Doi, Kamiyama and 16 sherpas to camp V on the South Col.

In spite of these modifications, progress on the South West Face did not improve considerably, whereas the progress on the South East Ridge was swift. On 10 May, they established camp VI at the same site as our last camp in 1965. On 11 May, Matsuura and Uemura left their last camp at 6.10 in the morning for the summit, and at 9.10 they stood on the summit of Everest. The following day, Hirabayashi and sherpa Chotare also reached the summit at 9.55 a.m. Progress on the South West Face was being made, though at a slightly slower pace. On 6 May, camp IV was established with a duralumin frame platform on a rock surface at 7,500 m. On 8 May, Konishi and Yoshikawa reached a height of 7,800 m. (25,600′) and two days later, Kano and Sagauo with two sherpas reached a height of almost 26,400′, just below the rock band by using fixed ropes. This is the highest point they reached on that Face. They, however, inspected this route and found that a narrow couloir would lead them to a huge rock band which would bring them to the Yellow Band and they were of the opinion that if they had ten days of good weather they would have certainly explored the route further to the summit via the South West Face.

The expedition was however marred by another accident on that day. Kano was hurt on the back by a falling stone while they were descending on the ice slope from camp III. Nakajima was also hit on his right knee by another stone near camp IV the same afternoon. Hiromi Ohtsuka recalls, "When I heard of their misfortune, I didn't want them to take any more risks. It seemed very difficult to pass over the rock of the Rock Band in the remaining ten days, but this accident was the main reason for calling off the assault via the South West Face. On 12 May with news of the successful second attack, I decided to abandon the South West Face project and put all efforts into making the third and fourth attacks from the South East Ridge a success." Having called off the South West Face attempt and concentrating on the South East Ridge to put two more assaults also enabled Miss Watanabe to establish the world record for women on the South Col.

Kano, along with 20 sherpas, completed the ferry on 16 May to the South Col. On 17 May, Yoshikawa and two other members reached South Col after leaving camp III. Fujita along with other members also reached South Col. Among the supporting members was Miss Watanabe. On 18 May, the weather took a turn for the worse and high winds began to blow. On 19 May, the weather deteriorated further with poor visibility. On South Col there was snow 30 cms deep, and there was no chance of clear weather. Fujita came to the conclusion that since the weather was not going to improve, the third and fourth ascent via the South East Ridge would be called off. On 21 May all members returned to base camp for the return journey.

In my opinion, after having made up their plans earlier, they should have stuck to it and not kept changing them. I am sure if they had concentrated their efforts on the South West Face and given it top priority, they would perhaps have done exceedingly well. It is notable that despite this they reached an altitude of 26,400′ on the Face. Had they remained on the Face they would have reached this point much earlier, and they could have devoted the rest of the period in exploring and opening the route further. They might well have made the summit had they decided to turn to the right and join at the South Summit, like the British post-monsoon Expedition of 1975. The team should have been more acclimatised which would have reduced the rate of sickness, as it was a very large team and was thus exposed to more accidents. Here is an extract from the diary of the Deputy Leader:

As a deputy leader of the expedition, I would like to state some of the characteristics and problems of our expedition and the possibility of the South-West Face. Our expedition was a large force consisting of 39 members, including 9 reporters and cameramen. At the Base Camp, the members amounted close to 120, including sherpas. There were more than 60 members living together even at camp I and higher. A 39-member expedition was too large to work as a cohesive unit. One leader should not have more than 12 members to work with, otherwise there may be a lack of common bond among the members. Furthermore, the pleasure of mountaineering is stifled.

Our expedition consisted of two distinct groups which had the same objective— to gain the summit of Everest, but with a different route and different tactics. This scheme has made the expedition into such a large size. The necessity of such a big expedition should be considered with restraint in the future. I want to pay a tribute to the American expedition which scaled the summit both from the South East Ridge and the West Ridge. I have come to know how hard it is to keep close coordination between two teams with different tactics.

If there is a need to set up an expedition with a similar set-up as ours, it is necessary to set up two distinct ones beforehand, under the powerful committee organisation of the expedition. And there are reasons to believe that even such an organisational set-up has its own setbacks.

The weather was unusual since there was scarcely any snow during the previous winter. Going over the records of our meteorologist who passed the winter at Periche (4,243m.), there was scarcely any snow during his stay. This unusual weather influenced our expedition. Ice, which we had expected, did not form on the surface of the South West Face. The rock surface, compared to ice, took us more time to climb. Furthermore, this lack of ice caused frequent falling rocks from the Yellow Band. As a result two of our members were injured.

As compared with the previous fall, the South West Face became harder to climb, although the South East Ridge was easier than expected. Blessed with good weather, we were able to complete two ascents. For the first summit trial, both our health conditions and the weather were at their best and they made an ascent in just three hours from Camp 6.

The Japanese returned with the firm belief that the climb via the South West Face was possible with the right kind of expedition.

1970 JAPANESE SKI EXPEDITION

In spring 1970 along with the Japanese Everest expedition, a ski expedition consisting of 34 members including two skiers and ten cameramen was also in the Everest region. The object of this expedition was to perform the descent from the South Col by the professional skier Y. Miura and to take a cinemascope film of the descent. On 5 April the expedition lost six sherpas in the ice fall due to an avalanche. On 6 May however, Miura, accomplished his descent by parachute from the South Col. Both these expeditions had no relation whatsoever with one another as they were sponsored by different organisations. The expedition later released their film which won an academy award in 1976.

May our five senses be pure, and may the weather on the
honourable mountain be fine.

—Japanese Pilgrims' Motto

9

1971 (Spring) International Expedition
1971 (Autumn) Argentine Expedition

Norman Dyhrenfurth, who had a noteworthy success as the leader of the American expedition to Everest in 1963, decided to launch an international expedition in 1971. Apart from climbing, it was also to be an experience in understanding and cooperation among nations. He had the experience of two international expeditions by his parents in 1930 and 1934, and his 1955 expedition to Lhotse. But times had changed and the international venture proved an utter failure. The expedition was composed of 33 representatives from 13 countries. With the inclusion of a B.B.C. crew of 9 and journalists, the strength of the team totalled 30 members.

The total budget of the expedition was a quarter million dollars with each member's personal contribution being only £500 each. The members of the team were: Lt. Col. James O. M. Roberts (U.K.), Wolfgang Axt (Austria), Major Harsh Bahuguna (India), F. Duane Blume (U.S.A.), John Cleare (U.K., B.B.C.), Gary Colliver (U.S.A.), Odd Eliassen (Norway), John Evans (U.S.A.), Dougal Haston (U.K.), Toni Hiebeler (West Germany), Ian F. Howell (U.K., B.B.C.), David Isles (U.S.A.), Ned Kelly (U.K., B.B.C.), Reizo Ito (Japan), Carlo Mauri (Italy), Pierre Mazeaud (France), Dr. J. David Peterson (U.S.A.), Leo Schlommer (Austria), Dr. Peter R. Steele (U.K.), Ian Stuart (U.K., B.B.C.), Jerzy Surdel (Poland, B.B.C.), Jon Teigland (Norway), Antony Thomas (U.K., B.B.C.), Naomi Uemura (Japan), Michel Vaucher (Switzerland), Yvette Vaucher (Switzerland), Don Whillans (U.K.), Bill Kurban (U.K., B.B.C.), Arthur Chesterman (U.K., B.B.C.), Sunday Times reporter: Murray Sayle (Australia), Liaison Officer: Capt. Vishnu Prasad Sharma (Nepal), Geologist: Dr Harka Bahadur Gurung (Nepal).

The aim of the expedition was to make a two-pronged assault, one team attempting the South West Face, the other ascending the West Ridge from the American Camp IV straight up and not following the American route of 1963. The members of the expedition were allowed to have the route of their choice.

The South West Face team comprised Americans Gary Colliver, John Evans and Dr. David Peterson, Britain's Dougal Haston and Don Whillans, Japan's Reizo Ito and Naomi Uemura, Toni Hiebeler from West Germany, and Leo Schlommer from Austria. The West Ridge team comprised Austria's Wolfgang Axt, the Swiss husband-wife team Michel and Yvette Vaucher, the Norwegians Odd Eliassen and Jon Teigland, the American David Isles, and India's Major Harsh Bahuguna.

Initially France's Pierre Mazeaud and the Italian Carlo Mauri joined the team to attempt the Face, but later joined the ridge party. All the members of the team assembled in Kathmandu on 16 February except Mazeaud and Whillans who joined later. Thirty-six tons of equipment came by sea to Bombay and was later transported by road to Kathmandu with the help of Harsh Bahuguna and two other members. The entire load was airlifted to Lukla. Base camp was established on 22 March and work to open camps beyond was taken in hand. Below is an extract from Norman G. Dyhrenfurth's diary:

> April 4: The team is magnificent! The men work exceptionally well together, and general morale couldn't be better. Yesterday camp I (20,500') was established, the entire route through the ice fall is fixed and secured. Today Dougal Haston, Don Whillans, Harsh Bahuguna, Reixo Ito and Carlo Mauri move up with eight sherpas to spend the night at camp I. Tomorrow they'll set up camp II (Advance Base) at about 21,600'. Everyone is relieved and grateful that the terribly dangerous route has been put in at last, and without any accidents. There continues to be complete harmony among the team members, not the slightest indication of any friction whatsoever.

While this expedition was making progress, the news media constantly spoke of the obvious inability and unwillingness of the team to cooperate. After establishing camp II, the two routes separated. On 9 April, the Japanese and the British established camp III on the South West Face at 23,000'. The ferrying of loads became slow and bottlenecks developed at camp I. Some members did not help at all in load carrying as is normally done in expeditions. They considered the work of load carrying as primarily the duty of the sherpas while they remained the 'stars'. The work on both the face and the ridge continued but trouble on the expedition started brewing. On 16 April, Wolfgang Axt and Harsh moved up and established camp III on the ridge at 22,600'. Carlo and Pierre deposited ropes and other material to construct a long horizontal rope-traverse which would shorten the route by almost an hour.

On April 17 after staying a night at camp III, Wolfgang and Harsh moved across to the crest of the ridge at a height of 24,000'. They saw no serious problems as far as the rocky portion of the ridge was concerned. During their descent, they discovered a comparatively good spot and shifted the position of camp III. Below is an extract from Norman G. Dyhrenfurth's diary:

> April 18: Radio contact at 8 a.m. Wolfgang is concerned about the weather. From his position he can see ominous cloud formations to the north west. He and Harsh plan to move camp to the higher location before rejoining us at advance Base. I try to get them some help from others of the Ridge team, but those not plagued by sickness and altitude problems are not very eager to move up. Pierre, Carlo and the Vauchers complain once again that much of their gear is still at camp I, and that the

sherpas are too slow in bringing up supplies. I suggest descending to the lower camp *en masse* to make a big carry ourselves but the four "Latins" consider this beneath their dignity. No 'sherpa-labour for them'. Disgruntled, I decided to set an example and pick up my Kelty-pack and head for camp I, where I discuss the supply problem with Dave Peterson, Dougal Haston, Leo Schlommer and Toni Hiebeler. Hiebeler had gone down earlier for some rest at Base.

With two oxygen cylinders—one each for Face and Ridge, in fairness to both teams—I begin the ascent towards camp II. The weather turns bad; soon the "Valley of Silence" is blotted out by a raging snowstorm. As I pass underneath the nearly vertical walls of Nuptse, I hear the ominous sound of a powder snow avalanche. No time to get out of its way! With crampons and ski poles I anchor myself to the steep slope. The snow masses swirl against and around me, but I can hold my ground. A few deep breaths, and I resume the climb through white-out and storm, groping my way along the route marked by willow-wands.

My sherpa Ang Lakpa has been much worried about his Bara Sah'b and meets me halfway. He shoulders my heavy pack, and together we move on. A couple of duffel bags lie alongside the trail, abandoned by a sick sherpa. Ang Lakpa intends to pile them on top of his load, but I don't let him. Once again I shoulder my own Kelty, and on we go. The red marker-flags are too far apart, for a while we lose our way among huge crevasses on the right, but then we get back on the right track. Suddenly there are screams from above, to our left. Harsh Bahuguna! Again and again we hear the screams, and we answer until our voices give out.

Meanwhile Wolfgang reaches Advance Base around five, alone, and utterly exhausted. His hands and feet are frostbitten. "Bahuguna is still up there!" Within minutes a rescue party of Odd, Michel, Don, Pierre, Carlo, Peter and Ang Phurba sets off. The storm is frightening, and night just around the corner! To double-time from 21,500′ to 22,300′ is torture at best, but in this weather! Odd is first to reach Harsh, then Michel. Michel recounts: ". . . His condition is desperate. He has lost one mitten, his face is covered by a thick crust of ice. His chest harness and carabiner are clipped onto the long fixed rope placed there by Odd and myself the day before. A few meters more, and Harsh would have reached easy going. But his state of exhaustion was so complete that he couldn't even get warm clothing out of his rucksack. Soon Whillans catches up with us.

Meanwhile I have put Harsh on a rope and managed to unhook him from the rope-traverse, while Odd belayed me. There are only three of us. The storm is more violent than ever. Night has fallen. To carry Harsh across the steep ice is impossible. We lower him towards a small crevasse which might offer protection from the wind. Our rope has run out. It would take many more of us to carry him . . . . Harsh is unconscious . . . . Odd begins to cry . . . . We have no choice but to retreat. On the way down we meet the others. What agony and terror, this descent through night and storm . . . ."

We meet in the big tent, a demoralized, dejected group. I ask for details of the rescue attempt. Pierre Mazeaud, lawyer and deputy of the French National Assembly, is quick to accuse Wolfgang of murder through negligence, but I warn him and implore everybody not to draw any hasty conclusions. Wolfgang himself—on the advice of Dr. Peter Steele—has taken sleeping-pills and knows nothing of the tragedy.

The following morning he is last to enter the big tent: "Wie geht es Harsh?" (How's Harsh?) he asks me. "Weisst Du es noch nicht? Er ist tot!" (Don't you know?

He's dead!). Wolfgang is thunderstruck. He and Harsh had become close friends. This terrible death hits him harder perhaps than any of us.

I conduct an official inquiry in several languages, which is recorded on tape, in anticipation of later requests from the governments of Nepal and India. Everyone has a chance to be heard. Then I ask Wolfgang: "Why weren't you roped together on your way down?" "There was no need, there were no difficulties at all. We had used our climbing rope the day before to secure a steep section on the way down. To save weight I left my harness and carabiner at the upper Camp III-West. At first Harsh went ahead. Around two o'clock the weather turned bad. Soon we were caught in a raging storm. When we reached the long rope-traverse, I took over the lead and got across it hand over hand. It was very long and tiring as hell. At the far end I waited for Harsh. Voice communication was impossible, the storm was too strong. I waited for a long time, perhaps an hour. My hands and feet had lost all feeling. Then I saw Harsh, moving very slowly. He was tied into the fixed rope with harness and carabiner. He groped his way around the last corner of the steep ice slope which separated us. He waved with one hand. Everything seemed O. K., no indication of any serious problems. By now I was really worried about frostbite and continued the descent. Just before I got into camp, I heard his screams and alerted everybody. I couldn't have gone back up, I was completely done in." "Why didn't you stay with him?" "I had no idea how badly off he was. And even if I had known, what could I have done without rope and carabiner? Harsh did take his gear, but I would have had to go back hand over hand across that long traverse! I wouldn't have had enough strength left for that, and my hands and feet felt like blocks of ice . . . ."

The tragic news did not reach Base Camp until the following day. In the continuing storm, radio communication broke down completely. Toni Hiebeler, himself fighting a losing battle with altitude sickness, wrote a farewell note: "My dear, kind Norman! You will be disappointed in me, but after Harsh's death I could not and cannot continue—I am a physical and mental wreck. I can't take a single step towards the mountain—forgive me. I must go home, because I am convinced that I can do more for you and the expedition in Munich than here, where I am nothing but a living bundle of misery . . . Dear Norman. I shall never set foot on the summit, but I have discovered a very dear human being in you, and I look upon you as my close friend—that is worth a great deal. My heartfelt thanks for every thing! My thoughts are with you and the others, but mostly with you. Your Toni." Shortly afterwards the world's news media falsely announced that Toni Hiebeler had deserted the expedition and turned his back on me!

The snow lasted for a week followed by threats of an avalanche. Provisions at advance base camp became very scarce. The West Ridge team was demoralised. The members wanted to switch over to the conventional South Col route. Dyhrenfurth tried to convince the members that the conventional route would not be worth it as a number of teams had gone that way and it may perhaps be worthwhile to use all the remaining strength to support the assault from the Face, but nothing worked.

Finally it was decided to vote and the majority opted for the conventional South Col route. Now it became a question of personal glory to reach the summit. The attempt on the Face was dropped and work on the conventional route began. Camp III was established. The "Latins" wanted to launch the summit attempt from camp VI which was not possible. Another setback was that members started feeling sick. Axt had influenza,

130

Facing: *Harsh Bahuguna*
Overleaf: *Camp IV West*

Michel Vaucher developed thrombosis in one leg. Three other members descended because of poor physical condition. Of the members, only Mazeaud and Mauri, both 42, remained to make the summit.

On 26 April, Bahuguna's body was retrieved and taken to Gorak Shep for the funeral. A commemorative carving was made on the stone and his ashes were sent to his home in Dehra Dun. There was a complete decay of morale in the expedition, and no one obeyed the orders of the leader. The leader, in consultation with Jimmy Roberts and others, decided to scrap the attempt via the South Col and to put everything as the last bid in climbing the Face: Some members were delighted at this decision, but the Italians did not take it sportingly. On 2 May, all the dissidents left the base camp.

On the other hand, camp IV on the Face was established at a height of 24,600' and on 2 May, Whillans and Haston moved to camp V which was established on 5 May at 26,000'. At this time, 7 men contracted a strange glandular fever followed by 3 others. The leader himself was sick and was ordered by the doctor to leave immediately and for him this was the end of the expedition. With the depleted strength in the team, Don Whillans took over and towards the middle of May, Haston and Whillans established camp VI at 27,200' supported by the Japanese and the sherpas.

The bad weather continued, and exceptional cold rendered technical climbing all but impossible. The flow of supplies dwindled to a trickle. Another camp would have been needed above the Rock Band. When Whillans—at the end of a traverse to the right—reached the crest of the South Buttress, he could see moderately angled slopes leading up to the normal route just below the South Summit. Should they abandon the Face for the sake of a summit "victory" at the last minute? The public at large would no doubt consider the expedition to be a full success, but mountaineers think differently. The 1970 ascent by way of the South Col was judged a failure in leading Japanese climbing circles, since the clearly stated objective of the expedition had been the Face. The 1971 expedition's goal too was the summit by way of the Face, and not "victory at all costs," by any route.

Whillans acted accordingly and returned to Haston. Together they climbed 300' up an icy couloir in the Rock Band, fixing ropes. But then they too had reached the end of the line. There was still some oxygen left at camp VI, but no more butane and precious little to eat. For more than three weeks they had lived at high altitude without coming down to Advance Base once—a world record and dramatic proof of their incredible toughness, as well as of the superb oxygen system developed by Duane Blume. The combination of snowstorm, intense cold, rockfall, avalanches and faltering supply lines put an end to the struggle. On 21 May news of the expedition's failure was announced to the outside world. Ken Wilson had this to say in "Post-Mortem of an International Expedition" in *Mountain,* 17 September 1971 :

For a public and press weaned on mountaineering success, this year's failure on Everest was unacceptable. The extensive advance publicity (particularly in the U. K.) made it inevitable that there should be an extreme reaction to the project's conclusion: scapegoats had to be found, and the expedition's failure had to be accounted for in suitably sensational terms. When the failure was announced, many newspapers referred to the affair as a 'fiasco' while the procession of experts delivering instant criticism to press and television added to the expedition's poor image. Some of these pundits had expressed grave doubts before the expedition's departure; others had stayed silent, however, just in case Whillans and Haston might have somehow spirited themselves to the summit over 1800' of hard climbing at extreme altitude. It was

Facing: Climbing on the West ridge.

not until the reality of the expedition's plight was finally revealed that they really let themselves go.

The main butt of all criticisms, of course, was Norman Dyhrenfurth. Naturally, as leader, it is he who has to bear the brunt of failure, just as in 1963 he bathed in the pleasant aura of success. But this time he has almost been crushed by the recriminatory back-lash that followed the expedition. He has borne all this with dignity, however, avoiding the type of untidy fracas that followed last year's Nanga Parbat episode. A generous man, he has been the first to excuse the outbursts made by his critics. He has done everything possible to provide the material for this article, despite the fact that the final verdict must inevitably go against him.

Every leader has to be prepared to face the realities of failure. Lord Hunt was in the same position after his catastrophic expedition to the Pamirs in 1963. The long knives were out then, and later, in 1971, Dyhrenfurth was the victim. To describe either Hunt or Dyhrenfurth as incompetent because their expeditions failed to justify the hopes invested in them would be wrong, but it is possible that a hitherto successful expedition leader might sometimes bank too heavily on his charisma, neglecting some of the painstaking attention to detail that brought him success in the past.

Despite suggestions to the contrary, it is clear that Dyhrenfurth's motive in organizing the expedition were completely altruistic and stemmed from an idealism traditional to his family and typical of his Swiss-American background. It is easy to forget the sheer workload involved in organizing an expedition such as this without strong national backing. It was a tremendous achievement in itself to get thirty people from thirteen different countries to the foot of Everest with all the food and equipment needed to climb it. The majority of those people speak highly of Dyhrenfurth and are deeply grateful to him for giving them the chance to go to the highest mountain in the world. The expedition's failure will leave him with a large personal debt to pay off.

Quite understandably, Dyhrenfurth has been deeply hurt by the criticism and cynicism levelled at the expedition, particularly as the whole affair represented an attempt to further the friendship and understanding of mountaineers the world over. Superficially, it failed, but on closer inspection it is clear that many international friendships were formed. It has also been a salutary reminder not only of the harshness of the big mountain environment, but also of the whole new range of pressures that face contemporary mountaineers as they step into the public arena.

Dyhrenfurth, who was ordered by the doctor to go home as he was unwell, had a brief halt in Delhi where I met him. There were a number of controversial reports in the papers to the effect that he returned from the mountain because he was unable to cope with the tragic events that had taken place. This is not true. He was unwell with a terribly bad throat and could hardly speak. I had known Dyhrenfurth since 1964 and his love for the mountains is unquestionable. I was fully convinced that Dyhrenfurth was not to be blamed for the circumstances which led to the failure of the expedition. Any leader in that situation would have reacted in the same manner as he did.

The tragic death of Maj. H. V. Bahuguna on the International Himalayan expedition to Mount Everest was a grievous loss to India. The Indian Mountaineering Foundation decided to set up a Committee comprising Brig. Gyan Singh as Chairman and myself as member to enquire into the circumstances leading to the death of Maj. Bahuguna on 18 April 1971 on the mountain. After going through the statements of various members,

Bahuguna's letters, transcriptions of tape recording of the proceedings of the enquiry conducted by Dyhrenfurth at the advance base camp and other available information, we submitted our report to the Indian Mountaineering Foundation. The committee stated, *inter alia*:

> According to Axt, he did not go back to look for Bahuguna because he had no harness or carabiner without which he would have been of little help. Presumably for the same reason he crossed the rope traverse quickly without waiting for Bahuguna to follow close behind. But even before he started, Axt knew about the existence and nature of the traverse and as an "ice-specialist" he should also have known that the harness and the carabiner would be needed on this obstacle. However, he chose to leave this essential safety equipment, weighing no more than a few hundred grams, behind for "reasons of weight". The Committee, therefore, consider that Bahuguna may not have lost his life if Axt had brought his essential safety equipment and travelled close to his rope-mate.
>
> The Committee find it difficult to agree that he did not realise that Bahuguna was in difficulty until he heard his shouts for help at 4.15 p.m.
>
> The Committee rule out wilful foulplay on anyone's part.
>
> The Committee are not certain if Bahuguna was, in fact, wearing silk or nylon gloves under his thick outer gloves. But, apart from this his clothing was appropriate for tackling the traverse, and in his rucksack he was carrying adequate insulated clothing. Unfortunately, after Bahuguna was incapacitated on the fixed rope, the clothing he was wearing was not sufficient to protect him from the elements and keep him warm.

AUTUMN 1971 ARGENTINE EXPEDITION

The Argentina Government sponsored expeditions to Dhaulagiri I in 1954 and in 1956. In 1971, they sponsored their first Everest expedition. It was led by Lt. Col. H. C. Tolosa with the following members: Carlos Comensarna, Capt. Nestor (Antonia) Azuage, Jorge (Teodore Carlos), Sqt. Juan Bautista Barrientos, Sqt. Edmundo (Cirilo) Burgos, Juan Serguio Fernandes, Jose Luis Fonrouge, Dr. Jose Maria Iqlesias, Lt. Juan Manual Llavar, Omar (Luis) Felleqrini, (Eduardo) Jorge Peterek, Sqt. Guillermo Robles, Alfredo (Carlos) Rosasco, Lt. Alberto Mario Serrano, Jorge (Juan) Skyarca, Guillermo Vieiro, Ulises (Sila) Vitale, and Jorge Eduardo Viton. The entire equipment of the expedition was transported from Delhi to Kathmandu but was held up in north India due to rains and heavy floods, and the trucks carrying the equipment had to be brought back to Delhi. It was then transported by air. This delayed the expedition considerably. During the post-monsoon period, there is always a risk in transporting the package by road due to heavy rains. On its way to Nepal, the expedition passed through Delhi and consulted us regarding technical difficulties and other administrative arrangements on Everest. I had a special association with the team as they regarded me more or less as their advisor. Even after the team had left Delhi, the leader would speak to me from the base camp on the wireless and seek advice.

The expedition left Kathmandu on 17 August and after spending one week of acclimatization at Thyangboche monastery, established base camp on 15 September, camp I at 6,200m. on 17 September, camp II at 6,500m. on 19 September and camp III at 7,000m. on 21 September. No further progress could be made because of bad weather which lasted almost eight days. The expedition had its share of illness in which one of the members got pneumonia and had to be evacuated by helicopter. On 1 October, one of their top climbers, Jose Luis Forrouge, left Nepal having quit the expedition apparently over differences with the leader. The expedition continued to face adverse conditions with temperatures going as low as minus 30° centigrade with very poor visibility. On 8 October, camp IV was established at 7590m. and camp V was established on 21 October. The expedition could not make progress, the deteriorating weather being the main factor. Their supply line was also affected due to bad weather. There was also illness and defections.

In spite of the deterioration in weather, the expedition climbed Lhotse face and reached South Col on 28 October. The next day, the leader spoke to us in Delhi to know if there was any chance of wind speed reducing. I had earlier carried out a study of the wind speed behaviour on Everest with the help of the meteorological department with data available for almost 20 years and found that on an average the wind speed starts increasing from the third but definitely from the fourth week of October. By the first week of November, the winds are rather high and well beyond 100 km. with the temperature well below freezing point. Because of the very bad weather and an unfavourable meteorological forecast, the leader decided to withdraw. The expedition had done extremely well but was delayed considerably which resulted in the setting in of high winds. Col. James Roberts commenting on the expedition said: "Perhaps the Argentine team's mistake was they pushed on too quickly in the beginning stages, not consolidating properly, so that when they got very bad weather they were not in a position to deal with it. The expedition left Kathmandu on 13 August and by 21 September had set up camp III at 22,960′. Camp V was set up on 21 October after delays due to bad weather. Everest is a siege mountain — for if you do try a quick, light bid for the summit, you have to have very good luck with the weather."

The team members were back in Delhi and at a function at their embassy they announced the highest award in the field of mountaineering, *Condor-de-Oro*, to be given to me. I was quite touched by their sentiments and felt that it was too much of an honour as I had only helped them in a very small way. Later the leader told me that following my advice they closed the camp at the base of the Lhotse face. Immediately after closing camp that night there was a huge avalanche. Had they not closed camp, the expedition would have been faced with a very serious disaster resulting in many deaths as almost ten members of the expedition were to spend the night at this camp.

10

1972 (Spring) European Expedition
1972 (Autumn) British Expedition

After the failure of the International Everest expedition Karl Herrligkoffer of West Germany stepped in to lead another band of climbers from various countries. He fully knew of the debacle of the international expedition which was primarily due to the fact that a number of leading climbers of various countries were included in it and that the leader himself had lost control over them. The other factors in the failure were the weather, the split objective, and the language problem. Dr Herrligkoffer had a long record of expedition organisation. He led the expedition to Nanga Parbat in 1953. His interest in mountaineering was confined to Nanga Parbat and he was known to have a very limited experience in climbing. He was essentially an administrator and organiser and would never go beyond the base camp.

His interest in Nanga Parbat began as early as 1934 when his step-brother Willi Merkl died in a disaster on Nanga Parbat when 9 climbers and sherpas were killed in a storm. In the 1953 expedition to Nanga Parbat, after he called off the expedition, Hermann Buhl, an Austrian climber, reached the summit in a solo attempt. This led to a great argument and controversy between Herrligkoffer and Hermann Buhl, which led them to a court of law. His interest in Nanga Parbat brought him back almost six times to Nanga Parbat where his team attempted the mountain from various faces. Although his team succeeded in climbing Nanga Parbat from the Diamir face, the Rupal Ridge, and the Rupal face in 1970, almost all the expeditions ended up in arguments, making Dr Karl Herrligkoffer a very controversial figure.

Chris Bonington, who was also a member of the 1972 expedition, met Herrligkoffer in November and was very disappointed as Herrligkoffer had no idea about the problems and the difficulties that an expedition would face on Everest, and the financial position also seemed very poor. Chris Bonington and Dougal Haston withdrew from the team. The other British members who stayed on were Hamish MacInnes, Doug Scott and Don Whillans. It became more or less a British, German and Austrian expedition. In the beginning, before the expedition could set off, there arose a serious problem as to the full copyright of the expedition, story and the photographs. Members were unhappy as they wanted to use their own pictures and also to be able to write for the press in their own countries.

With these differences the expedition set off and reached Kathmandu on 12 March. Some members flew to Lukla in order to open the base camp. Herrligkoffer arrived later. The British contingent was quite unhappy with Herrligkoffer and when they reached Lukla with him, they found that the base camp had already been opened. He ignored the period of acclimatisation for any member as perhaps he did not believe in it. This to my mind is the first sign of the failure of any expedition. Acclimatisation, apart from making you fit for higher climbs, also gives you a chance to know the other members of the team which is rather important on an expedition of this nature. Herrligkoffer wanted to make a straight dash to the base camp and if anyone wanted ever a day's rest on the way, he bluntly refused. This resulted in Prof. Huttl having high altitude sickness and he had to be evacuated back to Lukla and then to Germany. The British members also did not take part for the first few days as Don was down with vertigo and Doug with dysentery.

At the base camp, the sherpas were not at all satisfied with the standard of equipment. There were insufficient mattresses, sleeping bags, and no down clothing for the ice fall sherpas. Herrligkoffer was used to climbing on Nanga Parbat with Hunza porters who are not as sophisticated as the sherpas. Instead of reasoning out and coming to terms with the sherpas, the Germans started shouting at them. The sherpas refused to go any further and the expedition got stranded. Eventually, Herrligkoffer rushed back to Germany to collect more equipment.

As soon as this problem was solved, another problem cropped up. The Germans felt that the Britishers were not helping them in opening the routes and that they were perhaps saving their energy to be used later for the summit attempt. Don explained to them that this was not true and that they needed to acclimatize before taking on a higher climb. The Germans refused to let the Britishers be in the front—they were particularly careful lest Don take the lead. The expedition had a surprise when Mischa Saleki from Persia joined the expedition. He was originally invited and had also helped Herrligkoffer to raise money for the expedition but was later dropped, about which he understandably felt bitter.

In the beginning the German members kept themselves in the lead and used others as load carriers in exactly the same manner as the British and the Japanese did in the International Everest expedition. The Big Four—Felix Kuen, Adolf Huber, Werner Haim and Leo Breitenberger—were the four Germans who stayed in the lead. Camp I was opened on 5 April. The Germans pushed to camp II and III and further established camp IV. The British team went up to build the "carry" at camp IV. This was allowed only on the condition that the British would go no further than camp IV. The expedition had made rather slow progress considering the fact that all the fixed roping was left by the International expedition and it was now almost the end of April. The British helped in putting up three platforms and two boxes at camp IV.

Herrligkoffer had just returned from Germany with the equipment for the Sherpas. The Deputy Leader called the entire team to base camp to welcome Herrligkoffer. This idea seemed quite stupid to the British and a waste of time, particularly when the weather was good. The British contingent along with the sherpas stayed back at camp II and wanted to go to camp IV in order to establish and stock camp V but because of lack of the availability of sherpas who had also gone down, this advance could not be undertaken. Doug Scott at this stage had this to say:

> The casualty list was now growing, and in theory at least, we were fortunate to have the Doctor back. Leo Breitenberger was sent back to Kathmandu in the helicopter which came to collect Hain. According to Herrligkoffer , Breitenberger had pulmonary oedema, but in fact, he turned out to be suffering from pleurisy, while Hain came back to Base Camp two weeks later, having recovered from a suspected shattered knee joint. However, the doctor did not tend many more patients before he, too, had to be evacuated. He had flown up to 15,000' and had a mild heart attack from the physiological strain this entailed.
>
> Horst Vitt, the German diplomat, had already died from pulmonary oedema, having tried to reach base camp too quickly to take over from the unfortunate Professor Huttl. Mischa Saleki also joined the list of evacuees, though for a different reason. Unable to stand the derision which came his way, any longer, he stowed away in a helicopter, according to German press statements. Considering the machines only seated two, he must have made himself very inconspicuous, if not invisible, and presumably almost weightless. (Incidentally these were the highest helicopter comings and goings ever recorded as far as we know.) Finally, Hans Berger had gallstone trouble and severe pain in his bladder, but with suitable treatment he was able to come back towards the end.
>
> On the credit side, Peter Bedner recovered from a wrongly administered cholera injection which had plagued him throughout the expedition. Luckily, a visiting band of German professors had diagnosed his problem and had treated him correctly. Peter was at last able to reach the Face after being posted for weeks at a time at the lonely camp I. Meanwhile, we went up to camp IV, and in the next few days fixed 500' of rope up to camp V, using the remainder of the International Expedition's rope which Dougal and Don had placed the year before. We dumped ropes, tents and oxygen at the site and chopped out a platform for two tents.

The staying back by the British contingent at camp V was severely disliked by Herriligkoffer and was described as sabotage. They blamed the British for having occupied that camp for ten days using up 15 large oxygen bottles at night and consuming a large number of provisions for laying a mere 40 meters of new rope between camp IV and camp V and setting up the platform box. Finally the English contingent withdrew from the camp. When Doug was in Delhi on his return from climbing Everest in 1975, I drew his attention at this accusation of using up the oxygen. He told me that the account of 15 bottles came about by including the old empty oxygen bottles used by the Japanese and the International expedition in the camp. In fact, they used very little oxygen. The British were rather calm and did their best to keep the expedition going, but the controversy continued. In Doug's words:

> Huber and Kuen arrived at camp IV, armed with a plan they had worked out at Base Camp. In effect it placed us in camp III, and sherpas in camp IV with Peter Perner or Adi Weissensteiner if the latter's cough would allow it. Horst Schneider and Adi Sager were to go to camp V and Kuen and Huber to camp VI. When all was ready, two of us were to be allowed to join them at the front in an attack on the summit. But just how we could get enough oxygen and other equipment up there to support our climbers was not explained, and we grew suspicious. We had a feeling that we

Members moving in Western Cwm

Don Whillans with other members of the Expedition at Camp II

Dr. Karl Herrligkoffer

Hamish MacInnes

were being edged out again. So we worked out a compromise plan, which put us in support of the summit pair, with one other Austrian accompanying us in camp V. After Kuen and Huber had made their bid, we four of the support party would have a go.

After some debate, this proposal was accepted and Kuen and Huber moved up to camp V. Unfortunately, Schneider and Sager were not satisfied with the new arrangements and they went to persuade Kuen to revert to his original plan. The crunch came when Schneider and Sager returned from their mission. Schneider said, 'You British are in trouble. Kuen says you must go down to camp III or he will come down, call off the sherpas and end the expedition'. Next day we went down to camp II and later to Base Camp. We had come to the end, and reached the point where personality differences could no longer be ignored. Both Schneider and Sager refused to carry for Don. Even the equable Peter Bedner said he was fed up with acting as a sherpa for the British.

After having opened a route to camp V the summit parties were discussed. A workable plan was agreed upon and it was decided that the British would be in support of the summit pair of Kuen and Huber. After the summit pair had made their bid the support party consisting of the British contingent would have a chance to go to the summit. The other members did not agree to this, particularly Schneider and Sager, and they wanted to have the British return. There was total confusion and no agreement with the result that everyone withdrew to camp II. The relations between the British and the Austrian members became very bad. The British were not prepared to come down from the position of second summit attempt, and they agreed to support the first pair from camp V. The expedition had reached a point almost similar to that of the earlier international expedition. After prolonged arguments and counter arguments, the British contingent moved to camp II on 15 May.

On the other hand, on 19 May, Sager, Bedner, Schneider, Huber, and Kuen moved into camp V and for support they had five sherpas. On 21 May, the five Austrians along with the sherpa support moved to camp VI. Unfortunately, the weather deteriorated at night. The expedition could not wait since the equipment was inadequate and on the 22nd decided to turn back. Doug Scott summed up the expedition as follows:

To me, the trip gave rise to few delusions of grandeur. I am simply glad to have been able to go up the ice fall unscathed, and to have entered the Western Cwm, that incomparable valley of snow lying between the iridescent ice of Nuptse and the hanging glaciers of the South West side of Everest. Each day I expected to succumb to the altitude; I examined myself minutely each morning for sore throat or other symptoms. Thanks to Don's guidance, all three of us acclimatised slowly, and after more than two weeks and four carries up to camp V, we went well to the end.

One of the driving forces was a personal curiosity to find out how high one can go before the stomach starts to heave, the legs fold under, the head aches and the mind hallucinates. Once back home the bad memories fade. One's slides and photographs bring back the haunting beauty of rock and ice swept by winds and avalanche and scorched by strong sunlight. It is an area of stark beauty where nothing grows— no trees, no flowers, no lichens even. It is a place where man's confidence is quickly shattered by a slight disturbance in the atmosphere which may transform the once-quiet Face into a whirling mass of spindrift, sending its insolent invaders scuttling to their tents, battered by the fury raging outside.

BRITISH EXPEDITION

An Italian millionaire Guide Monzino had booked Everest for both autumn 1972 and spring 1973 as he had planned to make the reconnaissance in the autumn for a full-scale attempt the following spring. Chris Bonington who was in contact with Mike Cheney, now living in Kathmandu, kept liaison in the booking of Everest. It was in the month of April 1972 that Monzino withdrew his reconnaissance expedition. This vacancy was offered to Chris Bonington. Indeed, the time he had was very short, as there would hardly be three to four months left to prepare before the team could attempt Everest in autumn. Chris Bonington was fully aware of the difficulties that one faces during the autumn climb. After giving considerable thought to both expense and shortage of time for preparations he examined a number of proposals like taking a very small expedition to climb Everest in the shortest possible time.

On a big mountain like Everest, it may be difficult to climb with a small number of climbers and sherpas even when one climbed from the conventional route of the South-East ridge. There has got to be a small contingent of the ice fall sherpas whose duty would be to keep the route open and the advance base camp fully supplied. The advance base camp has got to be manned by one or two sherpas who would help ferry loads for higher camps. In case of bad weather or accident, a small party on Everest exposes itself to greater danger and risk of life. This would also be true for a very large party like that of the Japanese in 1970.

The workable solution would be ideally around eight climbers and eight sherpas with two sherpa cooks. In such a situation, the members should carry as much as the sherpas. This would make for effective cooperation between the two and promote good relations. Chris Bonington kept working on his four-man expedition with Dougal Haston, Nick Estcourt, and Mick Burke. He later added two more members, Mike Thompson and Peter Steele as doctor. With all the members selected, Chris Bonington began his preparations but he was not too happy at the prospect of climbing Everest by the South East ridge, and by mid-June he changed his plans and decided to make an all-out attempt on the South West Face, knowing fully well that the odds were against him. They were left with only 8 weeks for preparations. He had to raise a large sum of money, almost £60,000. He also added Doug Scott and Hamish MacInnes and a support climber, Kelvin Kent. He appointed Jimmy Roberts his Deputy Leader. Don Whillans, who had been to Everest on two previous expeditions, was not selected although he was rated as an outstanding mountaineer. The main reason for his not being included was perhaps that he never integrated with the team. Later, Mick Thompson and Dr. Peter Steele withdrew from the expedition and were replaced by Dave Bathgate and Barney Rosedale as doctor.

On 21 August, Chris Bonington with his team flew from London to Kathmandu. Considering the fact that the permission was only granted in mid-April it should be considered a creditable performance. The expedition did not fly to Lukla air-strip but as a part of acclimatisation, started their approach march after staying two days in Kathmandu, reaching Thyangboche monastery on 7 September. They left Thyangboche on 11 September for the base camp when the monsoon clouds were still over them. The approach march during this period is most depressing in the Himalayas, as crossing through fields, forests and villages, dust and leeches are a constant menace. I remember in one of my own Sikkim climbs, we had to camp at a place called Bakkin approximately 7,000' in the middle of a bamboo forest. It rained heavily throughout and when we tried to slip into the tent at night, there were thousands of leeches all over. They were dangling from the inner walls of the tents and were horrible to look at. We kept awake trying to put salt and burnt match sticks to remove them from our bodies. We literally had to make a kind of wall with salt around us, as the leeches would not crawl over salt.

On 14 September, the expedition established its base camp. On the 16th, Doug and Hamish along with 5 sherpas started to open a route in the ice fall. By 20 September, the expedition succeeded in cutting a route through the ice fall in about five days. The weather had been good and the expedition seemed well ahead of schedule. But for a week after opening the ice fall, they could not push further in the Western Cwm because of bad weather and strong winds. It was only on 30 September that they established camp II and on 2 October made the first ferry to camp III. Doug and Mick took over in making a route beyond camp III at a height of 22,000' on the South West Face.

There was a second spell of bad weather with high winds which put the expedition back by four days. It was only on 9 October that Doug and Mick moved up to camp III again and started opening the route beyond, while the sherpa support started clearing and making platforms for boxes at the camps. During this time, unlike the summer climb, the days tend to get shorter and shorter and become horribly cold as soon as the sun drops behind the mountains, and the temperature goes down to minus 10° to 20° or below during the night. Working time is greatly reduced and this is a great setback in winter.

The pair started fixing the rope and made laborious progress. A large rope 300' long supplied to Mick and Doug by sherpas Anu and Ang Phurba was fixed leading to the centre of the face. The higher they climbed, the greater were the gusts of winds tearing at them. At the site for camp IV, they found a few items left by a previous expedition. It was a creditable job forcing a road to a height of 24,600'. Supplies across the ice fall were not coming in time from the base camp as the route kept changing. During the post-monsoon period, the ice fall does not remain static which results in crevasses opening up and closing. You may put up a ladder to go across a crevasse but the next day the crevasse becomes so large that there would be no sign of the ladder.

Since Doug and Mick had been on the Face for a long time they needed to be replaced. Dougal and Hamish with sherpa support pushed up to replace them on 12 October. The location of camp IV was on a slanting surface as there was no level space. It was always dangerous to keep things loose as they would roll down and go like a missile. On 12 and 14 October, Hamish and Dougal pushed up towards the rock band and they succeeded in pushing the route to camp V, which seemed rather good progress, but as luck would have it, the post-monsoon winds started. On 16 October, the expedition had its first taste of winter winds, blowing at a terrific speed. The nights were usually stormy with the deafening roar of avalanches. One of the members, Kelvin, was severely frost-bitten in the fingers and had to be evacuated. Chris, who had reached camp IV, was trying to watch and wait if the weather would improve. Due to bad weather the box at camp IV collapsed and Dougal and Hamish came down to Camp II and suggested withdrawal till the weather improved. Chris, who was at camp IV, had a difficult decision to make. There was no change throughout the night or the next morning. But, later, suddenly, the weather cleared. There was no more wind and so Chris, who was already at camp IV, decided to move up along with sherpa Ang Phurba.

With great difficulty, Chris Bonington plodded up and finally reached camp V with the ferry of loads. After leaving the loads, the party returned to camp IV pushing Nick and Dave upwards to camp V but this could not be done because the altitude began to tell upon Chris and his sherpas. All hope of stocking camp V was, therefore, abandoned. On 22 October the wind rose and there was no activity for almost two days. The team

146

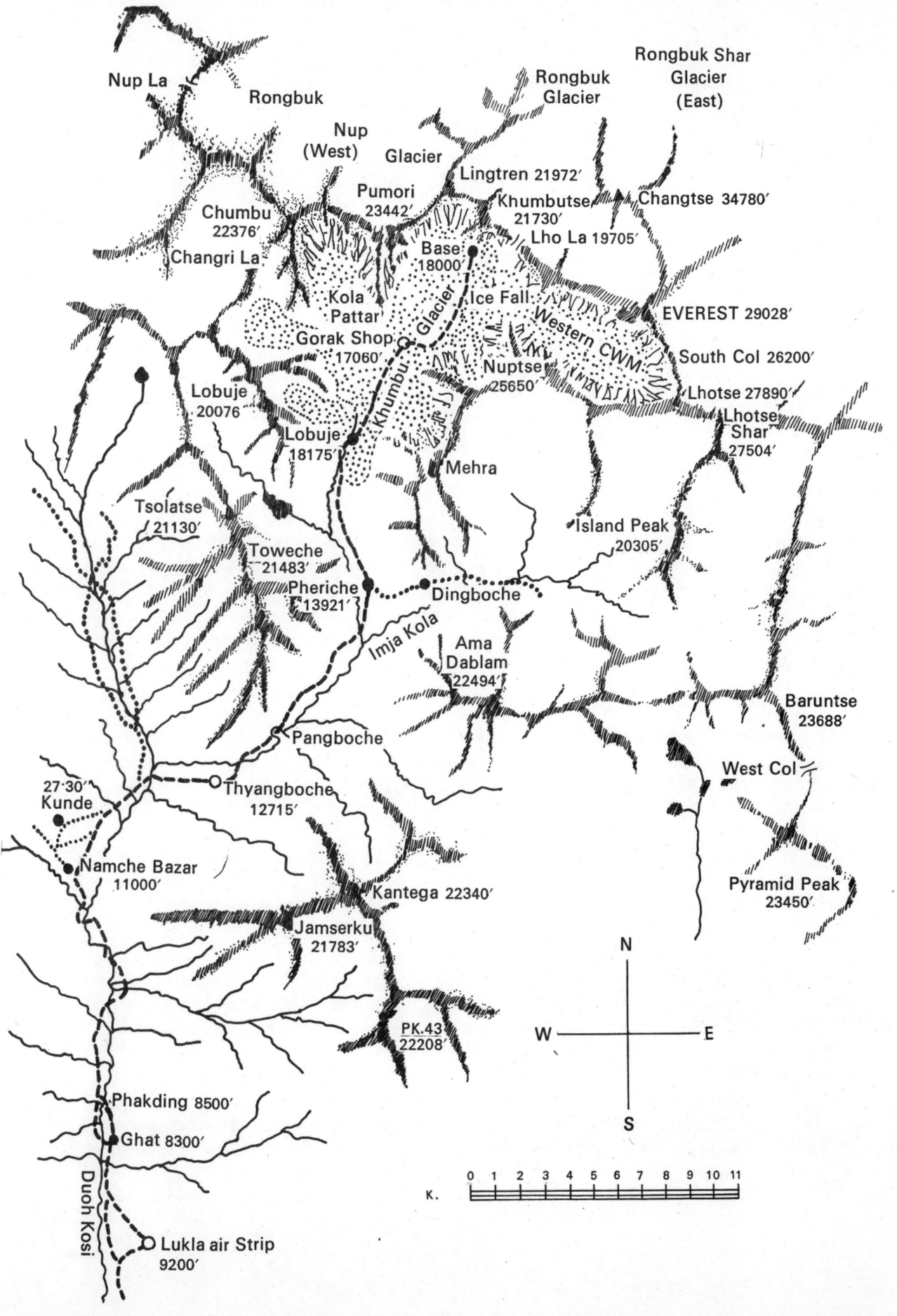

moved down, and the weather, even at the Western Cwm, was frightening. The higher camps were closed later. There was a slight improvement on the 28th, but later the wind rose.

The expedition had not yet made up its mind to withdraw completely and was still hopeful of having some sort of a short spell of good weather which they got. Activity in the higher camps was resumed and on 1 November, Nick and Doug again moved up to camp IV with the hope of moving to camp V on 2 November. But they could not do so because of the repairs to the route, and could only reach camp IV on 4 November. On 5 November, Nick and Dave started moving up camp V to join Mick and Doug to establish camp VI. According to plan, the leader had decided to use Mick and Doug to establish a route to camp VI and then replace them by putting Hamish and Dougal straight up to push to the rock band. Unfortunately, Mick and Doug said over the radio that they could not move ahead as Mick was suffering from a bad case of piles and Doug had mild frost-bite, so they had to come down. The other problem was that if Dougal and Hamish came up to camp V, straight from camp I, they may not be able to stand it because of the lack of acclimatisation, and may not be able to work efficiently.

At this point, the members of the expedition had arguments and counter-arguments with the leader as to who would open up the route to the rock band, as this was the aim of every climber before attempting the summit. The arguments rose to such a pitch that the leader had to tell them that in case they did not agree with his decision they could return to Kathmandu. I doubt if there is any expedition which has not faced differences between the leader and team members. As a climber, I feel it is better to let off steam than to supress one's feelings.

Meanwhile, work continued in opening camp VI and stocking camp V with oxygen and other equipment. On 7 November, Nick and Dave, along with two others, were ready to leave the camp at 10 a.m. to attempt reaching camp VI. It was a big day for them. They were using oxygen which was constantly troubling them. The valve of Dave's cylinder did not function and so Nick set out with the two sherpas leaving Dave. Dave improvised and harnessed the oxygen cylinder and set out to catch up with the others. But he lagged far behind. Nick made good progress. While they were making towards the rock band they could see Dave plodding up at an extremely slow pace. Dave, in spite of his best efforts, could not make his oxygen work, so he had to return. Nick and party however succeeded in establishing camp VI.

The sherpas who were following Nick as the support party were going without oxygen, and they showed great stamina indeed. Nick's oxygen apparatus also started giving him trouble and he discovered that he had run out of oxygen. On the other hand, without oxygen, though much lighter, his progress was hampered greatly, for he felt much colder. By now he had reached almost half way across the final slope. He anchored the rope used for fixed roping. Nick soon discovered that he would get incredibly late as the sun was dropping on the horizon. They had reached a point where they would establish camp VI but had now to hurry down. It was pitch dark and they had to handle their carabiner with numb hands. The wind had also risen. They were greeted by Dave and Janbo who had some hot drinks ready for them. At this height, everyone carries sleeping pills, vitamin tablets, iron tablets, salt tablets and headache pills.

I do not remember having taken any pills on our expedition except the multi-vitamin tablets with breakfast every morning. The sherpas on this expedition were well looked after by the members and this was the reason they had such a cordial relationship. Both Nick and Dave were completely exhausted. Nick's hands from the previous day had been frost-bitten and so were Dave's feet, and they had to go back. For them the expedition was over.

While Dave and Nick moved down, Chris and Ang Phurba moved up to camp V. The idea was to open camp VI after resting for a night at camp V. It was mid-day before Chris and Ang Phurba left camp V. On all occasions at this camp it takes almost three hours more than at the lower camps to get ready. Although, the going was slow they reached the foot of the rock band carrying loads for camp VI, and soon reached the last point reached by Nick's party. An immediate problem now was to find a suitable camp site which would not be unduly exposed to the winds and also to find a place where there was bright morning sun which would hasten the morning activities before the team set out.

Chris managed to reach a place which was approximately 27,000′ and looked across the South Col and the Lhotse. It was already three in the afternoon, and after setting up camp VI, they rushed down. Now having opened camp VI, the chances of making an attempt on the summit were certainly brighter, but only if the weather helped. Graham, who was hurt by a stone which fell on his forehead, became unconscious for a while and was later moved down to camp II where the doctor stitched his wound. Chris and Ang Phurba were getting ready to make another ferry of loads to camp VI. At this stage of the climb, it becomes rather important to work out the oxygen loads available and its requirements. In fact, in every expedition during the last stages, every litre of available oxygen is worked out, and is checked and rechecked. Chris Bonington became conscious of the oxygen requirements and started to work the available oxygen at various camps. To do so, he kept in constant touch with lower camps, as Mick warned him of depleting stocks of oxygen. It was 10 o'clock next morning and Chris had to work out the entire oxygen stocks available which meant that he would not be able to take the ferry up to camp VI. He decided, therefore, to send Ang Phurba alone to take the ferry. Ang Phurba left without any hesitation. Since they had already laid the fixed ropes, there was no undue danger in Ang Phurba ferrying by himself. But it is always advisable to have two men.

The oxygen position was not very bright. He could at the most send only one summit party. Meanwhile around 1.30 Ang Phurba returned taking approximately three hours to reach camp VI and come down. This was very creditable. The next morning Ang Phurba was to go down and Chris was to do the ferry to camp VI all alone, but because of the very bad condition as reported by Ang Phurba, Chris decided to wait and clean up the tents for Hamish and Dougal who would arrive in the evening. The plan was that on the 13th, Chris would carry the load to camp VI while Mick and Doug moved up to camp V so that the next day they could ferry the loads to camp VI.

On the 13th, Chris set out alone to camp VI. The oxygen did not work well. His progress was very slow and by 3 p.m. he was still a long way from the rock spur but managed to reach camp VI where he dumped the loads and started down and reached camp V in a completely exhausted state. After having hot tea at camp V, he had to move to camp IV as decided earlier. It was a terrible descent. The sun had gone down and the light had faded. It was pitch dark when he reached camp IV. It had been a very tiring journey for him. Next day, Dougal and Hamish moved up to occupy camp VI, supported by Doug and Mick. They moved up the fixed rope but Hamish turned back fairly early because of a faulty oxygen set. The other three also came back and could not reach camp VI because of high winds. The condition had almost become unbearable and Chris as a leader had finally to take a decision to go back, as he himself had experienced such bad conditions at camp VI the previous day. In Nick's words, "My own feeling—emotional I know— is to wish that they had at least spent a night at camp VI, and tried—somehow. I feel cheated and let down. I know this is stupid; it's partly Base Camp frustration. In some ways it's better, in some ways worse, for the front four. I feel sorry for Chris."

But this is what mountaineering is. The entire mountain was in the grip of winter winds and the expedition had to return hastily. The higher camps were closed and the expedition moved down on 16 November which was fairly late. Tony Tighe, who spent his last eight weeks at base camp, went up the ice fall in great excitement and was killed in an avalanche and his body was never recovered. It is bad luck for an expedition to have such a disaster when the expedition is called off. Chris Bonington had a similar disaster on his earlier expedition to Annapurna in the tragic death of Ian Clough. It was a cruel loss for an expedition to go back unsuccessful and then to leave behind one of the dear climbers buried on the mountain. But this must be accepted as a part of mountaineering.

Facing: Camp V with boxtents partially collapsed after the big storm. Cho-Oyu in the background.

Climbing near the Rock Band, around 8,000 m

Load-carrying in the Ice Fall region

Camp III at about 7,000 m

11

1973 Italian and Japanese Expeditions
1974 Spanish and French Expeditions

A 64-member expedition, the largest so far to Everest, led by Count Guido Monzino left Kathmandu around the second week of February to climb Everest through the conventional South Col route. The expedition was supported by 70 sherpas led by Sirdar Lakpa Tenzing. The important members of the expedition were: Guido Monzino (leader), Piere Nave and Giuseppo Pistino (both deputy leaders), Roberto Stella (director of the climbing group), and Paolo Corretelli (director of the medical team). The expedition's total load was seventy tons as compared to twenty-five tons of the Indian expedition of 1965. The team included press men, helicopter pilots, and technicians. Eight members of the expedition flew to Lukla on 11 February followed by the rest of the team. The entire load of seventy tons of equipment was also flown to Lukla.

The expedition could not open base camp until 22 March due to very heavy snowfall in the Everest region. The expedition established camp I on 28 March. On 2 April, they opened camp II at a height of 21,325 . The Italian air-force helicopters undertook the task of air dropping supplies to the camp in the Western Cwm. Air-dropping is relatively new in Nepalese mountaineering. The major air-dropping undertaken earlier was for the British Army expedition on Annapurna in 1970. On 16 April the expedition established camp III at 22,960 . The Nepalese Foreign Ministry, however, objected to the Italian air-force helicopters being used for dropping supplies. It is understood that except for the dropping of medical supplies, other items are prohibited and this could be taken to be in violation of the Nepalese Foreign Ministry's permit. On 18 April, a helicopter of the expedition crashed in the Khumbu ice fall. The helicopter was completely destroyed. The pilot, however, escaped with a shoulder injury and was evacuated to the base camp.

Sir Edmund Hillary, who was in this area, visited the base camp of the expedition

155

Sherpa boy

which looked so different from the base camp he had seen before. The leader, Guido Monzino, was living in camp in style. He had a very large tent complete with office, bedroom, toilet, shower and dressing room. The entire area was carpeted and furnished with brass studded leather chairs and desk.

The expedition was making slow progress due to bad weather conditions: There was a high wind and heavy snowfall which was giving the Italians a tough time. After continued bad weather for two weeks, the expedition succeeded in establishing camp IV on 29 April and camp V on 30 April. The expedition succeeded in putting a total of 5 Italians and 3 sherpas on the summit. They could not break the Indian record of putting 9 members as they had hoped. Due to bad weather, the leader decided to withdraw, and unwilling to take unacceptable and unjustifiable risks, ordered the return of the entire expedition. Sir Edmund Hillary, commenting on the Italian expedition, said, "As a mountaineer I think he [Monzino] would have been much better carrying it out in the European Alps. It has been a very competent military operation, but it has nothing to do with mountaineering . . . . I hope in future that Everest will be left to mountaineering parties composed of small groups of enthusiastic climbers. It's now reached the height of the ridiculous."

AUTUMN 1973 JAPANESE EXPEDITION

A 48-member Japanese team led by Michio Yuasa, the largest ever to attempt Everest, arrived in Kathmandu on 22 July in a post-monsoon attempt on the South West Face. The expedition was sponsored by the Japanese Rock climbing club and was assisted by 33 sherpas. The expedition was divided into various parties. An 11-member advance party led by Jiro Endo established base camp I at 6,000 m. on 4 September, and on 18 September, camp III was established on the Face. Camp V was established at 8,000 m. on 10 October. The expedition could not move beyond this camp due to bad weather. On 17 October, there was a big storm which damaged the tents at camp IV and camp V. Since the weather deteriorated no progress could be made on the South West Face. Another party, however, started via the traditional South Col route and succeeded in climbing Everest on 26 October.

The members to reach the summit were Hisahi Ishiguro, an office worker from Tokyo, and Yasuo Kato, a student from Omiya, Saitama. When they reached the summit at 4.30 p.m. Kato realised that his oxygen cylinder was empty, his middle finger of the right hand and several toes were frost-bitten. While descending they were overtaken by darkness as their progress was extremely slow due to the lack of oxygen. They decided to spend the night on a rock shelter slapping each other to ward off sleep. They had no water or food. They kept awake and renewed their descent early next morning. They reached the camp fully frost-bitten and temporarily blinded by exposure. With this Japan became the first country to have scaled Everest in the post-monsoon season. The party on the South West Face continued to make slow progress and reached an altitude of 8,300m. The expedition also tried to find the body of the sherpa guide Tangbu of Namche Bazar who was killed here by an avalanche on 12 October. The expedition succeeded in reaching a height of 8,380 m. in spite of bad weather, and then finally decided to abandon the attempt on 30 October due to bad weather.

SPRING 1974 SPANISH EXPEDITION

A 16-member Spanish expedition to Everest for spring 1974 was financed by Tximist, makers of famous storage batteries. The leader of the expedition was Juan Iqna cio 157 lorente Zugaza who was also the doctor of the expedition. The other members of the expedition were: Angel Alexandre Valleio Rosen, Angel Landa Bidarte, Felipe Uriarta Camera, Alfonso Alonso Dies, Luis Abalde Alzuart, Juan Cortazar Larrea, Luis Ignacio Domingo Uriarte, Luis Maria Saens de Olazagoitia, Juan Carles Fernandez de la Torre, Francisco Lusarreta Grumeta, Rodolfo Kirch Uqarte, Julio Villar Gurruchaqa, Ricardo Gallardo Senosiain, Fernando Larruquert Aquirre, and Angel Lerma Herrero. The expedition attempted the mountain from the conventional South East Ridge route, and succeeded in opening camp VI at a height of 8,500 m. but could not go beyond due to very bad weather and strong winds. Two members, Angel Alexandre Valleio Rosen and Felipe Uriarta, reached camp VI and were 350' below the summit when they returned due to stormy weather. This was the second summit attempt. The first attempt by Ricard Gallardo Senosiain and Luis Abalde Alzuart was foiled by strong winds. They were both very badly frost-bitten and were flown back from the Lukla airstrip. On their return Felipe Uriarte said that he and Angel "had reached Camp VI in very good condition despite my swelling fingers which were painful on the following morning, the day of the first of three proposed summit assaults."

They were ready for an early morning start on 13 May, but the high winds drove them back inside the tent. As the wind slackened at 1100 hours, clouds started coming up from below and they decided they had to beat a retreat. As they descended, the snow started. "No one ever occupied camp VI again. Two days of good weather on 22 and 23 May were of no use because there was no one left fit enough in the top camps to make a summit attempt," said Felipe Uriarte.

AUTUMN 1974 FRENCH EXPEDITION

A 10-member team led by G. Devouassoux, a guide, leader of the French expedition to Annapurna South in 1970 and Deputy to the Mayor of Chamonix, left Kathmandu on 2 August. All the members of the expedition were highly experienced mountaineers and guides in Chamonix. This was the first French Everest expedition and was sponsored by Maurice Herzog, Depute-Maire de Chamonix who climbed Annapurna in 1950. The team comprised Gerard Devouassoux (leader), George Payot (deputy leader), Claude Ancey, Daniel Audibert, Fernand Audibert, Jean-Paul Balmat, Denis Ducroz, Dr. Eric Lassorre (doctor), Christian Mollier, and Pierre Tairraz. The aims of the expedition were: to put every member of the team on the summit of Everest; to open and climb *via* a new route, the entire West Ridge. The Americans in 1963 did not begin climbing at the base of the West Ridge (at the Lho La Pass, 6,000 m.) but joined the ridge at a height of 7,300 m. from the Western Cwm. The Americans, then, went left onto the North face and rejoined the ridge very close to the summit to attempt the peak without oxygen, and to study the high altitude effects on the human heart. With these aims in mind the expedition set out for the mountain.

The expedition could not go very far in achieving their objectives as they were met with disaster when the leader and five sherpas were killed in an avalanche between their first and second high altitude camp on September 9. This demoralised the entire expedition and they decided to abandon it. George Payot, deputy leader, and Pierre Tairrez, who were with the leader when the tragedy occurred, said that even experienced sherpas had told them that they had never seen an avalanche of such a magnitude. A rolling thunder lasting just 30 seconds on 9 September crushed the leader and five sherpas.

Payot said that after the tragedy they had no heart to go on and it was the opinion of

*Looking up the
Lhotse Face from Camp 1*

*Advance Base
Camp*

Rinaldo Carrel, Mirko Minusso, and Lhakpa Tenzing on the summit

Capt. Fabrizio proudly displays a momento at the Summit

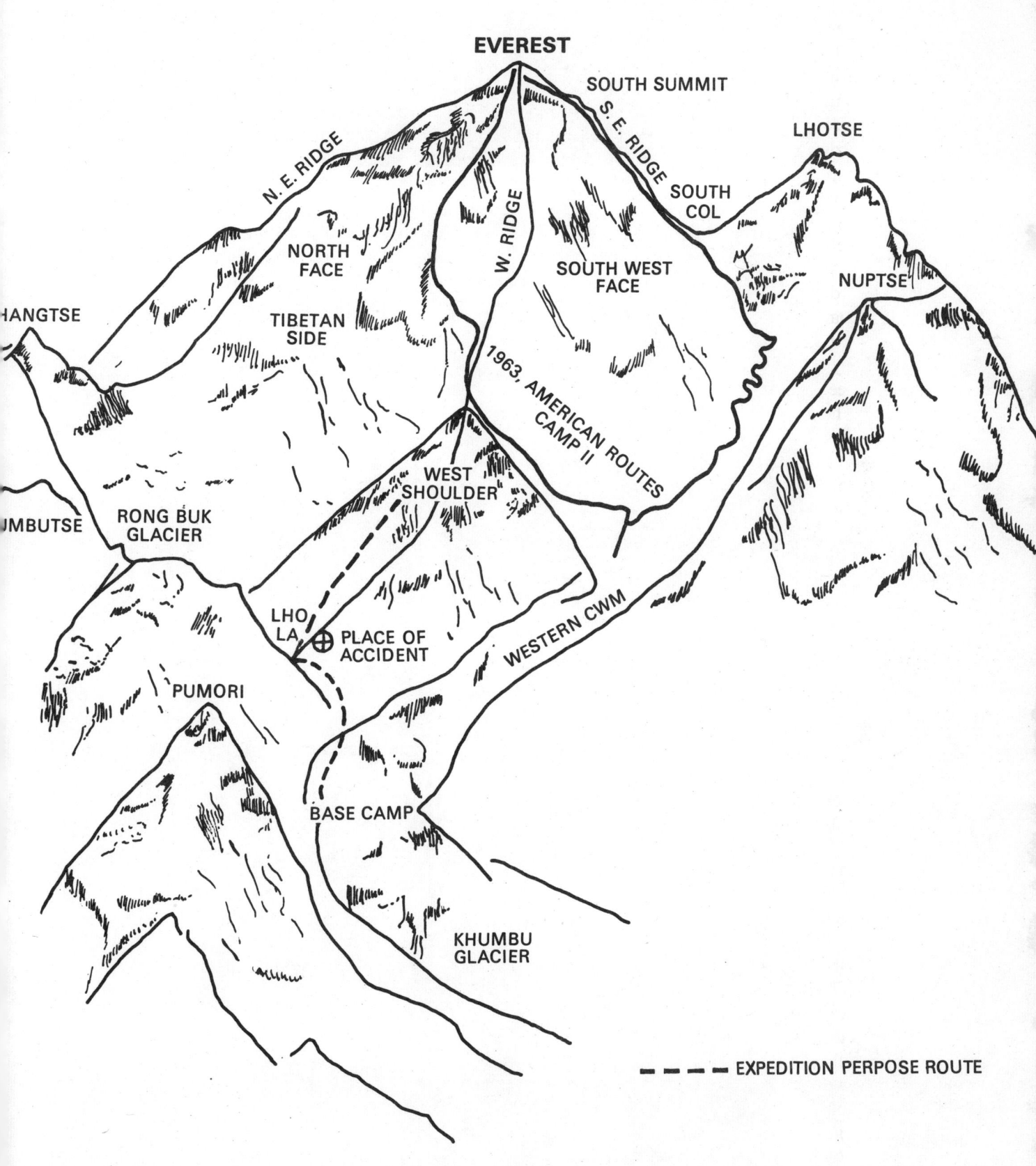

EVEREST

SOUTH SUMMIT

LHOTSE

N. E. RIDGE

S. E. RIDGE

NORTH FACE

W. RIDGE

SOUTH COL

TIBETAN SIDE

SOUTH WEST FACE

NUPTSE

HANGTSE

1963, AMERICAN ROUTES CAMP II

RONG BUK GLACIER

WEST SHOULDER

MBUTSE

LHO LA

⊕ PLACE OF ACCIDENT

WESTERN CWM

PUMORI

BASE CAMP

KHUMBU GLACIER

– – – – EXPEDITION PERPOSE ROUTE

all the members of the expedition and sherpas that the attempt should be called off. In fact, Pierre Tairrez was so shocked by the disaster that he spoke halting even in French and in between used to switch over to broken English while talking to the press.

George Payot commenting on the disaster said, "The leader, 5 sherpas, and myself were buried deep under the snow sent by an avalanche. Fortunately I was buried only up to my neck. With tremendous effort I extricated myself and dug out one sherpa. Then both of us started digging for the others. By the time we could gather our wits and part of our equipment it was 10.30 in the night. There was no trace of the missing members even on the next day." The next day they continued the search in spite of heavy snowfall but they were aware of the fact that it was impossible to recover any of the party members as it was a massive avalanche. The expedition, to begin with, should have had a humble approach and a low key plan rather than an ambitious one.

12
1975 (Spring) Japanese Women's Expedition

Women in the past performed great feats in mountaineering. Around 1808 the first woman stood on the summit of Mont Blanc and almost a century ago Lucy Walker climbed the Matterhorn. There are hosts of other women who have stood on the summit of various mountains. Then we have the famous all women International expedition to Cho-Oyu led by Claude Kogan in 1959, of which Tenzing's two daughters, Pem Pem and Nima, and a niece, Doma, were members. This expedition met with disaster in which the leader, a member and a sherpa were lost. In India women climbers have undertaken a number of climbs and in 1977 an all-woman expedition succeeded in climbing *Kamet*, the highest mountain to be climbed by women in India. The team was led by Dr. Meena Aggarwal.

The Japanese Everest team of 1970 included Setsuko Watanabe who became the world's first lady 'eight thousander' as she reached Geneva Spur on Everest and then South Col. Mrs. Yvette Vaucher, 34, a parachutist from Geneva, had come very close to becoming the world's first woman on Everest in 1971. She had joined the West Ridge team of the International Everest expedition along with her school teacher husband, Michel Vaucher, and Maj. H. V. Bahuguna. She had climbed up to camp IV, 23,622', in spite of heavy snowfall and bad weather. The West Ridge team then withdrew and opted for the traditional South Col route and succeeded in setting up camp III at 23,458' on the Lhotse Face. Everything was set for Yvette to step on the summit, but unfortunately the leader suddenly decided to abandon this route in favour of the South West Face. With this her hopes of becoming the first woman Everester ended.

The Japanese Everest expedition actually had attempted a Himalayan summit in the summer of 1970 when Mrs. Junko Tabei, Mrs. Hiroko Hirakawa and sherpa Tenzing and Pasang Nima reached the summit of Annapurna III (24,787′) on 19 May. In fact, it was the first ladies expedition from Japan to attempt such a major climb to Nepal and it was the success of this expedition which enhanced the climbing prestige of women from Japan and their eyes were now set on Everest. It was in 1971 that permission for them to climb Everest was given in the spring of 1975. The preparation for the expedition started immediately with Mrs Hisano as the leader. The expedition was sponsored by the Tokyo Women's Mountaineering Club. A Japanese newspaper and T. V. company provided most of the expenses and also deputed three journalists and four cameramen to cover the expedition. Mrs Hisano raised almost £50,000 from the *Yomiuri Shimbun* (a newspaper), Nikon T. V., and with contributions from various commercial firms. She had 23 sherpas and about 500 porters. The sherpa Sirdar Ang Tshering had climbed with the Japanese Rock Climbing Club expedition to Everest in 1973 and had done extremely well. The expedition had 14 Japanese women climbers and a doctor: Mrs Eiko Hisano, Mrs Junko Tabei, Michiko Manita, Fumie Nasu, Mrs Yuriko Watanabe, Setsuko Kitamura, Mrs Masako Naganuma, Mrs Sumiko Fujiwara, Teruyo Hirashima, Yoko Mihara, Reiko Shioura, Fumiko Arayama, Sachiko Naka, Yumi Taneya and Dr. Masako Saka-guchi. The expedition left Kathmandu on Feb 9. They followed the same route as previous expeditions to reach Thyangboche Monastary. The expedition spent almost two weeks at Thyangboche acclimatising and on March 16 they set up their base camp at the foot of the Khumbu glacier. The expedition took almost two weeks to open the route through the ice fall and established camp I on 3 April on the top of the Khumbu ice fall. On 14 April Fumie Nasu, Michiko Manita and two sherpas set up camp III at approximately 21,000′. "So many people had camped thereabouts that we hardly gave a thought to the choice of the site," said Mrs. Hisano. "Judging by the empty spaghetti tins we were about 15 metres from where the Italians had camped, on a small hammock of ice."

On 27 April they established camp IV, and on 2 May they succeeded in establishing camp V at Lhotse Face. The expedition was doing extremely well when they were struck by a disaster on the night of 4 May when a big avalanche came thundering down the Lhotse and Nuptse wall and hit seven members and six sherpas in camp II. Junko and two sherpas were very seriously injured. Junko recalls: "I was sharing a sleeping bag with Yuriko and heard a wild sound like a big explosion, followed by huge blocks of ice hitting our tent. One block landed on my chest and another on my legs. I felt suffocated and felt that we were going to die." In spite of the heavy pressure which immobilised her, she managed to pull out a knife from a pocket and pass it on to a sherpa, before losing consciousness. The sherpa cut through the tent to rescue them. "On regaining consciousness, I realised I had a bruise on my chest. My first question was about the safety of the team. Luckily we were all safe and alive," said Junko. According to Ang Tshering a delay of two or three minutes would have meant the end of both Junko and Yuriko.

This accident made their summit attempt extremely difficult. The sherpa guide insisted that it would be useless now trying to make the summit and that they should turn back, but they gave this thought a deaf ear and continued their climb. But the mishap compelled Junko to spend two days in the oxygen tent and four more days for rest under medical care to recover from the shock and the injury. Her chances to climb further now seemed remote, but the way she picked up soon made her the fittest member of the team. This mishap put the expedition behind schedule as they had lost a lot of equipment, tents, and oxygen. The team could now not afford to put two summit pairs as planned and had to reduce it to one only. The team resumed their climb on 7 May. On 13 May, Junko and Ang Tshering moved to establish camp VI at 27,887′: On 15 May they were to make an

164

Facing: Japanese women's expedition.
P-167: Junko Tabei being greeted by the members of the team at the base camp.

Junko Tabei on the summit

Crossing the ice-fall

attempt on the summit but were beaten back by foul weather. They stayed back in the tent and on the 16 morning at 5 a.m. they took off for the summit. Junko carried a load of 14 kg. which comprised cameras, coffee flasks, the flags of Japan and Nepal, and oxygen cylinders. The pair negotiated the Razor's Edge and the portion of loose rocks. At 8.30 a.m. they reached the South Summit at the base of which they left their partially filled oxygen cylinder. Junko describes the climb as follows:

> We checked our equipment and resumed the climb at 8.30 a.m. It took us about four hours from there to reach the top. The route was too steep and too long for a woman. Ang Tshering was climbing faster and often urged me to move on by pulling my hand. I was tired and we progressed slowly towards the summit, sometimes on our elbows. It was a very hard climb.
>
> Ang Tshering was all along telling me to hurry, but I was going on slowly. I looked up towards the summit and felt it was quite a difficult climb. When we got very close to the peak there was deep, soft fresh snow. I had to crawl very slowly. Tshering first got on top and then pulled me up. There was snow all around. I planted the Japanese and Nepalese flags there, buried a thermos full of coffee in the snow and then we took a number of still and movie pictures.

While the pair moved up, the wind speed rose. They were now walking over the big boulders between the South Summit and Hillary's Chimney. Hillary's Chimney was a difficult hurdle but the pair managed to cross it in spite of the high winds. Junko's short height must have posed a problem while crossing it. "Tall people have an advantage in hurdles of this nature," said Junko. "After crossing the Chimney, it was sturdy going. The way was narrow and the summit too was narrow and small. Ang Tshering stepped up first and I followed. The snow on top was soft and dangerous. It took me a few minutes before I could stand properly." Mrs. Junko collected 27 rock pebbles as mementoes. One of the pebbles was given for a test in Tokyo. She writes:

> Dr Joyo Kosaka, Professor of Geomineralogy at Tokyo Institute of Technology, has since examined a one mm. thick slice of a rock under polarising microscope. He has found in it parallel layers of semi crystallised limestone with quartz and a very small amount of feldspar placed between them. It was formed by sedimentation under warm and shallow sea water, 20 to 30 million years ago. The sea bed has been pushed upward by convulsions of the earth's crust to become its highest point.
>
> When I thought of descending through the same steep and dangerous route I was a little scared. I was afraid of climbing down.

On the return they did not stay at the last camp but came down to South Col and then to base camp which they covered in four days.

After staying for four days at the base camp, the team returned to Tokyo after a brief halt in Delhi. While Eiko said, "Success was due to co-operation from all sides," Junko stated, "Four years of continued efforts and the will to get to the top led to success." *Himavanta* magazine wrote in the issue of May 1975:

> In spite of strains between some Japanese teams and their sherpas, the ladies had no unpleasant incident and their relations were very good. This leads to another question—whether this was an all-ladies' expedition? Most of the plans were worked out earlier in Tokyo and the members were 'full of confidence and determination.' So in spite of Ang Tshering and his men it was a ladies expedition. That she went through

Razor's Edge with last camp and Makalu at the back.

*Mrs. Tabei and sherpa A
Tsering returning from t.
summit of Everest*

the traditional route does not rob Junko of her greatness. Her grit, courage and determination in the face of near catastrophe and against tremendous odds can only be matched by a select few and the 36th Everester will go down in history as a class of her own. She now ranks among such greats as Tenzing Norgay, Edmund Hillary, Amelia Earhart of aviation fame, Sonja Heniein the Olympic figure skater, Suzanne Lenglen the tennis star and Valentina Tereshkova the first woman cosmonaut.

Born on 22 September 1939, Junko graduated from Showa Women's University, Tokyo and became a middle school teacher. She gave up the teaching job in 1973 and invested her retirement benefits in the present expedition, in which participants bore half of the expenses. A climber with 15 years experience, she is a member of the Japanese Alpine Club. Shortly before leaving for the Annapurna expedition, she married Mosanobu Tabei, whom she met while climbing in Japan, and they have a three-year old daughter. She does not think that household chores clash with mountaineering, although a married woman with a child needs some assistance from her husband. Bespectacled, just five feet tall, Junke weighs only 42 kg. and has immense stamina. A colleague said of her, "I wonder where her power comes from!" Her husband nicknamed her the "Beaver." She is disarmingly frank and can speak in halting English. She is a member of the editorial staff of the Journal of the Physical Society of Japan.

Ang Tshering was born in Namche Bazar in 1946. Having acted as Sardar in two previous expeditions, this was his third Sardarship. He has become the sixth Nepal-born sherpa to climb Everest after Tenzing Norgay, Phu Dorji, Chotare Sherpa, Sambhu Tamang and Lhakpa Tenzing. Sambhu, however, continues to be the youngest on Everest. He was only 19 when he achieved this outstanding feat on 5 May 1973. This is the third ascent of Everest by the Japanese—the only country to do so. While Gombu still remains the only double-Everester, no other nation has achieved a double, not to speak of a triple, or has put a woman up on Everest or climbed in autumn.

13

1975 (Spring) Chinese Expedition

The Chinese had claimed on 25 May 1960 of putting 3 climbers on the summit by the North Face. The summiters were Wang Fuchou, Kobnu (Tibetan) and Chu Yin-Hua. Now exactly 15 years after the Chinese have again claimed putting nine members on the summit including one woman on 27 May at 14.30 hours Peking time, from the North West Face of Everest. The Chinese had erected a 3 m. high red metal surveying pole with a five-star red flag on the summit. Doug Scott and Dougal Haston, the first summit pair of the British Everest expedition (autumn 1975) by the South West Face, claimed to have seen this on the summit. The red flag must have been made of very strong cloth to withstand the high monsoon winds on Everest.

The expedition began its activities in mid-March 1975 when they set up their base camp at Rongbuk Monastery (5,000m). Camp I was set up at 5,500 m., camp II at 6,000m., camp III 6,500m., camp IV 7,007 m., and camp V at 7,600 m. These camps were established between 15 March and 15 May. On 17 May, they established camp VI at 8,300 m. and the final camp at 8,680 m. The Chinese mountaineering expedition decided to send two summit parties which set off from Rongbuk Monastery on 17 and 18 May in two groups. The summit parties reached camp V on 20 and 21 May when the weather deteriorated. The expedition reported that the weather was so bad that they could not light their gas stoves for cooking or go out to get the ice and snow for boiling water. There was no movement for almost four days. On 24th May, Sodnam Norbu, Darphuntso, Tsering Tobgyal, and Kunga Pasang left the camp and reached the final assault camp at 8,680 m. on May 25.

On 26 May Sodnam Norbu and the 3 other climbers left the camp with ropes to establish the route to the summit. The weather was bad and they could not make any headway. Meanwhile, the 5 other members of the assault team—Lhotse, Phanthog,

Chinese on the summit ridge

Our great leader Chairman Mao has taught us: "I am for the slogan 'fear neither hard-ship nor death.'"

The Summit

Marx said: "There is no royal road to science, and only those who do not dread the fatiguing climb of its steep paths have a chance of gaining its luminous summits."

Hou Sheng-fu, Samdrub, and Ngapo Khyen—reached the camp at 8,300 m. on 25 May, but failed to reach the final camp at 8,680 m. due to very high winds. Since the weather continued to be bad, the summit plan was re-arranged and the summit attempt was now planned to be made on 27 May. The assault team constructed a route on a 3 m. high vertical wall on the southern side below the summit and reached the assault camp during the late hours in the evening. On the morning of 27 May, the summit party left the assault camp while it was still dark in the morning, after taking some water and food. They carried with them a five-star red flag, a metal surveying pole, cine cameras, oxygen cylinders, and other equipment. I reproduce an account of the expedition as reported by the *Peking Review No. 23*:

> The final assault camp was only half a kilometre away from the summit. But because of the extremely oxygen-poor air at altitudes above 8,600 m., members of the assault team had to stop at some places and draw a dozen deep breaths at each step while leaning on their ice-axes. In the 1960 expedition, Wang Fu-chou and two other comrades who set out from the final assault camp at 8,550 m. reached the summit after 19 hours' march. This time, though Phanthog, Sodnam Norbu and the seven other members had spent much of their energy after ten days' climb at high altitudes, all gave a good account of themselves as staunch fighters in the face of difficulties.
>
> Throughout the entire March, Sodnam Norbu was always foremost. Carrying an oxygen cylinder and an eiderdown sleeping bag, Phanthog, the woman climber, never lagged behind. Marching in a line, they steadily pressed forward along the steep ridge. At 9.30 that morning when they reached the top of the Second Step by way of a metal ladder, the wind began to gain force. Braving a force 6–7 strong wind, they continued the climb and soon found themselves at the foot of the pyramid-shaped Qomolangma Feng summit. Between them and the summit were two 150 metre-long stretches of steep slopes covered with ice and snow. Following a short pause for oxygen, they put on their crampons, picked up their ice-axes and resumed the march.
>
> After more than three hours of herculean efforts, they got over the two stretches of ice and snow slopes and came within about 50 metres of the summit. It was one o'clock sharp in the afternoon. When they began the final assault after a short rest, the way was blocked by a virtually perpendicular ice slope. Wielding his ice-axe, Sodnam Norbu cut a flight of steps on the slope but failed to climb up. The team had no alternative but to make a detour to the north of the slope, cross a rocky cliff, march westward and then head straight for the summit. At that moment, palls of haze again rose over the summit and a howling wind of force 7–8 blew up. It took the assault team nearly one and a half hours to cover the last 50 metres.
>
> At 14.30 hours Peking time, all nine members of the assault team finally reached the top of the Qomolangma Feng. When Hou Sheng-fu on behalf of all the assault members, reported the glad tidings to the base camp over the Walkie-talkie, cheers of 'Long Live Chairman Mao!' and 'Long Live the Communist Party of Red China!' resounded on the peak and below.

After reaching the summit Phanthog said:

> I was very excited when we stepped onto the summit of Qomolangma, I stood beside Hou Sheng-fu as he reported our success to the base camp over the walkie-talkie and when we heard the cheers of our comrades at the base camp I joined them in shouting 'Long Live Chairman Mao! Long Live the Chinese Communist Party.'

Chinese on the summit from the North Face

Overleaf—Chinese on the summit with a woman climber, Phanthog, (second from the left) conducting scientific studies

The success of the expedition stems from the members' collective effort. On the acclimatization marches the women ascended shoulder to shoulder with the men, carrying their share of the equipment and supplies. Each woman had a load of about 15 kg.—foodstuffs, tents, cylinders of oxygen and cooking gas, and other things necessary for setting up camp at the various altitudes—and not a word of complaint was heard. In addition there were scientific instruments, for the women climbers also played an important role in scientific survey. We have lived up to our pledge: Chinese women have a strong will, difficulties can't stop us. We climbed the highest peak in the world. We really hold up half the sky.

After reaching the summit, they took photographs, shot films, planted a 3 m. high red metal surveying pole and conducted scientific research according to plan. After staying one hour and ten minutes on the peak, they left for the final assault camp at 8,680 m. and safely reached it at 21.00 hours the same night. Originally, four summit parties were to make the summit attempt which comprised 3 women and 15 men. But after reaching a height of 8,618 m., due to fatigue 2 women and 7 men dropped out from the summit team. Descending from the final assault camp the following day, they were met by Chen Jung-Chang, deputy leader of the expedition, and two other mountaineers at camp V, 7,600 m. above sea level. Upon reaching camp IV at 7,007 m. they were greeted by Wang-Fu-Chou, Secretary of the Expedition's Party committee, and two other mountaineers. The descent that day continued until they were back at camp III which had been set up at 6,500 m. above sea level. On 29 May, they went down to camp II at 6,000 m. It is interesting to note that of the nine members who scaled the peak, eight were Tibetans belonging to lower middle class peasant families. Phanthog is an office worker who has climbed many peaks before. She went to the top of Everest including Muztagh Ata. Sodnam Norbu is an electrican in the Chinese Army. Lotse, age 37, is a Tibetan who was a member of two expeditions earlier. Hou Sheng-Fu was also a member of many scientific surveys in the mountains. Samdrub, a Tibetan, is an army man and began mountaineering in 1974. Darphuntso is a Tibetan paint sprayer in the Tibet Motor Vehicle Repair Works. Kunga Pasang, also Tibetan, is an army man and has taken part in many mountaineering and scientific surveys. Tsering Tobgyal is Tibetan, and an electrician in the Shigatse Grain and Oil Processing Mill. Ngapo Khyen, a Tibetan, was the youngest member and belongs to the army.

The Chinese not only had a success on the mountaineering side but also brought back some valuable records as a result of their scientific study conducted in the Everest region. Alongwith the climbers there was a team of almost 70 scientific workers from 13 Research Units to conduct a study of survey-cartography, geology, high-altitude physiology, atmospheric physics and other fields. The studies were mainly conducted on the East, Central and West Rongbuk glaciers where they carried out triangulation, EDM traverse, gravity surveys and astronomical determinations over an area of 140 sq. km. This laid a sound foundation for an accurate determination of the position and height of the peak. They also studied the gravity in the vicinity of the peak and the surveyors made repeated trips to North Col to make gravimetrical measurements. Reproduced below is an extract from the *China Reconstructs,* September 1975.

The 3 m. red metal surveyor's beacon planted on the top of Qomolangma by the assault team on 27 May made possible precise measurement of the height of the summit and its position. Surveyors posted at 10 stations located between 7 and 21 km. from the peak, at altitudes from 5,600 m. to 6,300 m. observed the beacon with their

theodolites for three consecutive days and obtained data for different periods of the day. The surveyors completed the precise measurement of the height of the summit.

China then became the first country to announce the accurate height of Everest based on scientific calculations as 29,029·24′ against the commonly used figure of 29,028′. The expedition also carried out geological strata observations by climbing the slopes and traversing glaciers in an area covering almost 300 sq. km. They collected 600 rock specimens from an altitude of 4,700 m. to the summit thereby working out a fairly systematic, detailed and complete geological profile of the north slope of Everest. An extract from this paper's scientific survey of the roof of the world is reproduced as:

In limestone beds corresponding to the stratum of the peak, fossils of brachiopods, crinoids and trilobites of the Ordovician period (c. 440 million to 500 million years ago) were found. The locations were the Chuhala and Chienchin valleys and a third valley east of the Rongbuk Monastery—all close to the Qomolangma area. The first such fossils discovered in this part of the world, these provide new facts for determining the age of the rocks at the peak.

In late Paleozoic rocks at Chubu, located along the profile under observation were discovered many fairly well preserved fossils of glossopteris and other plants previously found only on the Indo-Pakistan subcontinent (part of the ancient Gondwanaland). These discoveries show that in the Paleozoic era the northern slope of Qomolangma was not separated from the Indo-Pakistan subcontinent by the "great wall" of the Himalayas. This discovery has extremely important significance for the study of the paleogeographical environment and geological development of the Qomolangma area.

Lastly they carried out study on high altitude physiology by studying the changes in the climbers' respiratory, cardiovascular, and cerebral functions at various altitudes. Electro-cardiograms made on the summit by the members were transmitted by radio to the base. They also conducted studies on atmospheric physics, and samples of ice and snow were gathered and studied. Water samples from an altitude of 7,600 m. to the summit were collected to determine the contents of the heavy water.

Among the highlights of the expedition were the use of yaks to ferry loads from base camp to a camp at 6,500 m. Six women were able to reach the North Col. 36 members of the expedition were women who included workers, commune members, P.L.A. soldiers, office workers, and students. Considering the fact that evidence was available of the Chinese having reached the summit from the route from which all pre-war expeditions had failed, this climb by the Chinese should be considered as one of the greatest in the history of mountaineering and should be held in no way less important a success than the British 1953 expedition.

...inese conducting a survey in the Rongbuk glacier

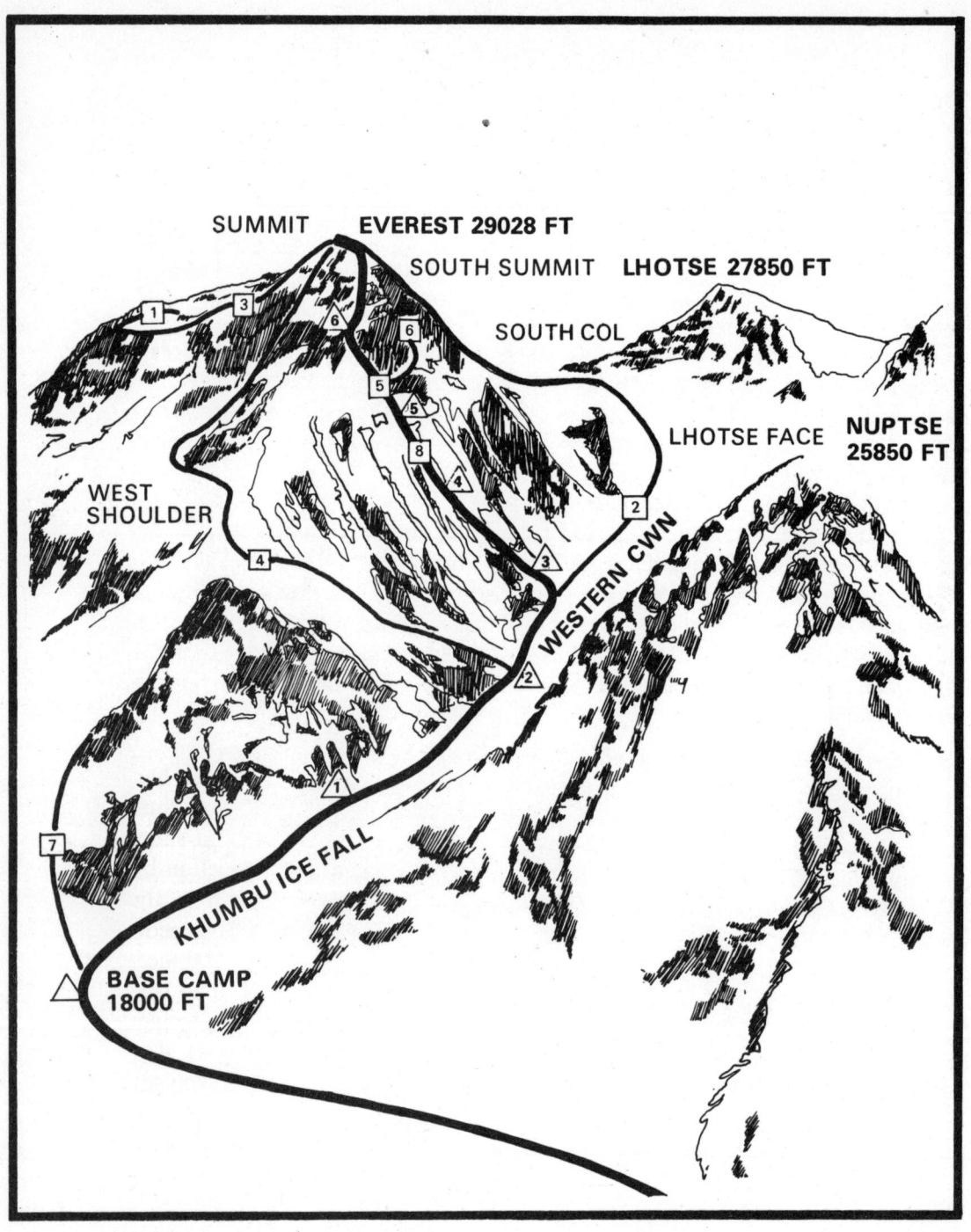

SUMMIT **EVEREST 29028 FT**

SOUTH SUMMIT **LHOTSE 27850 FT**

SOUTH COL

LHOTSE FACE **NUPTSE 25850 FT**

WEST SHOULDER

WESTERN CWN

KHUMBU ICE FALL

BASE CAMP 18000 FT

Routes Camps
□   △

1
Pre-war North Ridge attempts.
2
South Col route taken by successful British Expedition led by Colonel Hunt. Edmund Hillary and Sherpa Tenzing reached the summit on 29th May, 1953.
3
Route claimed to have been climbed by the Chinese in 1960.
4
American Expedition 1963. Hornbein and Unsoeld reached the summit from the West Ridge and descended the South Ridge, thus traversing the mountain.
5
Japanese reconnaissance of the South West Face in Autumn 1969 and first full attempt Spring 1970.
6
Point reached by International Expedition Spring 1971 and European Expedition Spring 1972.
7
French Expedition West Ridge route in Autumn 1974.
8
Route of the British Expedition 1975.

Facing: Pumor
Overleaf: Crossing the longest man mad
bridge on the Khumbu ice fal
P-185: Member being belayed at th
entrance of the Western Cwm
P-186: The Ya

14
1975 (Autumn) British Expedition

It was early in 1974 that Chris Bonington came to know that the country which had booked Everest for autumn 1975 had dropped the expedition. There was very short time to prepare for such a big expedition, but he was used to organising expeditions at short notice. I was in England in October 1974 and was invited for the inaugural function by Lord Hunt. Barclays Bank International had agreed to finance the expedition to the extent of £ 120,000. As compared to this colossal amount, Emmic Shipton's British expedition of 1938 cost a meagre £ 3,000. The expedition was also supported by about 200 local suppliers of equipment and food. The equipment taken was very much superior to that used on the earlier expeditions. Among the other items carried by them were ten tonnes of food, 1,000 gas cylinders for cooking, 30,000 tea bags and 2,000 hand towels. The expedition used 8,000 m. of rope and had 60 aluminum ladders each 6′ long. The oxygen apparatus of a much improved quality was originally designed for use by the aircrews.

I understand that a special kind of tent was developed for the expedition, particularly for the Western Face and the last camp which had bullet proof covers. This provided protection from rock falls which are a constant hazard on this part of the climb. The specially designed tents consisted of aluminum tube frames which could be joined together without much difficulty to form a platform—developed by the British Aircraft Corporation and used in the Concorde. This summit box tent for two members weighing 16 lb. can be erected in two minutes even if the weather is extremely bad with high winds and the temperature much below freezing point.

India supplied the expedition four Bell type tents especially manufactured in Indian Ordnance factories, and which were designed to withstand the heaviest snowfall in the Everest region. If one compares modern equipment with that of earlier expeditions, one

187

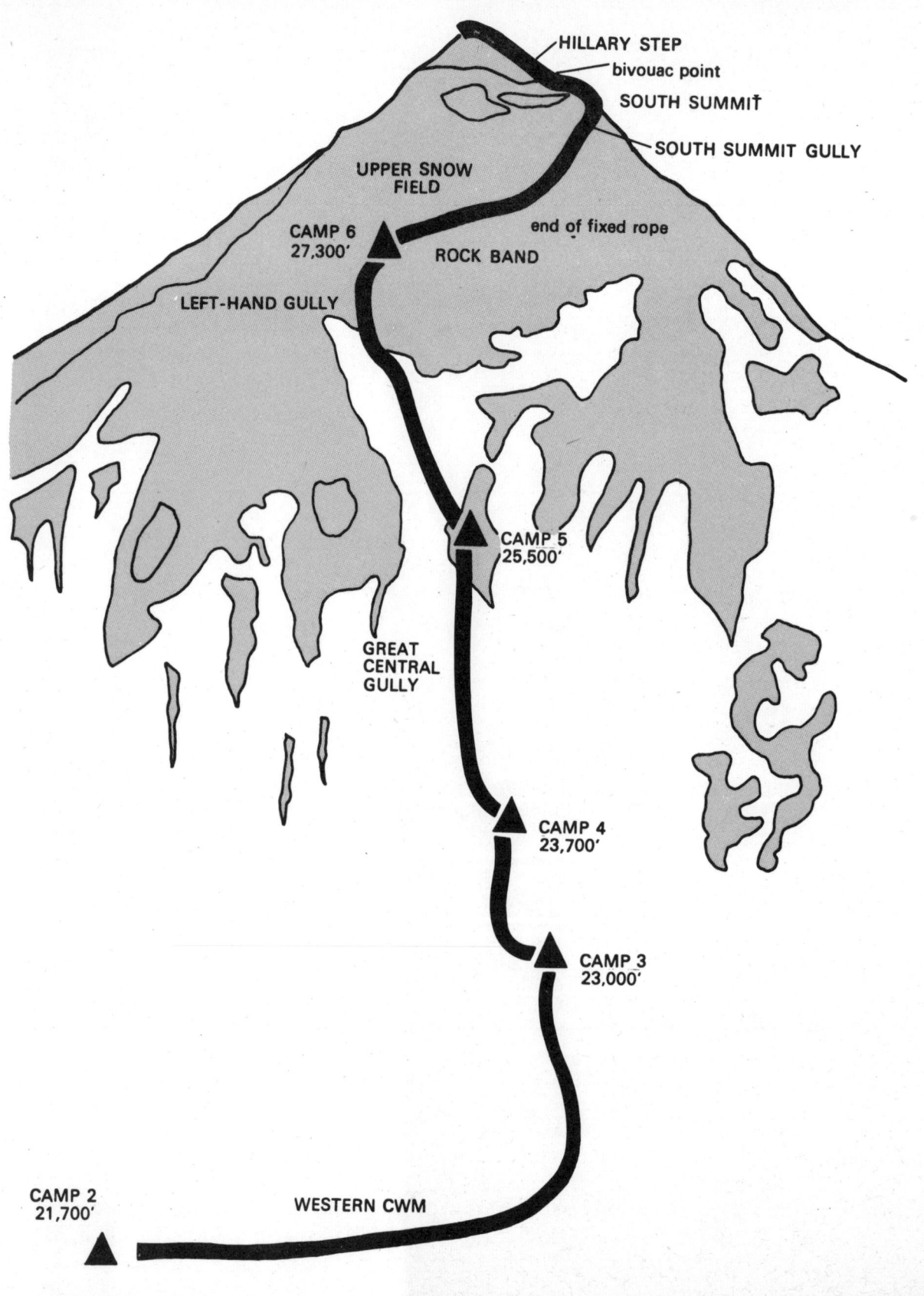

HILLARY STEP
bivouac point
SOUTH SUMMIT
SOUTH SUMMIT GULLY

UPPER SNOW
FIELD

end of fixed rope

CAMP 6
27,300'

ROCK BAND

LEFT-HAND GULLY

CAMP 5
25,500'

GREAT
CENTRAL
GULLY

CAMP 4
23,700'

CAMP 3
23,000'

CAMP 2
21,700'

WESTERN CWM

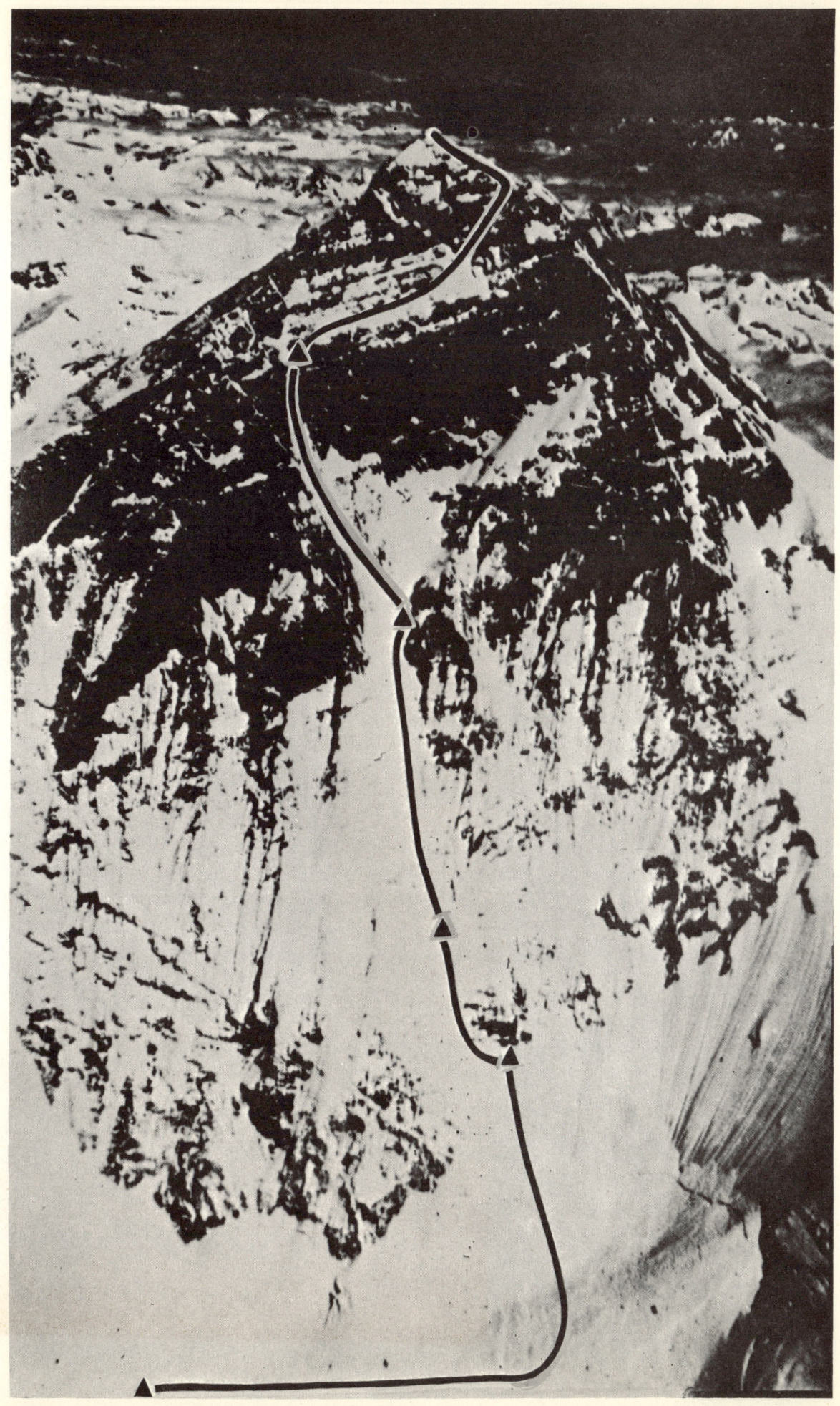

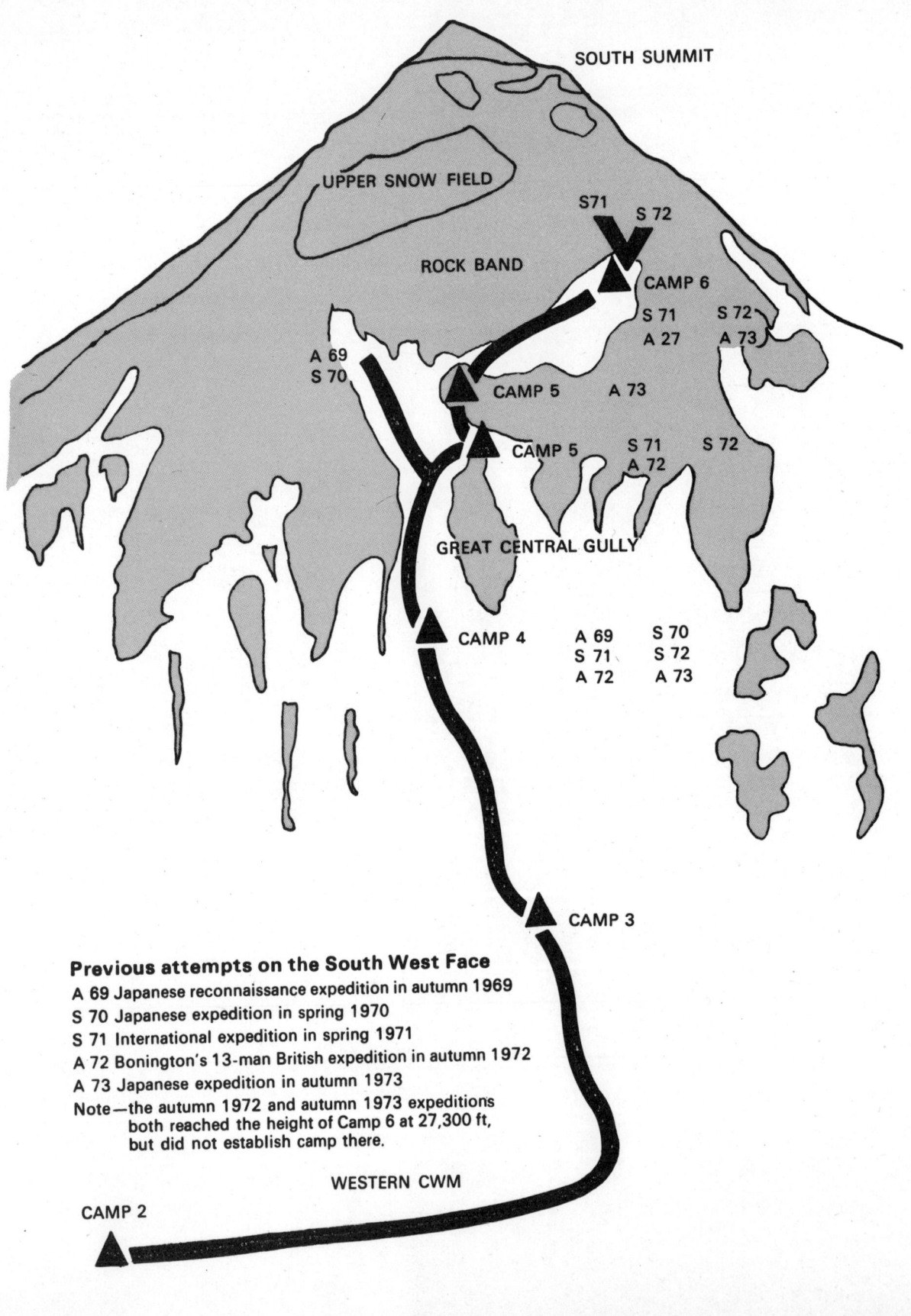

SOUTH SUMMIT

UPPER SNOW FIELD

S71 S 72

ROCK BAND

CAMP 6

S 71 S 72
A 27 A 73

A 69
S 70

CAMP 5 A 73

CAMP 5

S 71 S 72
A 72

GREAT CENTRAL GULLY

CAMP 4 A 69 S 70
S 71 S 72
A 72 A 73

Previous attempts on the South West Face

A 69 Japanese reconnaissance expedition in autumn 1969

S 70 Japanese expedition in spring 1970

S 71 International expedition in spring 1971

A 72 Bonington's 13-man British expedition in autumn 1972

A 73 Japanese expedition in autumn 1973

Note—the autumn 1972 and autumn 1973 expeditions
both reached the height of Camp 6 at 27,300 ft,
but did not establish camp there.

WESTERN CWM

CAMP 3

CAMP 2

Negotiating a difficult crevasse on the Ice fall

realises how far below standard the equipment used to be. The earlier climbers lacked light-weight oxygen breathing equipment and their clothing was unsophisticated. In 1924 when George Mallory and Andrew Irvine disappeared at a height of 28,000 they had on only tweed jackets, over four cardigans, ordinary walking boots with four pairs of socks, knicker-bockers, woolen mittens, felt hats and waterproof topcoats. I wonder if they ever realised how sophisticated the equipment would become half a century later.

Chris Bonington's team consisted of 18 climbing members (total members 25) as against 11 members during his last expedition of 1972. The team certainly can be called one of the best in the world. The members of the team were Hamish MacInnes (deputy leader.), Martin Boysen, Peter Boardman, Mick Burke, Mike Cheney, Charles Clarke, Nick Estcourt, Allen Fyffe, Dougal Haston, Ronnie Richards, Doug Scott, Mike Thompson, Paul Braithwaite, Arthur Chesterman, Dave Clarke, Jim Duff, Adrian Gordon, Ned Kelly, Chris Ralling, Mike Rhodes, Keith, Fan Richardson, and Ian Stuart.

Chris Bonington followed a different strategy of flying the equipment before the monsoon, so as to have a very early start for the autumn climb. The equipment was sent in two large Ford lorries in early April. They passed Delhi on their way to Kathmandu collecting the tents manufactured by us. The equipment was then flown from Kathmandu to Kundi. where it was stored right through the monsoon under the supervision of a few sherpas. They had the entire handling of the equipment right from Kundi, till they arrived at base camp independently. The leader had made a deal that if the equipment was kept safe and handed over at the base camp, they would be paid a commission on every kilogram of the equipment which was a good incentive for the sherpas. By doing so, not only did the sherpas feel involved but they also felt a sense of responsibility.

Fifteen members of the team, including Chris Bonington, arrived in Delhi on 30 July and left for Kathmandu the same day. I was at the airport and met the entire team. Chris Bonington handed over to me a set of fibre glass sticks which he had brought from England for a tunnel tent. They had just enough time to change planes. They stayed in Kathmandu for two days and left for the base camp on 2 August. The team established base camp on 21 August 1975, while in earlier expeditions the base camp was established much later. While everything was going well with the expedition, it was struck by a tragedy immediately after establishing base camp. A young deaf and dumb sherpa, Mingma, was lost on the glacier while coming from Gorak Shep to the base camp. The moment it was discovered that he was missing, all the members of the expedition including the sherpas fanned out down the valley to search for Mingma. His body was later discovered by Adrian in a stream of icy water. He was perhaps trapped under the moraine debris and could not shout for help. Since some of the members had stayed with Mingma's family in Phariche in 1972, they had developed a great liking for him. The members were so disturbed that they wept like children. In an expedition while one has happy moments there are some such sad moments also. Immediately the advance party opened the route through the ice fall and within a matter of 5 to 6 days, the ice fall was completely opened and camp I established on 28 August. Camp II at 22,000' was established on 4 September at the foot of the South West Face. There was a lot of snow which resulted in a number of avalanches coming down the Face. On the evening of 9 September, part of an overhanging serac broke away from one of the ice fields of the west shoulder of Everest and rumbled down, disrupting the ropes of ladders. Luckily no one was injured.

Every member of the team on this expedition worked extremely hard. They would usually start their work rather early in the morning, at times as early as 3 a.m., and continue to work till midday. Chris Bonington's plans worked well and so did his leadership

Facing: Looking up the Western Cwm from camp I. Tent in the foreground manufactured by the Indian Ordnance Factory.

Dougal Haston, Doug Scott, Peter Boardman and sherpa Pertemba

Chris Bonington

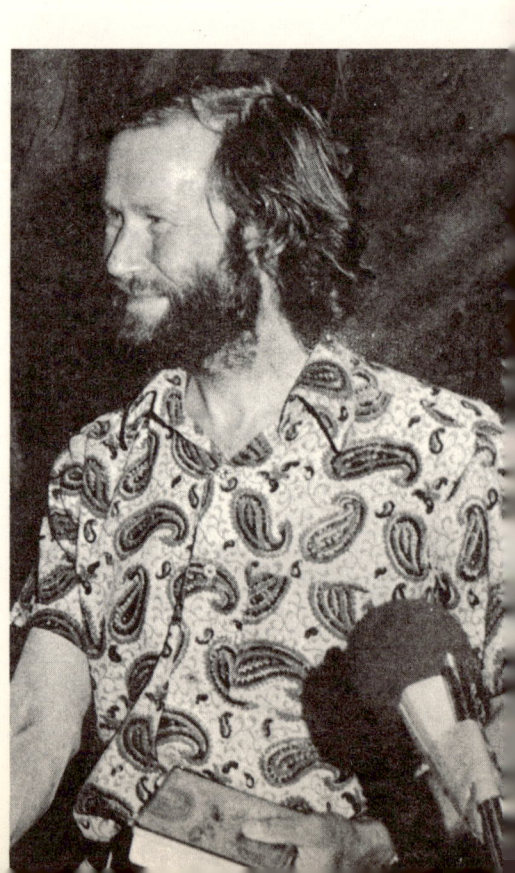

in controlling almost a hundred men in various camps. He wanted to ferry 10 to 15 tonnes of equipment to higher camps as fast as he could so that in case of bad weather, his plans would not be affected. He was fully aware of the disaster due to bad weather in the French expedition of 1974, when the leader, G. Devouassoux, along with 5 sherpas was killed by a huge avalanche. Then there was the fear of monsoon rains and damp weather which can be a death-trap where thousands of tonnes of snow could slither across the bed of moisture at any time. He also feared jet streams—even worse than an avalanche. With the onset of winter, the winds begin to rise and reach a terrific speed of almost a 100 miles an hour, pushing down the already sub-zero temperatures. These icy winds hit the face like a knife of ice and can rip a tent in no time.

Camp II was established at 23,000', and camp IV (which is half way up the Face) was established on 11 September by Doug Scott, Ronnie Richards, and Bonington. The angle to the Face here is between 40 to 50 degrees, and beyond this it becomes difficult to pitch tents. Camp IV was pitched almost 245 m. lower than those pitched by previous expeditions. Chris Bonington decided to do away with camp III and established camp IV much lower so that it was safe from avalanches. There was, however, one disadvantage to the plan—the "carry" between camp IV and V by the sherpas without oxygen would be an extremely difficult task. For this he gave a special incentive to them by raising the daily carrying rate from Rs 100 to Rs 150. Camp V was also established in early September at a height of 25,000' at the foot of the rock-band. Work for camp VI started on 20 September. There was a deep gully near this camp which required very hard climbing through these hard rocks.

Nick Estcourt and Tut Braithwaite made a great contribution by opening a route beyond camp V through the rock band and sheer cliffs which were full of loose and dangerous stones which had beaten all the previous expeditions. They moved to the base camp because the weather had deteriorated and could not be included among the first six members of the assault team. Hamish MacInnes was also not among the first 10 members chosen to go to the summit. He had known Chris for almost two decades and had a major hand in organising the expedition, spending months designing the tents and the ladders.

He had been hit by the powder-snow avalanche while climbing with Dougal Haston on 17 September around camp V and had since been resting at the foot of the mountain. He said that he was almost suffocated by an avalanche of powdered snow. He was unconscious for a while but was able to collect himself and get back to camp IV. Had the avalanche been slightly stronger than it was, he would perhaps have lost his life. Dougal Haston, who was moving ahead with the oxygen mask, did not know anything about this accident. He never fully recovered from the accident and went home early before the end of the expedition. The reason for Hamish MacInnes decision to quit the expedition at an early stage is believed to be his dissatisfaction at Bonington's decision on the selection of the summit parties.

On 22 September, a camp was established above the rock-band with sherpa support and the leader, who were followed by the summit pair Doug and Dougal. The leader along with the sherpas came down to camp V. The first summit party of Doug Scott and Dougal Haston who had already arrived at the last camp, left to open the route by laying out the fixed ropes through the rock-band which took almost seven hours of hard work. The summiters returned to the camp for the night.

On 24 September at 3.30 a.m. they left for the summit with the wind still threatening to blow hard. They crossed the first part of the hurdle with the help of fixed roping which they had laid the previous day in just two hours. They were near the corridor of the South summit when they discovered that Dougal's oxygen apparatus was giving trouble—it was frozen. His breathing became difficult. At one point they thought of returning, but while fiddling with the oxygen apparatus with a sharp knife it suddenly started to work again. So they resumed climbing with wind speed ranging from 40 to 50 miles per hour. There was 60' of steep rock and snow which they had to cut through and were very tired when they reached the Col below the South summit. It was almost 3 p.m. when they sat down to prepare some hot water to quench their thirst. Later they ascended the ridge on the south summit. From there they followed the conventional route which led them to Hillary's Chimney. After crossing Hillary's Chimney with a fixed rope they reached the summit at 6 p.m. and got an incredible view of the sunset. They found telescopic poles made into the tripod with a ring on top on which a Chinese red flag was still flying. Doug Scott in the book *Everest, the Hard Way* wrote:

All the world lay before us. That summit was everything and more that a summit should be. My usually reticent partner became expansive, his face broke out into a broad happy smile and we stood there hugging each other and thumping each other's backs. The implications of reaching the highest mountain in the world surely had some bearings on our feelings. I'm sure they did on mine, but I can't say that it was that strong. I can't say either that I felt any relief that the struggle was over.

In fact, in some ways it seemed a shame that it was, for we had been fully programmed and now we had to switch off and go back into reverse. But not yet, for the view was so staggering, the disappearing sun so full of colour that the setting held us in awe. I was absorbed by the brown hills of Tibet. They only looked like hills from our lofty summit. They were really high mountains, some of them 24,000 feet high, but with hardly any snow to indicate their importance.

I could see silver threads of rivers meandering down between them, flowing north and west to bigger rivers which might have included the Tsangpo. Towards the east Kanchenjunga caught the setting sun, although around to the south clouds boiled down in the Nepalese valleys and far down behind a vast front of black cloud was advancing towards us from the plains of India.

It flickered lightning ominously. There was no rush though, for it would be a long time coming over Everest—time to pick out the north side route—the Rongphu Glacier, the East Rongphu Glacier and Changtse in between. There was the North Col, and the place Odell was standing when he last saw Mallory and Irvine climbing up towards him. Wonder if they made it? Their route was hidden by the convex slope—no sign of them, edge out a bit further—no nothing. Not with all the monsoon snow, my external mind pointed out.

The only sign of anyone was the flag, it was some time before I got round to looking at it. It was an unwelcome intrusion and there had been more to do than look at manmade objects. Still, you couldn't help but look at it, seeing as how it was a tripod and pole nearly five feet high with a rosary of red ribbons attached to the top. Take a photograph. Ah, yes! Dougal ought to get some of me. He hadn't taken a single photograph on the whole trip. 'Here, you are, youth. Take a snap for my mother.' I passed him my camera. 'Better take another one, your glove's in front of the lens. Now a black and white one.' He's never been keen on photography, but he obliged.

196   After staying for a while on the summit, they descended. By 8 p.m. they reached the

Facing: Negotiating top of the ice fall.

The summit view slightly south of east with Dougal Haston and Makalu on the right

face of the south summit. While they were hoping to have a full moon, it became cloudy with poor visibility. It was evident that in the dark it would be impossible to descend and they decided to bivouac as they had already brought the tent sac with them. The visibility was still very poor. They then carved out a small cave and had some hot water at a height of 28,700'. The oxygen had already finished, so they kept awake the whole night keeping themselves warm. They took off their boots and socks and kept rubbing their toes to avoid frost bite, their biggest worry. The temperature was well below minus 30° centigrade. I can imagine the cold seeping into the very marrow of their bones. It was their strong will power and utmost vigilance which kept them going the whole night.

At 6 a.m. they left for camp VI which they reached at 9 a.m. They were tired and dehydrated. They fell in their sleeping bags, warmed themselves up and looked around for something to eat. It is amazing that they reached back without suffering any kind of damage to themselves. Otherwise in such a state of climb, especially taking into consideration the time that they had spent in the mountain without any food, fruit juice or oxygen—a very minor frost-bite or even a major one would have been possible. This shows how extremely well the summiters were acclimatised.

At camp VI they were joined by the second summit party consisting of Martin Boysen, Pete Boardman, Mick Burke, and Pertemba who erected another platform for a box tent as the second summit party would be of 4 members on 2 ropes.

On 26 September at 4.30 a.m. the second summit team consisting of Peter Boardman, Mick Burke, Martin Boysen, and sherpa Sirdar Pertemba left for the summit. Martin Boysen and Mick Burke were on one rope followed by Peter Boardman and Pertemba. There was a gentle breeze and a haze of clouds rising from the valley. While they were making good progress, climbing the initial stretch with fixed ropes, Martin suddenly discovered that his oxygen set had packed up and one of his crampons was loose and had fallen away. This meant an end of his climb and he had to return to camp VI.

Peter Boardman along with Pertemba made brisk progress and reached the South summit well before noon. At the South summit they had some trouble with oxygen which they rectified, changed their oxygen bottles and started climbing. The clouds by now had risen quite high with the wind speed rising steadily, but they kept going and reached the summit around 1 p.m. After staying on the summit for half an hour, taking photographs of the Chinese emblem and having some chocolates and cakes they started moving down.

On the return, just before Hillary's Chimney, around 2 p.m. they saw Mick Burke coming up by himself as his partner Martin Boysen had returned to camp VI. Mick Burke, who was an excellent cameraman, decided to climb alone. He crossed by fixed roping the corridor to the South summit, then finally Hillary's Chimney. Peter Boardman reported in the *Hindustan Times,* New Delhi, 18 October 1975:

> It was 2 p.m. on 26 September, I was descending, Burke was ascending. I was surprised to see him. He wanted me to go with him to the top of Everest. I told him that I would wait for him at the south summit. Then I left him. And that was our last meeting. We waited for him at the south summit for over an hour. The weather started deteriorating. The temperature fell below zero degree centigrade. Visibility was poor. It was beginning to grow dark. We knew we couldn't have survived the night out in the blizzard. So we had to take the agonising decision to descend without him. Search was impossible.

Peter Boardman and Pertemba waited at the South summit till half past four. The weather had deteriorated and visibility was becoming poor. They had to fight for their own lives and took the painful decision to move down immediately without waiting any more for Mick Burke. While going down they had a narrow escape on more than one occasion. They came in a powder snow avalanche, Pertemba lost one of his crampons, and at one point a section of the rope broke away. They perhaps thought that they will never be able to make to the camp. Around 7.30 they stumbled into camp VI where Martin was waiting for them and they all burst into tears at the loss of Mick Burke.

It is almost certain that the climber on the last stretch of the climb on Everest confronts no problem whatsoever and traverses a gradient not more than 30 to 40 degrees. This would have been very easily covered by Mick Burke in a matter of 15 to 20 minutes. There is no question of his slipping as he would have followed the footsteps of the earlier summit parties. He would have stayed on the summit for half an hour and in all probability started his descent around 3 p.m. when the weather started to deteriorate and visibility became poor. I fully believe that after reaching the summit, he misjudged his direction due to very poor visibility and perhaps walked too much to the left, stepping on a cornice which dropped him down the northern face of Everest.

On our climb Harish Rawat climbed all alone from a height 28,000′ to the base of the south summit. To cross the Razor's Edge and the loose rocky portion beyond is by no means easy, particularly when there were no fixed ropes at all and there was every chance of his slipping down on the Tibetan side. There is however a big difference between the Indian climb and that of the British. We spotted Rawat when we were at the base of the south summit on our way up while the British summit team met Mick Burke on the down. We stopped at the cost of depleting our stock of oxygen and of moving at an incredibly slow pace by having another member on the rope. It is well known that a rope of two moves much faster than a rope of three.

Among leading mountaineers, Rawat's decision to do it all by himself became a subject of great controversy. But I remember having asked myself while we were waiting for Rawat to join us, whether I would have done the same thing as him and the answer was "yes." I feel any mountaineer at that height would have taken the same decision. Mick Burke had not only been to the south face of Annapurna but had also reached camp VI on the British expedition in 1972 to Everest. Apart from climbing, he had a passion for photography. I had taken to the mountains because I loved photography. To me photographing mountains is loving them and is the expression of an inborn passion. I think Mick Burke's climb will be remembered as one of the greatest that any mountaineer has undertaken. On the next day, 27 September, the roaring winds made it impossible for anyone to go up and look for Mick Burke and so he, like many others, lies buried on the shoulder of Everest.

Akes Kunaver, leader of the Yugoslavian expedition to Mount Makalu, a neighbouring mountain, met me in Delhi on his way back after successfully climbing Makalu through the unclimbed South West Face. Kunaver, commenting on the tragic death of Mike Burke, said, "Now I can recall it was about the same night that we were also caught in extremely bad weather. We were lucky. We survived. The expedition, however, did not escape its share of mishaps. On the night of Mick Burke's death in another part of the Himalayas, a snow storm destroyed some and badly damaged other camps set up by our expedition. This delayed our final climb which otherwise would have been undertaken much earlier." Chris Bonington in his book *Everest, the Hard Way* wrote:

We were rather like the mourners after the funeral; glad to be alive, getting on with our own lives, the memory of Mick held with sadness and regret, yet accepted as an act that had happened; one of the risks of our climbing game. Is there a self-centred selfishness in this attitude? For those of us who are happily married and have children, there must be or we should not have carried on our life of climbing aware, as we are, of the risks involved. In our own single-minded drive and love for the mountains, we hope that the fatal accident will never happen to us, are freightened to contemplate the cruel long-lasting sorrow suffered by the widows, parents and children—an endless tunnel that for them must never seem to end.

To anyone who takes up climbing, the risk of losing one's life is always there and this factor is accepted by all of us. No matter how many precautions one takes, the element of luck will always be there. It can come any time—at the beginning of the climb, during the middle or towards the end. If it comes after one's success, it becomes most unfortunate. We are reminded that there is just a thin margin between life and death. Indeed, the risk factor is an integral part of mountaineering.

It was a glorious achievement for Chris Bonington, particularly when 5 previous attempts on the Face from many nations failed to reach the summit including Chris Bonington's earlier attempt in 1972. Everest has been climbed from almost all the available routes, but in no way has its popularity diminished. More and more mountaineers will go to Everest to satisfy their yearning to stand on the highest point in the world. I am sure that in the near future there will be an expedition trying to reach the summit of Everest straight from camp VI on the Western Face without going to the South summit. This would be a great challenge.

THE 1976 JOINT BRITISH AND ROYAL NEPALESE ARMY EXPEDITION

A thirty-five member expedition led by Lt Col. Tony Streather, M.B.E. of the Gloucester Regiment, left Kathmandu on 27 February 1976 to attempt an assault on Everest by the conventional South East ridge route. The expedition was unduly delayed in establishing camp V and VI due to abnormal weather conditions. At one stage it seemed doubtful if the summit attempt could be made before the start of the monsoon, but the decision to do so was finally taken, and on 16 May Sergeant Brummy Strokes and Corporal Bronco Lane reached the summit at 15.15 hrs. The weather was extremely bad and they were forced to bivouac above camp VI on the way down. Both were badly frost-bitten. Corporal Lane, who had frost-bitten fingers, feet, and face, describes his descent as follows:

We were still under way and well above our top camp at 7 p.m. The clouds were still thick and our steps made on the way up were hard to find. We only had one bottle of oxygen each for the whole climb and were in danger of running out. We sat it out until morning, but if the wind had strengthened, if we had not accidentally found that oxygen, there would have been a very different story.

The success of the team, however, was not achieved without the grievous loss of five of its members—David Brister, Gerry Owens, Richard Summerton, Pasang Tamang, and Terry Thompson.

AMERICAN BICENTENNIAL EXPEDITION

The post-monsoon period of 1976 witnessed the success of the American Bicentennial Expedition. It was a 12-member expedition including two women and was led by Phil Trimble. The expedition followed the South Col route and was successful in putting Bob

Cormack and Chris Chandler atop Everest on 8 October. Due to very bad weather, subsequent attempts were called off.

1977 NEW ZEALAND EXPEDITION

This expedition, led by Keith Wood-Ford, had only 8 members and introduced a new concept in climbing Mount Everest—the Alpine style. The mountaineers will climb without the help of porters and high altitude sherpas who have inevitably formed part of every big Himalayan expedition in the past. The climbers were a small band unaided by massive logistical support. The members would move together in a kind of self-contained capsule from one camp to the other. "With only eight of us," said Keith, "we will drastically reduce our equipment and also try and cut down on the number of camps. Usually, on the South Col route which we will be taking, they have six camps. We intend to have only five. We will carry a walkie-talkie with us and plenty of oxygen."

The plan to cut down the sixth and final camp may pose a few problems. "Our final push to the summit from the fifth camp will be over a steep climb of 3,000′. At that altitude every step counts," he added. Commenting on the risk factor, he said, "Life is very precious to all of us. We don't intend to risk our lives unnecessarily in attempting the summit of Everest." The expedition did not make any head way and had to abandon the attempt.

AUTUMN 1977 SOUTH KOREAN EXPEDITION

A 16-member South Korean expedition led by Young Do Kim, a member of the South Korean National Assembly, left for Kathmandu on 2 August to establish base camp. The team would be attempting to climb Everest via the traditional South Col route.

Due to continuous bad weather the expedition could not make any headway. Their first summit also failed to reach the summit. Towards the middle of September the weather improved and the summit party constituting Song Don Ko and sherpa Pemba Norbhu reached the summit on 15 September 1977. Song Don Ko later told the reporters in Kathmandu that his first thought on reaching the summit was one relief and happiness. He said that for a few minutes he and his companions were not sure whether they had reached the summit but soon located the surveying tripod left behind by the Chinese expedition in 1975. He buried a small Bible on the summit given to him by his wife alongwith the photographs of three Korean climbers who were killed in Korea during their practice for the Everest expedition.

He described his climb from the South summit onwards up to Hillary Step as very difficult and precarious. It involved climbing along a "knife ridge" in high winds. On reaching the summit he radioed his leader, "This is the summit. There is no higher place."

15
Why Mountains are Climbed

Mountaineering is a dangerous game and one has to recognise and minimise the dangers and come to terms with them. Everest has been climbed a number of times. More and more climbers will continue to go up, compelled to undertake the mighty adventure. It is this ambition which accounts for Everest being so heavily booked till 1983. Below are given some of the future climbs

1977 autumn	South Korean.
1978 spring	Austrian Expedition led by Wolfgang Nairz—South West Face probably.
1978 autumn	West German-Austrian team led by Dr. Karl Herriligkoffer—South West Face.
1979 spring	Yugoslav—perhaps West Ridge.
1979 autumn	British granted permission but the man who was the driving force has died and the expedition is now in doubt.
1980 spring	U.S.S.R.—probably South Col-Southeast Ridge.
1980 autumn	Nepalese attempt.
1981 spring	Japanese from Maiji University.
1983 spring	West German Expedition.

Why climb mountains? It is not easy to answer this question. For me the mountains are nature at its best and their beauty and majesty pose a constant challenge. Many of us believe that they are a means of communion with God or the creator.

But why Everest? Because it is the mightiest. It takes the last ounce of energy—a brutal struggle with rock and ice which once taken up cannot be given up even when one's life itself is at stake. With the peak climbed, there is joy and a sense of achievement, exaltation, triumph, of a battle won, which is very difficult to describe. The physical conquest of a mountain is, I think, only part of the achievement. More than that it is a sense of fulfilment, of satisfaction of that deep urge within every man which impels him to rise above his environment. It is part of the eternal quest for adventure, the passion for exploring the hazardous and the unknown. The experience is not only physical, it is also intensely emotional and even spiritual.

American mountaineers have called climbing "nine-tenths hell, one-tenth beauty". I am inclined to endorse this graphic description. Consider a typical climb, especially at the higher altitudes and within a short distance of the summit. You are sharing a rope with another climber. You firm in and he cuts the steps ahead in hard ice. Then he belays you and you proceed inching your way up. The climb is grim. You strain every nerve as you take another step. I am reminded of an interesting episode about Norton, the famous mountaineer, while he was climbing Everest with Somervell. He recalled, "I had to cross a patch of snow lying thinly over some sloping rocks. It was neither steep nor difficult, and not to be compared to the ground I had just left, yet suddenly I felt that I could not face it without help, and I shouted to Somervell to come and throw me the end of the rope. Here again I remember the difficulty I had in making my voice carry perhaps 100 yards. Somervell gave me the required aid, and I could see the surprise he felt at my needing it in such a place."

Breathing is very hard and as you gasp for breath, you curse yourself inwardly and wonder why you ever undertook the ascent. These are moments when you feel like turning back and dwell on the sheer relief of going downhill. But almost at once you snap out of this momentary mood. There is something in you that does not let you give up the struggle. And you go on. Just another 50', you think, or perhaps another 100'. The slope leads on and on and you ask yourself, "Is there no end?" You look up at your partner and he looks at you, and each seems to draw inspiration from the other. You feel all is not lost yet and keep plodding on. And then, suddenly a shape emerges in dim outline which becomes clearer as you approach it. What a joy to find yourself at last on the summit! Was it not worth all the effort and the agony of the climb?

Once on the top you look around. Other silvery peaks appear through the clouds. If you are lucky, you may find the sun shining on them and turning them into so many jewelled necklaces around the mountain. Below you are vast valleys, sloping far away in the distance as far as the eye can reach. It is an uplifting, ennobling experience. Carried away by all the beauty and the glory of the panorama surrounding you, you bow down and make your obeisance to whichever god you worship.

I left on Everest a picture of Guru Nanak, and Rawat a picture of the goddess Durga. Phu Dorji, who accompanied us, offered the mountain a relic of Buddha. Some years earlier Edmund Hillary buried a cross under a cairn in the snow. These offerings are not symbols of conquest but of trust and reverence. Climbing a mountain peak is loving it and constantly wondering if it will let you come nearer and closer. When at length you reach the peak, you are overwhelmed by a deep sense of joy and thankfulness. It is a joy which lasts a lifetime.

The experience changes you completely. The man who has been to the mountains is never the same again. He gains immensely from the mountains. He becomes conscious of his own smallness and loneliness in the immeasurable universe. The lure of Everest is as immortal as the great mountain itself. Like the sun and the moon it belongs to the whole of humanity and crosses national barriers as nothing else does. It will continue to attract the aspiring climbers young and old wanting to stand on the highest point of the earth.

Appendices

I Climatology of Everest by the Director General of Observatories

As the Himalayan peaks are situated above the permanent snow line and lie in the path of disturbances in middle latitude westerlies, an account of the climatology of the southern slopes of the Himalayan region would be of particular relevance. Freezing temperatures, land frost, snow-storms and blizzards resulting in avalanches and strong winds are common hazards that plague mountaineering expeditions in the Himalayas. A brief account is given in the following paragraphs of the incidence and frequencies of such hazards.

TOPOGRAPHY

The topography of a region exercises a profound influence on the weather and climate. The Himalayas present some remarkable physical features. They have some of the loftiest mountain ranges of the world radiating from the famous Pamir knot near the intersection of 38° N and 74°E where the territorial boundaries of Afghanistan, China, India, Pakistan and USSR come very close to one another. Mountains and plateaus exceeding an elevation of 3 km. cover nearly 3 million sq. km. The Tibetan plateau which is the highest and most extensive plateau in the world lies almost over the centre of the Himalayas.

CLIMATE OVER THE HIMALAYAS

Weather over the Himalayas follows the broad seasonal patterns as over north India. Strong westerly winds at 20,000' in winter and heavy monsoon precipitation in summer are not conditions favourable for mountaineering expeditions. Such activity is therefore largely confined to the transition periods of spring (pre-monsoon) and autumn (post-monsoon). The winds in autumn are comparatively stronger than in spring and periods of weak winds (lulls) are more frequent in spring. However, autumn has more settled weather than spring.

Monsoon sets in over the eastern Himalayas in the first week of June and extends to the western Himalayas by the end of June. The date of setting in of the monsoon easterlies over the Everest region has been found to vary from mid-June to mid-July. By the third week of September, the monsoons withdraw from the Himalayas.

METEOROLOGICAL PARAMETERS

It is the temperature and winds at the levels of 6 and 9 km. which are crucial for mountaineering expeditions. Weak winds, fair weather, with no accumulation of fresh snow are the favourable weather conditions for climbing.

In figs. 1 to 4 are shown temperature distribution at 6.0 and 9.0 km. for March–June and August–November. Figs. 5 to 8 depict the corresponding wind flow. The chief features of weather, temperatures, and winds are summarized in the following table. (Charts are reproduced at the end of this text).

DIURNAL VARIATION OF WINDS

Apart from the variation of mean winds described above from month to month a knowledge of day to day variations of winds for selecting the periods of assault on the summit will be of vital operational value to mountaineers. In the absence of data from a station in the Himalayan range itself, New Delhi (Lat. 28° 35′N; Long. 77° 12′ E) has been chosen to describe conditions in the free atmosphere over the Himalayan region as nearly representative.

Daily upper wind data for a recent five year period for the months March–June and August–November have been taken and daily averages of winds were calculated. Figs. 5 to 8 contain the time altitude cross-sections of average winds at 6 and 9 km. levels with isotachs (lines of equal wind velocities) drawn at intervals of 10 knots. The following are some of the salient features of these cross-sections:

(i) The wind directions are predominantly westerly from March to the third week of June. Thereafter, the winds tend to veer and assume an easterly component. The highest speeds, exceeding 70 kts, occur at 9 km. in frequent spells during March and early April. Wind speeds then gradually decrease to 60 kts. by the first week of May and then rapidly decrease to 20–25 knots in the first half of June. In the second half of June, a few days before the onset of the monsoons over northern India, wind speeds decrease significantly to around 10 knots. Large wind shears occur in the vertical between 6 and 9 km. in brief spells up to the first half of May; thereafter the shear also decreases.

(ii) The upper winds are variable in August and rarely exceed 10 knots. Winds assume a steady westerly direction by the second half of September and strengthen to around 35 knots by the last week of the month. Thereafter in October the vertical shear between 6 and 9 km. builds up with the wind speed reaching 50 knots by the last week of the month. Steady westerlies exceeding 60 knots generally and a moderate shear in the vertical are the salient features of November.

OPTIMUM PERIOD FOR ASSAULT

In end-May or beginning June before the onset of monsoon over northern India, the upper westerlies weaken significantly and lulls occur more frequently. The frequency of convective disturbance shows a tendency to decrease. Upper air temperatures are moderate and attain levels of easy acclimatisation. In view of the foregoing the pre-summer period just before the onset of the monsoon seems to be more suitable for successful mountaineering expeditions over the Himalayas than other periods.

WEATHER FORECASTING FOR MOUNTAINEERING

Knowledge of the normal seasonal features of weather helps in planning mountaineering expeditions, but for day-to-day progress, particularly in the final stages of the assault, weather forecasts are critical. Such forecasts can at present be issued for periods extending up to 3 days.

The Himalayan regions are affected during a large part of the year by extra-tropical weather systems. These systems are tracked and their movements are predicted by the Northern Hemispheric Analysis Centre (NHAC), Meteorological Office, New Delhi. Both conventional methods as well as computer techniques are used to forecast weather. Satellite cloud pictures covering a large part of the globe and obtained from the polar orbiting satellites of both USA and USSR are also utilised for this purpose.

Special weather bulletins giving the expected weather are issued by NHAC through All India Radio for the benefit of each mountaineering expedition which makes a request for the same. The weather man is handicapped by the lack of detailed weather information from the inaccessible areas for which he is required to forecast. It would, therefore, be good if expeditions could send copies of their weather diaries to the above centre.

SURFACE FEATURES

Month	Rainfall	Clouds	Thunderstorms	Duststorms
March	Generally less than 20 mm. but increases to 20–60 mm. on west slopes.	About 10 days a month, increasing to about 15 in west Himalayas.	Generally 1 per month increasing to 5 on west side.	1 day a month.
April	Between 10–40 mm. increasing to 60–100 mm on west side.	Less than 10 days, increasing to 15 on west slopes.	1 to 5 days.	1 per month. 5 days a month on west side.
May	Increases to 40–60 mm. on south slopes, decreasing to 10 mm. northwards to Tibetan Plateau.	Generally less than 10 days a month.	5 days a month increasing to 10–15 on west slopes.	1 per month and increasing to about 5 per month on west slopes.
June	Decreases from 100–200 mm. at foot-hills to less	15 days a month, increasing to 20 days on west	5 days a month increasing to 10 in west Himalayas.	1 per month.

Month	Rainfall	Clouds	Thunderstorms	Duststorms
	than 20 mm. on south face.	slopes.		
August	Decreases from 200–300 mm. in southern foothills to 20–40 mm. northwards to Tibetan Plateau. West Himalayas record up to 500 mm. and in some areas up to 1000 mm.	20–25 days are cloudy, decreasing to less than 15 further north to Tibetan Plateau.	Generally less than 5 days a month.	1 per month.
September	Small decrease. Rainfall in southern foothills is 100–200 mm., decreasing to less than 20 mm. northwards into the Plateau.	About 10–15 days a month.	1 to 5 a month increasing to about 10 along west slopes.	1 per month.
October	Rapid decrease. Rainfall on south slopes is 40–60 mm. decreasing to less than 10 mm further northwards. Relatively greater along western slopes.	5 days a month, increasing to 10 on south east and north west slopes.	1, increasing to 5 along west slopes.	Rare. Less than 1 per month.
November	Very low, less than 10 mm. a month.	Less than 5 days a month.	Rare, about 1 per month, increasing to 5 in the west.	Rare. Less than 1 per month.

UPPER AIR TEMPERATURES

Level	March	April	May	June
6 km. (20,000′)	Decreases from −13°C to −15°C along south slopes. Warmer in south east as	Warmest over south east Himalayas. About −8°C over Assam Himala-	Relatively warm, −5°C, over south east Himalayas, decreasing to	South east slopes warm up considerably. 0°C to −1°C in south east Hima-

Level	March	April	May	June
	compared to west Himalayas.	yas; −11°C over central Himalayas; −14°C over north west Himalayas.	−9°C over north west Himalayas.	layas, to about −3°C in north west Himalayas.
9 km. (30,000′)	−37°C to −41°C	About −35°C over south east slopes, decreasing to −40°C along north west Himalayas.	−31°C to −36°C	Warmest over south east slopes. Temperatures decrease from about −25°C over Assam Himalayas to −35°C over Punjab Himalayas.

Level	August	September	October	November
6 km. (20,000′)	With the seat of sub-tropical high pressure area south Himalayas, the region experiences the warmest temperature of the year, around 0°C to −1°C.	Monsoon withdraws from north India, and temperature falls from −2°C to −4°C.	Post monsoon circulation drops temperature from −6°C over south east slopes to −11°C over north west slopes.	Further fall in temperature. −8°C over south east slopes to −17°C over north west slopes.
9 km. (30,000′)	With the seat of sub-tropical ridge over south Himalayas, temperature varies from −23°C over south east Himalayas to −29°C over north west parts.	Warm temperatures continue at this level. South slopes have a temperature of −25°C decreasing to −31°C along north west slopes.	−30°C over south east slopes, and around −35°C over north west slopes.	−34°C over south east slopes and −41°C along north west slopes.

Level		March	April	May	June
6 km. (20,000')	Direction	Generally westerly.	Generally westerly becoming west-north westerly over Assam Himalayas.	Generally westerly	Generally westerly becoming west south westerly over Assam Himalayas.
	Speed	25–30 kts. decreasing to 10 kts over north slopes.	20–25 kts. decreasing to 10 kts. over north slopes.	20–25 kts. decreasing to 10 kts over north slopes.	5–10 kts.
9 km. (30,000')	Direction	Generally westerly.	Generally westerly.	Generally westerly.	West-south westerly becoming westerly over Assam Himalayas.
	Speed	50–60 kts. decreasing to 35–40 kts. over north slopes.	40–45 kts. decreasing to 25–30 kts. over north slopes.	35–40 kts. decreasing to 20–25 kts. over north slopes.	15–20 kts. increasing to 40 kts. to the north-east.

Level		August	September	October	November
6 km. (20,000')	Direction	Generally south westerly, becoming west-south westerly over north slopes.	Generally south-south westerly becoming westerly over northern slopes.	Generally westerly.	Generally westerly.
	Speed	5 kts. increases to 10 kts. over north slopes.	5 kts. increases to 10–15 kts. over north slopes.	10–15 kts.	25–30 kts. decreasing to 20 kts over north slopes.
9 km. (30,000')	Direction	Variable direction.	Generally westerly.	Generally westerly.	Generally westerly.
	Speed	Weak winds gradually increasing to 30–35 kts. over north slopes.	5–10 kts. increasing to 35–40 kts. over north slopes.	40–45 kts. decreasing to 30–35 kts. over north slopes.	67–70 kts. decreasing to 40–50 kts. over north slopes.

Facing: Indian Everest Expedition, 1965.

Last camp adjacent to the Razor's Edge

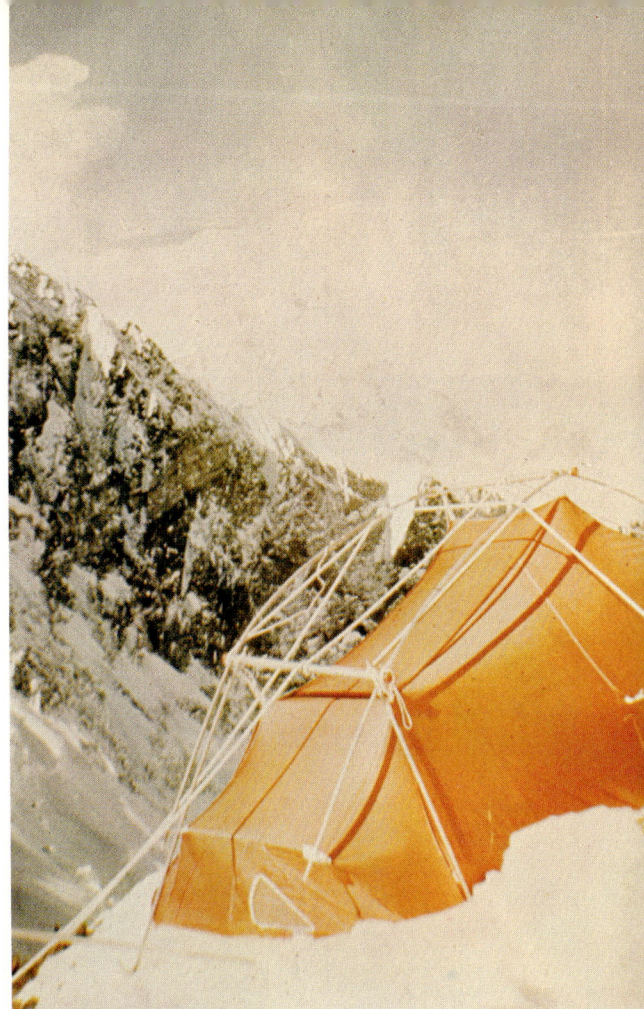

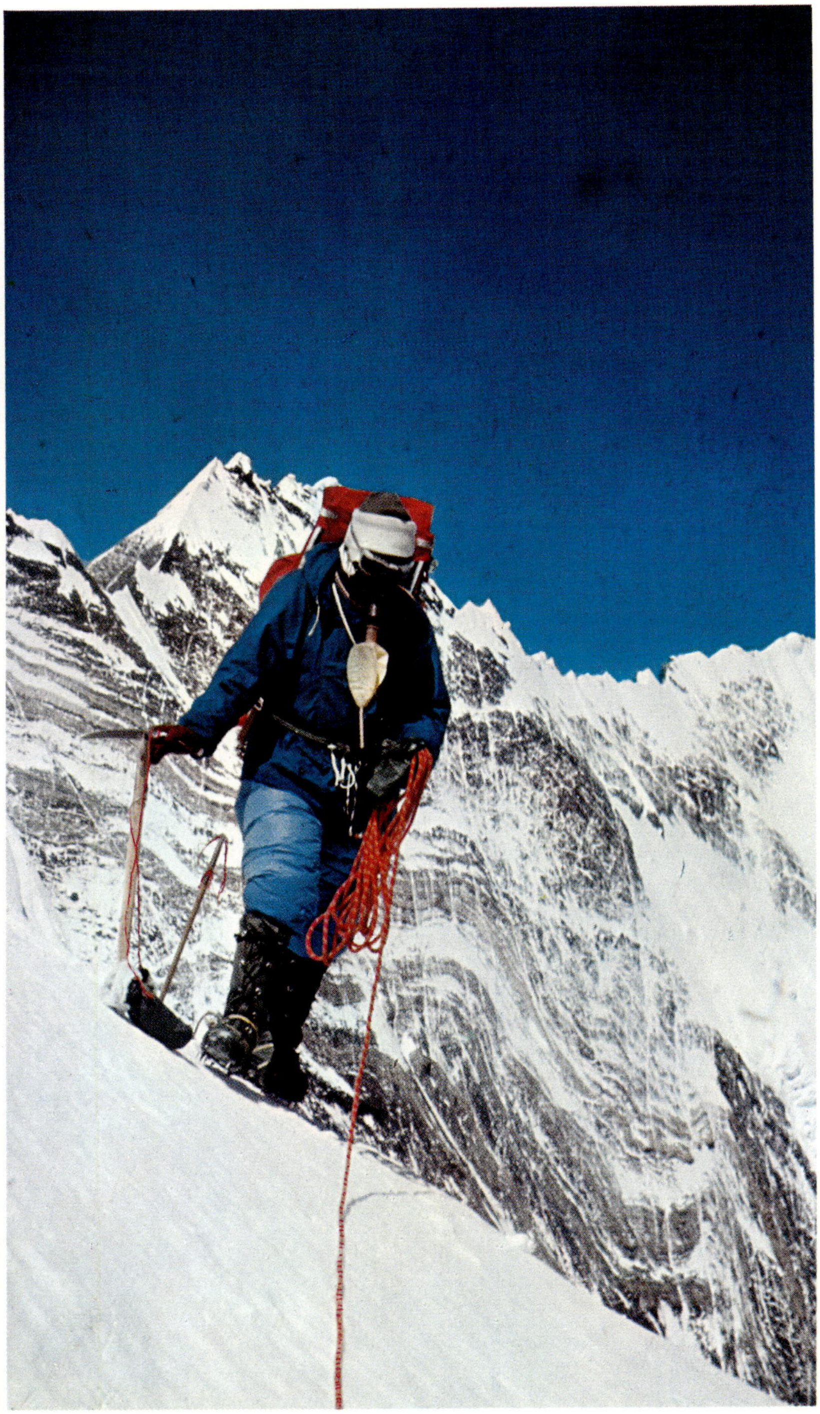

Cheema on the summit Ridge

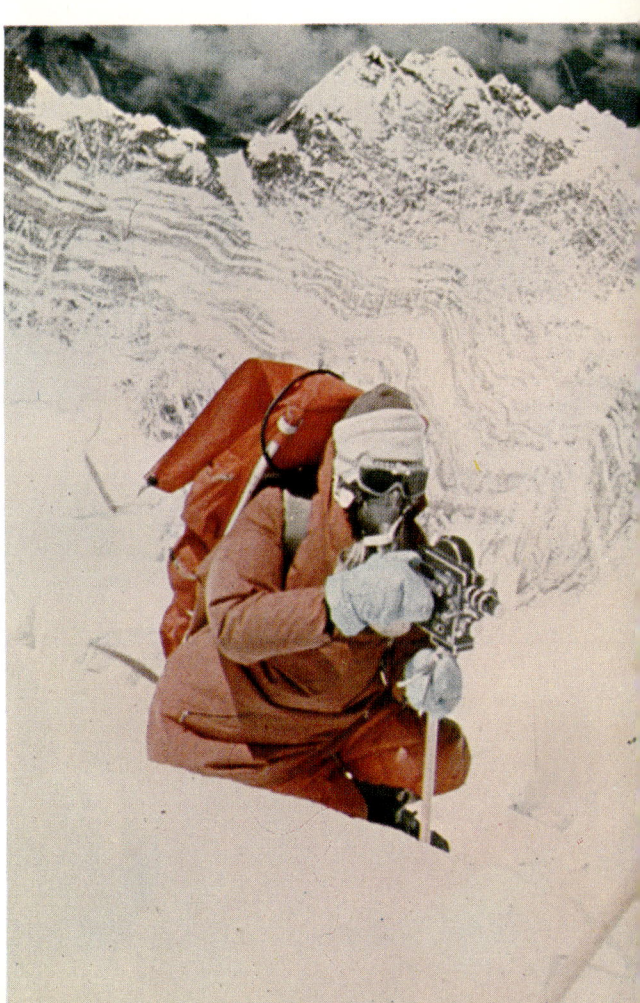

Last shot before the camera fails

Harish Rawat on the summit

Ahluwalia on the summit with his Corps flag (Electrical & Mechanical Engineering)

Rejoicing L to R: Cheema, Sonam Gyatso, Balakrishnan, Kohli,
Kumar, Ahluwalia and Ang Kami
Top: Bidding good-bye to the summit

Sherpa family

Upper air temperatures at 6 Km (20,000 feet) above mean sea level

MARCH

APRIL

MAY

JUNE

Upper air temperatures at 6 Km (20,000 feet) above mean sea level

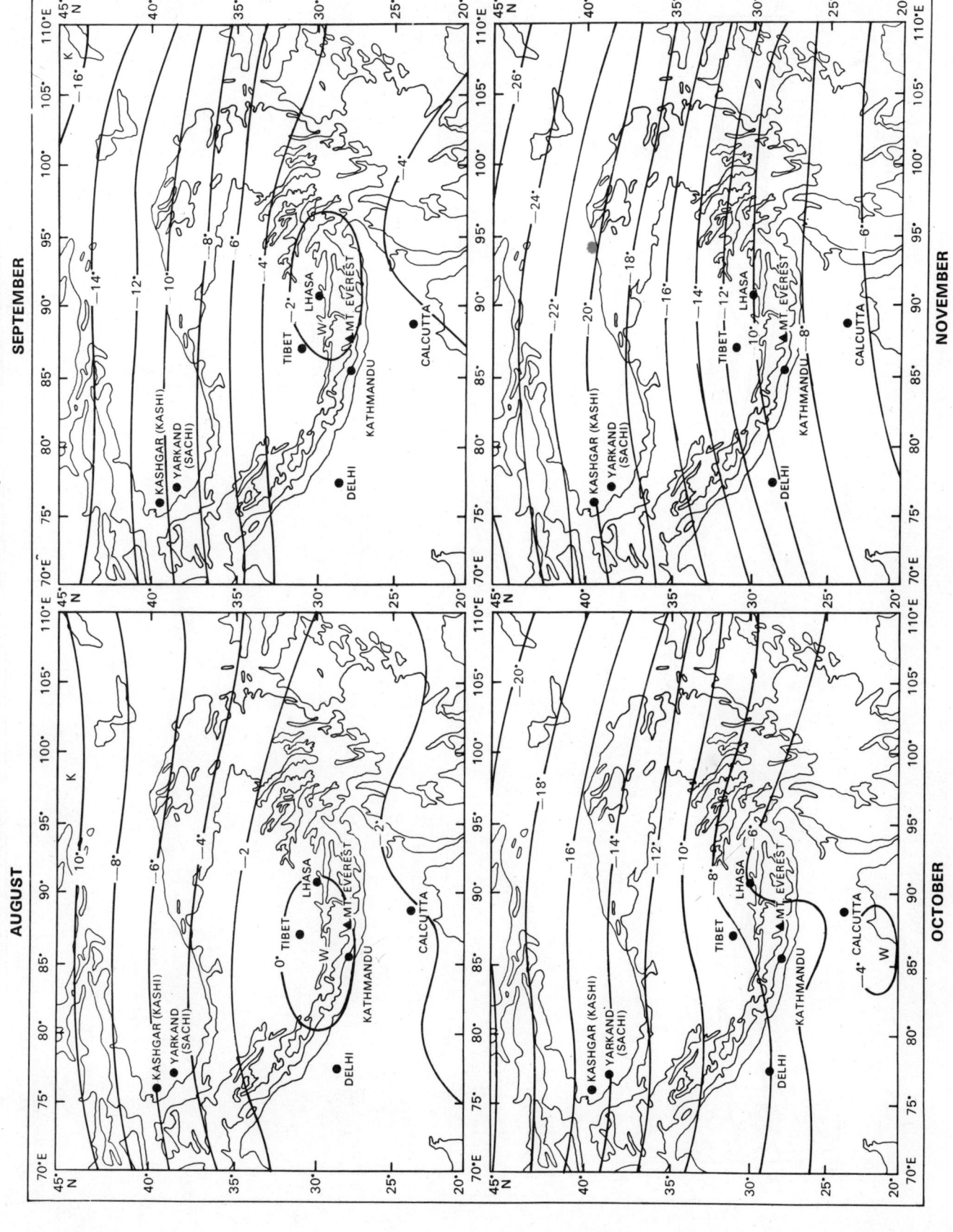

AUGUST

SEPTEMBER

OCTOBER

NOVEMBER

Upper air temperatures at 9 Km (30,000 feet) above mean sea level

MARCH

APRIL

MAY

JUNE

Upper air temperatures at 9 Km (30,000 feet) above mean sea level

AUGUST

SEPTEMBER

OCTOBER

NOVEMBER

Wind flow at 6 Km (20,000 feet) above mean sea level

MARCH

APRIL

MAY

JUNE

Wind flow at 6 Km (20,000 feet) above mean sea level

AUGUST

SEPTEMBER

OCTOBER

NOVEMBER

Wind flow at 9 Km (30,000 feet) above mean sea level

Wind flow at 9 Km (30,000 feet) above mean sea level

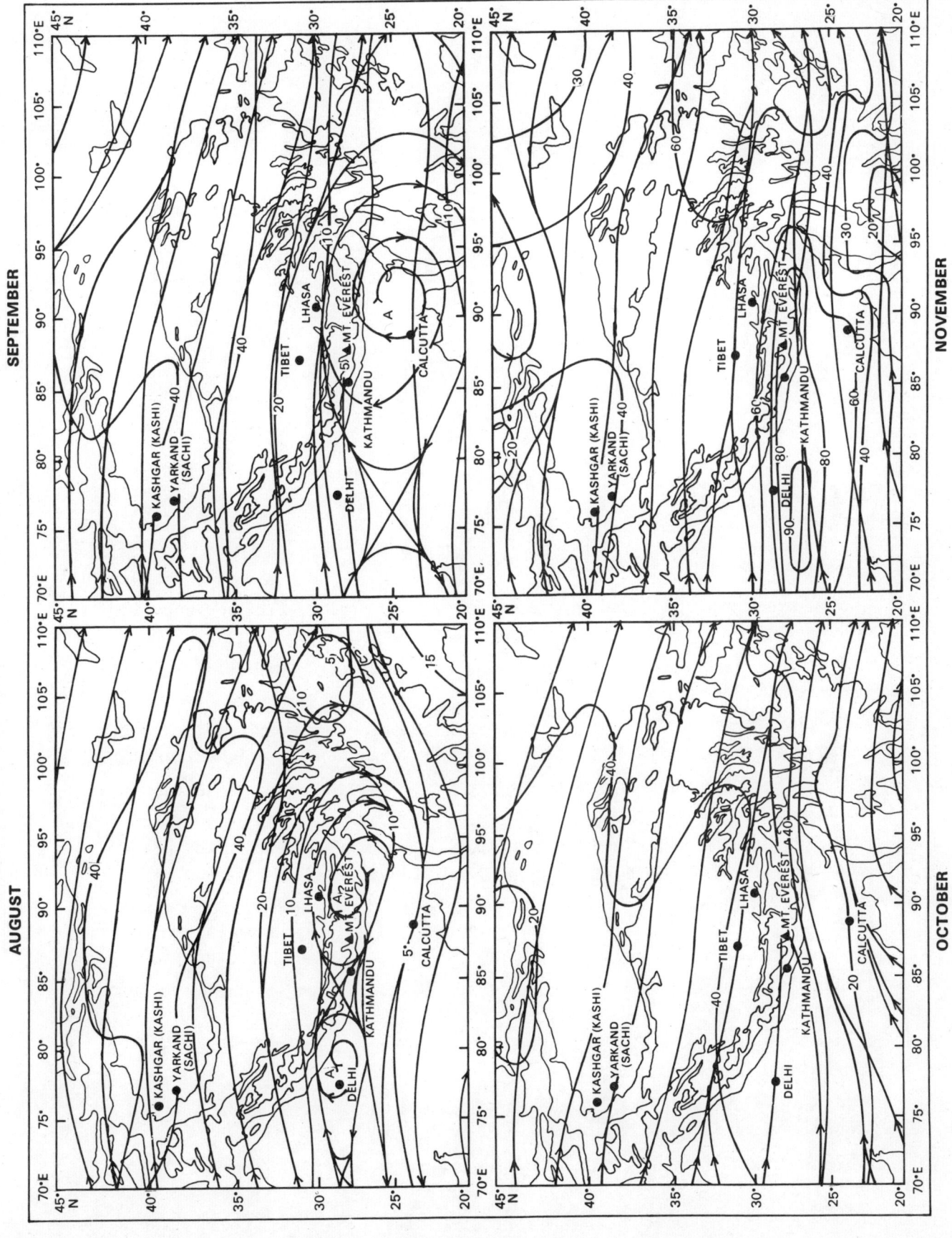

II Important Dates

The following historical summary gives a brief outline of the sequence of events in the exploration of Mount Everest and subsequent expeditions:

1711: Chinese lamas, instructed by the Jesuits made a survey of Tibet under the orders of the Peking Government.

1717: Jesuits in Peking drew a map of Tibet from the lamas' surveys and on the southern border of this map showed a mountain range 40 miles long, named Tchoumou Lancma.

1733: D 'Anville, the famous French geographer, published his map of Tibet in Paris basing it upon the lamas' survey.

1749: The Survey of India discovered and fixed a high peak in the Himalayas by means of observations taken from the low-lying jungle plains of India.

1852: The computations of the Survey indicated that this newly discovered peak was of a height greater than that of any other known mountain. There was no evidence whatever that this peak fixed from the south was standing on the lamas' range fixed from the north.

1852 to 1865: The names Devadhunga and Gaurishanker were put forward for the peak but not accepted.

1865: The height was finally determined by scientific calculations as 29,002′ and the name Mount Everest was selected.

1904: Col. Waddell and Sarat Chandra Das heard the name Chomo Kankar applied to Mount Everest by Tibetans in Tibet.

1907: An officer of the Survey of India, Natha Singh, who was allowed to survey the

Nepalese slopes of Mount Everest, heard the name Chholungbu applied by Tibetans to Mount Everest.

1909: Gen. Bruce was given the name Chomo Lungmo by sherpa Bhotias, whose home was high up in the Dudh Kosi valley of Nepal.

1920: Sir Charles Bell, the British representative in Lhasa, received an official order from the Tibetan Prime Minister, sanctioning the Mount Everest expedition, and in this order it was stated that the sahibs wished to see Chha-mo-lung-ma.

1921: Col. Howard-Bury, leader of the first Mount Everest expedition was given the name Chomo Uri for Mount Everest. He was also given the name Chomo Lungma for both Everest and Makalu.

1922: The first British Expedition in which oxygen was used for the first time. An avalanche caused the death of 7 sherpa porters.

1924: British Expedition in which Mallory and Irvine disappeared while climbing above 28,000 feet.

1933: British Expedition reached a point beyond 28,000'.

1934: Solo attempt by Englishman Maurice Wilson who died below North Col.

1935: British reconnaissance-in-force reached the North Col.

1936: British Expedition hampered by bad weather and could climb slightly above the Col.

1938: British Expedition reaching above 27,000'.

1947: Solo attempt by Canadian Earl Denman who reached short of the North Col.

1950: First approach to Everest from the South. H. W. Tilman and Charles Houston reached the foot of the Khumbu ice fall.

1951: British reconnaissance to south side; reached the entrance of Western Cwm at the top of the ice fall. Solo attempt by a Dane, R. B. Larsen, who started climbing from south side and crossed over to the north reaching the North Col.

1952: First Swiss Expedition. Pioneer route to South Col and summit ridge, reaching 28,200'. Swiss return in autumn for second attempt, but could only reach 26,300'. British pre-Everest Expedition under Eric Shipton crosses over to the northern side via Nepal.

1953: First ascent of Everest. Tenzing Norgay and Edmund Hillary.

1956: Second ascent of Everest by the Swiss, who place four men on the summit in two teams.

1960: First Indian Everest Expedition under Brig. Gyan Singh. The Chinese claim that three of their climbers had reached the summit, but western mountaineers discount the claim.

1962: Second Indian Expedition under Maj. John Dias. A group of three Americans and one Swiss make an unauthorised attempt from the North, reaching 25,000'.

1963: Third ascent of Everest by the American Expedition led by Norman G. Dyhrenfurth, reaching the summit in three successive bids—two from the conventional South Col and one from the unclimbed western ridge.

1965: Third Indian Mount Everest Expedition, led by Lt. Cdr. M. S. Kohli creates mountaineering history by making the ascent four times and putting nine members on the summit.

1969: Everest re-opened. Japanese Alpine Club reconnaissances.

1970: Japanese Expedition first unsuccessful attempt on South West Face. Japanese Ski Everest Expedition accomplished first descent with parachute on skiis from South Col. Expedition lost 6 sherpas.

1971: International Everest Expedition led by Norman Dyhrenfurth in which Maj. Harsh Bahuguna died. Unsuccessful Argentina Government sponsored expedition led by Lt. Col. H. C. Tolo sa.

1972: European Expedition led by Dr. Karl Herriligkoffer unsuccessful. British Expedition led by Chris Bonington unsuccessful.

1973 64-member Italian Expedition led by Count Guido Monzino successfully put 8 climbers on the summit. 48-member Japanese Expedition led by Michio Yuasa reached 8,380 m. via South West face.

1974: Unsuccessful Spanish Expedition suffered heavy frostbite. French Expedition via West ridge and to scale without oxygen resulting in the death of the leader and 5 sherpas.

1975: Chinese claimed to have put 9 members on the summit including one women. Japanese Women Expedition led by Mrs. Eiko Hisano. Junko Tabei reached the summit with a sherpa. British Expedition reached the summit via South West Face for the first time.

1976: Joint British and Royal Nepalese Army Expedition to Everest via South Col. Lost 5 members. American Bicentennial Expedition.

1977: New Zealand Expedition—first Expedition to Everest on Alpine style of climbing.

III List of Accidents on Everest

Year	Expedition	
1921	British	Dr. Kellas (member)
1922	British	Seven sherpa porters
1924	British	Two members, Mallory and Irvine.
1934	British (Unauthorised)	An Englishman, Maurice Wilson.
1952	Swiss	One Sherpa Two Porters on Ice fall.
1952	Russian	Leader Dr. Pawel Datschnolian and Five members.
1962	Indian	One Sherpa by falling rock on Lhotse face.
1963	American	John E. Brietenbach (member) on Khumbu Ice Fall.
1969	Japanese Reconnaissance Expedition	Phu Dorji (member) on Ice Fall.
1970	Japanese Everest Expedition	Narita (member) due to heart attack. One sherpa.
1970	Japanese Skiing Expedition	Six Sherpas on Khumbu Ice fall.
1971	International Everest Expedition	Harsh Bahuguna (member) due to Exposure & Exhaustion.

1972	British Everest Expedition	Tony Dighe (member) on Khumbu Ice fall.
1973	Japanese Rock Climbers Club	Sherpa guide, Tangbu due to avalanche.
1974	French Everest Expedition	Leader Gerard Devouassoux and five sherpas due to avalanche.
1975	Chinese Expedition	WU TSUNG YUEM (Cameraman).
1975	British Everest Expedition	Mick Burke (Member).
1976	Joint British and Royal Nepalese Army Expedition to Mount Everest 1976.	Members: David Brister, Gerry Owens, Richard Summerton, Pasang Tamang and Terry Thompson.

EVEREST TARRIF (NEPALESE CURRENCY)

S.No.	Item	Year	Year	Year	Remarks
		1963	1969	1976	
1.	Royalty Fee	Rs 4,800.00	Rs 10,000.00	Rs 15,000.00	To be deposited at the time of booking—non refundable.
2.	Insurance coverage (compensation for death)				
	(i) Liaison Officer	Rs 5,000.00	Rs 50,000.00	Rs 2,00000.00	To be paid in case of death on the mountains.
	(ii) Sherpas/ Porters	Rs 2,000.00	Rs 30,000.00	Rs 1,50,000.00 (above 6,600 metres) Rs 75,000.00 (between base camp 6,600 metres)	
3.	Daily wages				
	(i) Sirdar	Rs 12.00	—	Rs 30.00	Food and clothing extra.
	(ii) Sherpas	Rs 8.00	—	Rs 28.00	
4.	Mail Runners	Rs 8.00	—	Rs 25.00	
	Porters	Rs 6.00	—	Rs 18.00	

Note: In 1963 1 Dollar = Rs 7.6; In 1969 1 Dollar = Rs. 10.5; In 1976 1 Dollar = Rs 12.45

IV List of Expeditions

S.No.	Year	Leader	Age	Country	Route
1.	1921	C. K. Howard-Bury	38	British	North
2.	1922	Charles G. Bruce	56	British	North
3.	1924	E. F. Norton	40	British	North
4.	1933	Hugh Ruttledge	49	British	North
5.	1934	Maurice Wilson*	36	British	North
6.	1935	Eric E. Shipton	28	British	North
7.	1936	Hugh Ruttledge	52	British	North
8.	1938	H. W. Tilman	40	British	North
9.	1947	Earl L. Denman*		Canadian	North
10.	1950	Charles S. Houston	37	American	North
11.	1951	R. Becker-Larsen*			North
12.	1951	Eric E. Shipton	34	British	South East
13.	1952	Eric E. Shipton*	35	British	North
14.	1952	E. Wyss-Dunant		Swiss	South East
15.	1952	Gabriel Chevalley		Swiss	South East
16.	1952	Dr. Pawel Datschnolian		Russian	South East
17.	1953	John Hunt	42	British	South East
18.	1956	Albert Eggler	43	Swiss	South East
19.	1960	Gyan Singh	42	Indian	South East

S.No.	Year	Leader	Age	Country	Route
20.	1960		32	Chinese	North
21.	1962	John Dias	34	Indian	South East
22.	1962	Woodrow W. Sayre*	43	American	North
23.	1963	N. G. Dyhrenfurth	44	American	South East & Western Ridge
24.	1965	Mohan S. Kohli	34	Indian	South East
25.	1969			Japanese Reconnaissance expedition	South West Face
26.	1970	Saburo Matsukuta	70	Japan	South East & South West Face
27.	1970	Akira Takahashi		Japanese Ski Expedition	South East
28.	1971	Norman G. Dyhren-furth		International Everest Expedition	South West
29.	1971	Lt. Col. Hector Cativa Tolosa	43	Argentina	South East
30.	1972	Dr. Karl Herrligkoffer		European Expedition	South West
31.	1972	Chris Bonington	37	British	South West Face
32.	1973	Count Guido Monzino	44	Italian	South East
33.	1973	Michio Yuasa		Japanese Rock Climbing Club	South East
34.	1974	Juan Uqua Cio Lorenta Zuqaza	35	Spanish	West Face
35.	1974	Gerard Devouassoux	33	French	West Ridge
36.	1975	Mrs. Eiko Hisano	42	Japan Women Expedition	South East
37.	1975	Chinese Expedition		Chinese	North
38.	1975	Chris Bonington	40	British	South West Face
39.	1976	Lt Col. Tony Streather		Joint British and Royal Ne-palese Army Expedition	South East
40.	1976	Phil Trimble		American Bicentennial Expedition	South East
41.	1977	Keith Wood Ford		New Zealand	South East
42.	1977	Young Do Kim		South Korea	South East

*Unauthorised attempts

ASCENTS

1st ascent—29th May, 1953	by Edmund Hillary Tensing Norgay Sherpa	via South Col—South East Ridge	*British* led by Col. John Hunt (now Lord Hunt)
2nd ascent—23 May, 1956	by Ernst Schmied Juerg Marmet Adolf Reist	—do—	*Swiss* led by Albert Eggler
3rd ascent—24th May, 1956	Hanscrudolf von Gunten	—do—	

(4th ascent claimed by Chinese from northern side, but this claim not generally recognised by mountaineering experts in the West)

4th ascent—1st May, 1963	by Jim Whittaker Nawang Gombu	—do—	*Americans* led by Norman Dyhrenfurth
5th ascent—22nd May, 1963	by Barry Bishop Lute Jerstad	—do—	
6th ascent—22nd May, 1963	by Dr Willi Unsoeld Dr. Tom Hornbein	Via West Ridge	
7th ascent—20th May, 1965	by Capt A. S. Cheema Nawang Gombu	via S. Col— S. E. Ridge	*Indians* led by Lt. Cdr. M. S. Kohli
8th ascent—22nd May, 1965	by Sonam Gyatso Sonam Wangyal	—do—	
9th ascent—24th May, 1965	by C. P. Vohra Ang Kami Sherpa	—do—	
10th ascent—29th May,1975	by Capt. H. P. S. Ahluwalia, H. C. S. Rawat, Phu Dorje Sherpa	—do—	
11th ascent—11th May, 1970	by Neomi Uemura Teruo Matsuura	via S. Col— S. E. Ridge	*Japanese*, Japanese Alpine Club led by Hiromi Ohtsuka
12th ascent—12th May, 1970	by Katsutoshi Hirabayashi Chotare Sherpa	—do—	

13th ascent—5th May, 1973	by Rinaldo Carrel Mirko Minusso Lhakpa Tensing Sherpa Sambu Tamang	Via S. Col— S. E. Ridge —do—	*Italians* led by Guido Monzino
14th ascent—7th May, 1973	by Capt. Fabrizio Innamorati, Virginio Epis, Sonam Benedetti, Sonam Gyalgen Sherpa	—do—	
15th ascent—26th October 1973	by Hisashi Ishiguro Yasuo Kato	—do—	*Japanese*, Rock Climbing Club led by Michio Yuasa
16th ascent—16 May 1975	by Mrs. Junko Tabei & Sherpa guide Sirdar Ang Tshering	via S. Col S. E. Ridge.	*Japanese*, women's Expedition led by Mrs. Hisano
17th ascent—27th May, 1975	by One Woman and Eight men (as reported)	North Col. via Tibeten side	Mountaineering Expedition of People's Republic of *China*
18th ascent—24th Sept. 1975	by Doug Scott & Dougal Haston	South West face	*British* led by Chris Bonington
19th ascent—26th Sept. 1975	by Peter Boardman Sherpa Sirdar Pertemba	—do—	
20th ascent—16th May, 1976	by Sergeant Brummy Stokes and Corporal Bronco Lane	S. Col. S. E. Ridge	*Joint British and Royal Nepalese* Army, Expedition led by Lt. Col. Tony Streather
21st ascent—8th October 1976	by Bob Cormack & Chris Chandleer	—do—	*American* Bicentennial Expedition led by Phil Trimble
22nd ascent—15th September 1977	by Sang-Don Ko & Sherpa Pemba Norbu	S. Col S. E. Ridge	

V Glossary of Mountaineering Terms

ALP	Green pasture-land on a mountain-side.
ARETE	A sharp, ascending ridge of a mountain.
AVALANCHE	A large mass of snow and ice sliding down a mountain slope.
BELAY	Securing of a rope by hitching it over a projection or passing it around the body.
BERG	A mountain.
BERGSCHRUND	A large fissure or crevasse separating the upper slopes of a glacier from the steeper slopes of ice or rock above.
BIVOUAC	A temporary impromptu camp.
CHIMNEY	A steep, narrow cleft in a wall of rock or ice.
COL	A pass, or the low point of a ridge.
CORNICE	A projecting mass of snow or ice, as on the leeward side of a ridge.
COULOIR	A gully, usually in an up-and-down direction.
CRAMPONS	Steel frames with projecting spikes that are attached to the soles of boots to prevent slipping on steep snow or ice.
CREVASSE	A deep crevice or fissure in a glacier, caused by its downward movement.
CWM	A hollow in a mountain; a deep ravine.
EIDER-DOWN	Small soft feathers from the breast of eider ducks,

233

	a northern species, used for quilting.
FACE	The steep aspect of a mountain between two ridges.
FIXED ROPE	Rope attached to a mountainside.
GLACIER	A 'river' of ice formed by the accumulation or consolidation of snow.
GOMPA	Buddhist monastery.
GLISSADE	Sliding descent over a steep slope of snow or ice.
HAVERSACK	A canvas bag with a shoulder-strap to carry up to 20 lbs or so.
ICE-AXE	A mountaineer's axe mainly used for cutting steps on ice and as a stout walking stick for keeping balance on snow and ice.
ICE FALL	The steepest section of a glacier, usually taking the form of a widely jumbled mass of ice.
KARABINER	A metal snap ring, usually used in conjunction with a piton through which a rope may be passed for greater security during difficult climbing.
KHUMBU GLACIER	The glacier which descends from the Everest ice fall on the head of which base camp is situated, and part of the main route in the ascent of Everest from the Nepalese side of the border.
MASSIF	A compact range or group of mountain heights.
MITTEN	A kind of glove with thumbs but no fingers. It is of three types viz. eider-down, woollen, and wind-proof.
MORAINE	Rock and debris carried down by a glacier, distinguished by their position as medial, lateral, and terminal.
NEVE	A snow-field lying above the snow line, usually the source of a glacier.
NYLON ROPE	A soft rope made of nylon material about $\frac{3}{4}''$ thick which has a breaking strength of about 3,000 lbs.
PITON	A metal spike designed to give support in steep climbing to hand, foot or rope. Pitons are made in varying sizes and shapes; some designed for use on ice, some for driving into cracks in rocks.
POWDER-SNOW AVALANCHE	Caused by freshly fallen snow on a steep surface before it has had time either to thaw or freeze; one of the most spectacular and dangerous avalanche conditions.
RAPPLE	Roping down; letting oneself down a steep place by means of supplementary rope.
ROCK BAND	On Everest the 1,000' wall of sheer rock that stretches across the South West Face around 27,000'.
RUCKSACK	A bag slung by straps over both shoulders and resting on the back for carrying a climber's accessories.

SADDLE	The low point of ridge, a col.
SERAC	A tower of ice, usually found on a glacier.
SLEEPING BAG	A type of quilt, very warm and light, filled with eider-down or kapok material, fitted with a zip in the centre, joining the sides of the quilt.
SOUTH SUMMIT	The subsidiary summit of Everest at 28,700'.
SOUTH WEST FACE	7,000' high from its base in the Western Cwm to the summit; the first 5,000' is not technically difficult, being an open gully system, but above this, the Rock Band, fixed roping has to be done as the climb is very difficult.
SNOW BRIDGE	An arch of snow joining two sides of a crevasse.
SPUR	Rib, or lateral projection of rock.
TRAVERSE	The horizontal or diagonal crossing of a mountainside; also the crossing of a peak or pass from one side to the other.
WESTERN CWM	On Everest the cwm above the ice fall, leading up to the start of the Face and extremely dangerous because of avalanches.

Index

236